HOUSING AND THE ENVIRONMENT: A New Agenda

Edited by

MARK BHATTI, JANE BROOKE and **MIKE GIBSON**

Chartered Institute of Housing
Policy and Practice Series

The Chartered Institute of Housing is the professional organisation for all those who work in housing. Our purpose is to take a leading and strategic role in the encouragement of the provision and management of high quality, affordable homes for all. The Institute has over 12,000 individual members working for local authorities, housing associations, the private sector and educational institutions.

CIH, Octavia House, Westwood Way, Coventry CV4 8JP.
Tel. 0203 694433 Fax: 0203 695110

The New CIH Housing Policy and Practice Series aims to provide important and valuable material and insights for housing managers, staff, students, trainers and policy makers. The Editorial Team for the series is: General Editor: Professor Peter Williams; Series Editor: John Perry and Production Editor: Alan Dearling.

ISBN 0-901607-73-8

Housing and the Environment: A New Agenda
Editors: Mark Bhatti, Jane Brooke and Mike Gibson

Published by the
Chartered Institute of Housing © 1994.

Printed by Hobbs the Printers, Southampton.
Typeset by EMS Phototypesetting, Berwick upon Tweed
Designed by Alan Dearling for the CIH

CONTENTS

FOREWORD

Jonathon Porritt

On 16 March 1993 Norman Lamont, the then Chancellor of the Exchequer, lobbed a hefty policy grenade into the heartland of environment and housing organisations in the UK. By sticking VAT on domestic heating fuels (ostensibly to assist the Government in meeting its target of stabilising CO_2 emissions, but in reality simply to raise additional revenue), he compelled those two important progressive movements to enter into a dialogue which had until then been sorely lacking.

Since then, that dialogue has involved individuals and whole organisaitons coming out of their own particular policy bunkers to explore the extensive common ground they share between them. Housing organisations have had to recognise the central importance of energy efficiency and the whole sustainable development debate, whilst environmentalists for their part have had to make far more explicit their often unstated concerns about social justice and the scourge of poverty in the UK today.

As an observer of that process, I would say the dialogue has yet to bear fruit properly. And I believe the 'new agenda' laid out in this admirable book could assist very significantly in accelerating the process.

There is now widespread agreement that housing policy and new housing provision have to be seen as key components of sustainable development – leaving to one side precisely what we may mean by that much used and abused concept! Improvements in environmental performance are all well and good, but they are unlikely to be truly sustainable unless they simultaneously address pressing social and economic needs in society today.

Time after time, the message in this book takes us back to one of the over-arching principles of the 1987 Brundtland Report: "poverty reduces people's capacity to use resources in a sustainable manner: It intensifies pressure on the environment". With more than 1.5 million unfit dwellings in the UK today, and with more people living in fuel poverty at the end of the 1980s than at the beginning, the social justice element of sustainable development has to be right up front in everything we now do.

With the best will in the world, one has to say that this message continues to pass government ministers by at every turn. It's painful having to revisit the startling incoherence of their energy efficiency policies over the last decade, with new initiatives coming and going like so many wisps of insulation material in the wind.

Of even greater impact on communities has been the ducking and diving over inner city policy, with many urban regeneration schemes failing to bring about lasting changes in people's real quality of life. And not just because of under-resourcing.

That's the gloomy side of it. By contrast, there are now clear indications of exciting new partnerships emerging from many different quarters, with local authorities once more back in a central position both as deliverers of services and as strategic planners.

This is crucial, for contrary to all the rhetoric about Earth Summits and global agreements, it is primarily at the local level that the descipline of sustainable development will have its most benign impact. It's only when people feel truly at home in their own homes and in their own communities that they're likely to feel at home in Planet Earth.

Jonathon Porritt

September 1994

PREFACE

This book was conceived in the period immediately after the Earth Summit in June 1992, and produced during 1993 when VAT on fuel and cuts in housing investment were high on the political agenda: It was completed just as the Energy Conservation Bill was talked out in April 1994. These events represent important landmarks in what has been a rapidly evolving subject. We were also acutely aware that compulsory competitive tendering, negative equity, and homelessness have preoccupied recent housing debates. At the same time, growing public concern over local and global environmental degradation raises questions about the role of housing in a wider context. These developments informed our thinking about the book and we have come to the conclusion that both the housing and environmental agendas need to merge and progress together. The subject matter is mainly concerned with British housing policy and practice, within a European setting. The book is specifically aimed at practitioners and those studying the housing system; it offers an introduction to the greening of housing by exploring emerging issues as well as traditional themes. If we have stimulated housing debate in the direction of the environmental challenges that we all face, then the book has served its purpose.

ACKNOWLEDGEMENTS

A venture of this type cannot be tackled alone. In Glasgow we would like to thank colleagues at the Housing Department for their support, particularly David Comley, Margret Vass, Gerry Gormal, David Webster, Alastair Kerr and David Hepburn. Phil O'Brien, Jackie Roddick, and Lesley Rowan organised the conference on 'Housing and Sustainability' at The University of Glasgow with financial help from the ESRC Global Environmental Change Programme; we appreciate the opportunity for discussion and their comments on earlier drafts. In London, South Bank University supported the project throughout with a term's sabbatical leave for Mark Bhatti. Marjorie Bulos, Sarah Barnes, and Mary Rogers always came to the rescue when help was needed; Andreas Goldner provided the figure on page 24; Alan Dearling, John Perry, and Peter Williams read the complete manuscript and guided us throughout; Bob Evans made helpful comments on a number of chapters and Hilary Parkey proofread. Needless to say the mistakes that are left are solely our responsibility. In particular we would like to thank all the contributors for their effort and efficiency, and without whom the book would not have been possible. Finally, a big 'thank you' to our friends and families, especially to the next generation, including Freddie, David, Isla, Mora, Christopher, Simon, Sophie, Charlotte, Alex, and Zoe, whose future was a constant reminder of the importance of these issues.

Yvonne Rydin wishes to acknowledge the research assistance of Kevin Lee. The research reported in Rydin 1992a and 1992b was supported by a grant from the Royal Institution of Chartered Surveyors' Education Trust.

Sue Barker-Wolff would like to thank Steve Bendle and Roy Thomas of SLFHA Development Department, David Turrent and Allison Crompton of ECD Architects and Energy Consultants, and to Roy Grimwade of Roy Grimwade Architects for information and comments about the Greenwrythe Lane scheme.

Jane Brooke is indebted to Lesley Rowan of Stirling University Department of Management and Organisation for assistance and Wendy Simpson-Lewis of the Canadian State of the Environment Reporting Unit for the 'Condition/Stress/Response' framework.

Brenda Boardman's position as Senior Research Fellow at St Hilda's College, Unversity of Oxford, is sponsored by PowerGen: their generous support is gratefully acknowledged. Geoff Milne provided helpful criticism and assistance with the graphics.

MB. JB. MG. September 1994

Notes on Contributors

SUE BARKER-WOLFF is Senior Lecturer in Environmental Design at Brighton University, Brighton. Sue has been an energy consultant for eight years, working for architects, tenants' groups, housing associations and local government. She, together with Alison Crompton, advised the contractors, Willmot Dixon in implementing the green brief for Greenwrythe Lane. Sue is also an assessor for BREEAM schemes for new offices.

MARK BHATTI is Senior Lecturer in Housing Studies in the School of Land Management and Urban Policy, South Bank University, London. Mark has researched into housing issues for over ten years and has worked as a policy officer in local government. He recently conducted a survey on environmental issues and social housing and is currently studying the role of tenant participation in the production of Local Agenda 21.

BRENDA BOARDMAN is Senior Research Fellow (Sponsored by PowerGen) at the Environmental Change Unit, Oxford University. Brenda's main research focus is fuel poverty and she has written extensively on the subject. She is head of the Energy and Environment programme and is currently involved in a major project funded by the European Commission and Energy Efficiency Office, looking at policies that would encourage the purchase of energy efficient appliances.

JANE BROOKE is Principal Policy Research Officer at Glasgow City Council Housing Department. She has been working in a number of areas ranging from urban renewal to youth homelessness. Jane has written widely on the subject of sustainability and housing management, and has recently presented some of the ideas contained in this book to the United Nations Commission on Sustainable Development in New York.

JON BROOME is a member of Architype CO-OP, a leading self build architect practice who have developed timber building with an emphasis on energy conservation and green design. Jon has been designing housing for over 20 years and in 1978 he was joint architect with Walter Segal for the pioneering Lewisham self-build schemes. He is co-author (with Brian Richardson) of The Self-Build Book and is currently building his own house to an ecological design.

TIM BROWN is Principal Lecturer in Housing Studies, De Montfort University, Leicester. Tim has been researching local housing strategies for a number of years and he has published numerous articles in this area. He is currently a member of a research team carrying out housing needs studies for a number of local authorities.

MIKE GIBSON is Professor of Urban Planning and Head of the School of Land Management and Urban Policy, South Bank University, London. He has over twenty years' experience of research, consultancy and teaching in the field of housing and neighbourhood renewal. His current work includes a study of recent developments in neighbourhood renewal and an assessment of the impact of the Brixton Challenge project.

JANICE MORPHET is the Secretary of SERPLAN. Before this she was Director of Technical Services at Woking Borough Council and has worked in a number of other local authorities including London boroughs, a county and the DoE. Between 1986 and 1990, Janice was Head of the Department of Planning and Landscape at the University of Central England, formerly Birmingham Polytechnic. Janice writes on a number of issues, including 'The Role of the Chief Executive in Local Government' and 'Greening Your Local Authority', both published by Longman.

YVONNE RYDIN is Lecturer in Geography, London School of Economics and is responsible for environmental policy and planning courses. She has written extensively on the nature of landed property markets and development processes including Housing Land Policy (1986 Gower), and The British Planning System (1993 Macmillan). Yvonne's current research is on sustainable cities in the European context, local governance and the language of environmentalism.

FIONN STEVENSON is Lecturer in Sustainable Design at Heriot-Watt University and previously taught at the Department of Architecture at Strathclyde University. Fionn has worked with 'Assist Architects' in Glasgow where she won first prize in the 1991 Energy Design Advisory Service competition for rehabilitation work. She is a committee member of the Scottish Ecological Design Association and is on the winning team for the commission to design 'Scotland's Home of Tomorrow' for Scottish Homes.

Chapter 1
Housing and the New Environmental Agenda: An Introduction

Mark Bhatti, Jane Brooke, and Mike Gibson

> *We are knee-deep and sinking fast in the quicksand of our unsustainable 'waste culture', generated by the loss of personal and local control over the production of the 'major goods of life', not least our homes and our immediate surroundings. Along with most everyday things that used to be home- or locally-made, our homes have turned into commercial or welfare products for passive consumers. This aspect of pollution is one which... very few would have connected... with the threat to nature and our own future existence.* (Turner, 1993, p.236).

Housing is one of the longest established and most important areas of state intervention aimed at improving and managing poor environmental conditions at the local level. But now there is a new environmental agenda which is global in its scope and has profound social and economic consequences. Ecological problems such as global warming, ozone depletion, accumulating wastes in the eco-system, loss of bio-diversity, and declining non-renewable resources are beginning to affect the ways in which societies will develop in the future. What is *new* about the current environmental crisis is not just that there is a deep concern about nature, or alarm about the impact of unhealthy conditions, for much of this goes back to the 19th century; but that today the problems are truly global in scope and require international solutions. Yet key economic processes such as housing markets operate in specific localities, and it is mainly at the local level that ordinary people can make their actions felt. This book therefore intends to open up the question: what does *'think globally – act locally'* mean for housing? We believe that housing is on the threshold of major changes whereby global environmental considerations will have a greater and greater impact on housing policy and practice at the local level. Our objective in this book is to locate housing issues within the wider environmental debate, and highlight the opportunities and barriers for change in the housing system.

There are a number of themes to be explored throughout the book: the first examines mechanisms which are necessary for the greening of housing; the second is a critical discussion of policies and practices within housing which seek to address environmental problems; the third theme identifies housing inequality issues within the context of tackling environmental problems. This is not a how-to-do-it manual, as there is now considerable advice in this area (see Pocock and

Gayland 1992, Harland 1993, Taylor 1993). In contrast this book pulls together a range of contributions from policy practice and analysis in order to set the framework for the development of a housing system that is sustainable for people and for the planet. In this chapter we introduce and highlight a number of key issues that require critical debate in the housing literature. We start by examining reasons why practitioners and policy makers have to respond to the new environmental agenda, and then suggest some of the benefits of a green approach. We go on to outline the ways in which housing and the environment interact, and propose four principles of sustainability. In conclusion we summarise the contributions in the book with a brief overview of the issues they seek to address.

The new environmental agenda introduces fundamental issues into current housing debates which must lead to a re-appraisal of traditional policy concerns. Firstly, it reveals the fragmented nature of housing policy planning and implementation. We argue for an integrated approach in order to address economic, social and environmental imperatives. Secondly, this new agenda raises questions about the kinds of policies which are currently given priority. Thus a housing policy based solely on the market, driven by privatisation and the weakening of local authorities, is not compatible with meeting needs or responding quickly to the environmental crisis. Thirdly, the flaws in the relationships presently central to the housing process are now being exposed. The dichotomies of provider/user, client/contractor, central/local government, and producer/consumer, are barriers to the development of an environmentally sensitive housing system. These divisions need to be reassessed as a matter of urgency. Finally, the new environmental agenda reveals the sterility of current housing measures of efficiency and effectiveness. Performance indicators concentrate on a restricted definition of efficiency and ignore the vital interactions between social, economic and environmental factors. Moreover current policies dealing with environmental issues are limited, fragmented and partial. This book provides a first step towards developing a holistic and environmentally informed view of the development and management of housing; an approach we believe respects social and economic imperatives as well as environmental pressures and problems.

One barrier to talking about sustainability is terminology, which can often obscure more than it reveals. For many policy makers and practitioners the word 'sustainable' has a specific and restricted meaning. A capital project may be 'sustainable' if future revenue funding is secure; if it stabilises tenancies or is immune to anticipated changes in the policy framework; **not** whether materials used accelerate loss of virgin rainforest, or the construction process causes pollution, or wildlife habitats are destroyed. Failure to explicitly consider environmental sustainability in local decisions makes global problems worse. We believe however that there is no necessary conflict between social, economic, and environmental objectives. Sensitively designed and well managed houses can contribute to all three objectives providing a better quality of life for users while ameliorating global problems. Long term stability of social and economic processes contributes to environmental sustainability. Indeed if a 'green' project fails to provide a long term solution to the problems of an area because it does not address income or employment issues, or fails to consider the needs and aspirations for local residents, then further investment will be required at some time in the future. This represents a greater drain on the planet because of wasted resources and opportunities forgone through misplaced investment. Also local communities will have their own view of what makes their life patterns stable and sustainable: warm, dry, affordable housing, in a safe neighbourhood with access to a range of facilities. Indeed this understanding could be seen to be the most important: if it fails to work in people's daily lives, then it won't work for the planet!

It is important to point out at the outset that as housing providers, managers, and consumers we do not start tackling environmental problems entirely from a clean slate. There is a long history of policy action and research around poor housing, effective management of deteriorating neighbourhoods, and concern for housing deprivation and health. In particular housing managers have been developing energy efficiency measures from the 1970s onwards. While these traditional themes remain important, they need to be re-examined in the light of current concerns for the survival of the planet, that is, debates around sustainability. We therefore argue for a green perspective to be incorporated into housing provision. The book demonstrates that a green housing policy and practice must be more durable and flexible, more in tune with users' needs and concerns, more economical to run, and capable of adapting to current and future environmental problems. For example, genuinely 'green' buildings will use fewer non-renewable resources and have lower capital costs for a given performance. Green approaches also utilize existing buildings and infrastructure and would be linked to economic development strategies. They use local people and local knowledge thereby reducing dangers of management at a distance, so that benefits to the local population are secured. We believe this approach is effective in lifting people out of poverty without incurring undue environmental damage. Even so, there is one point at which green approaches are bound to be more expensive. It takes time and effort to work closely with service users, to nurture grass-roots initiatives and to develop and implement new approaches to purchasing, design, management and decision making. However, as many of the contributors to this book suggest, this is amply rewarded both through improved user satisfaction, and the lower long term costs of having buildings and management systems which do a better job.

Our main concern is that the current Government's obsession with privatisation, reducing costs, and exposing services to the disciplines of the market will not allow hard pressed housing providers and managers sufficient space to develop and implement environmentally sensitive policies. We hope that pressure both from the European Union, consumers, and housing organisations working at the local level will be effective in bringing about changes in direction. The alternative is that both the provision and management of housing remain part of the problem, instead of being a major factor in the search for a solution.

A Green Approach to Housing?

Homelessness, poverty and crime on housing estates, rising housing costs,community care, and compulsory competitive tendering (CCT) are at the top of today's housing agenda. Many practitioners feel that concerns about the natural environment and global sustainability distract attention from their efforts to cope with these problems. For example, 'environmentally friendly' products may seem too expensive when budgets have been squeezed by years of relentless pressure for 'value for money'. Similarly, gas central heating systems may generate lower levels of carbon dioxide emissions than electric systems, but if the electricity company is offering an attractive financial package which means that more houses get central heating, then the needs of the tenants will invariably come first, and the environment second. In these circumstances the development of green housing policies may be given a lower priority because they represent an extra burden on an overloaded system. However there are a number of reasons why practitioners, policy makers and academics need to take environmental issues on board as a matter of urgency.

First, international concerns over global environmental problems and world poverty have re-emerged in recent years with the publication of 'Our Common Future' by the United Nations World Commission on Environment and Development (WCED 1987). Commonly known as *'The Brundtland Report'*, this introduced the idea of 'sustainable development' as a way of reconciling solutions to global environmental problems with meeting basic human needs. Much of this activity culminated in the United Nations Conference on Environment and Development (The Earth Summit) in Rio De Janerio in June 1992. The signing of conventions on climate change, bio-diversity and forests, committed over a hundred and fifty national governments to specific actions and targets to protect the environment. By far the most important document to emerge from the Earth Summit is *'Agenda 21'* which identifies key problems and the groups most affected; promotes action by governmental and non-governmental organisations, and emphasises participation by the community. Agenda 21 provides the basic framework for environmental action at the international, national and local levels. The document sets goals, priorities, resources, and responsibilities, with monitoring and evaluation mechanisms regarding key environment and development issues which will be crucial for the future of 'spaceship earth'. In Britain the Local Government Management Board has produced a guide to help local authorities to develop their own 'Local Agenda 21' (LGMB 1992, 1994). The impact of Agenda 21, and its localised version, has yet to be determined but it could be the most important vehicle for local authorities to promote environmental action in the area of housing management and development.

Secondly, there are strong pressures on housing from the European Union. The European Commission has embarked on the 5th Action Programme on the environment entitled 'Towards Sustainability' (EC 1992a). Regulations and directives from Brussels will make increased demands on the environmental outcomes of housing and planning systems. National policy changes (DoE 1990, 1994a) suggest that housing may have a major role in tackling global environmental problems, though it is strong commitment at this level that appears to be missing.
Thirdly, the changing role of local authorities from being direct providers to enablers has major implications for environmental action. Increasing numbers of 'green' charters are a sign that local authorities wish to gain a new legitimacy around issues which affect the whole population in their areas. These ideas will permeate housing provision as people in run-down neighbourhoods, as well as in affluent areas, are looking for safer local environments. Users will wish to know the energy efficiency of their homes, seek information on the toxicity of chemicals used in construction or refurbishment, and pursue legal means to deal with dampness and other health hazards inside and outside the home. Thus the enabling role of local authorities in housing must include a new emphasis on environmental management and integrated local housing strategies.

Fourthly, there is a growing acknowledgement within the housing profession of the need to incorporate green thinking into housing policy and practice. The Chartered Institute of Housing, for example, lists fifteen proposals ranging from higher standards for energy efficiency, energy labelling, to provision of facilities for recycling in new homes. (CIH, 1991 p.30-32). Housing organisations will need to provide assurances about the environmental quality of their activities to consumers, investors, and their employees. They will increasingly be expected to improve their environmental performance (whilst offering value for money); which they can now do by gaining accreditation under BS 7750 or the European Union's Eco-Audit scheme. Housing organisations will have to respond imaginatively to growing environmental concerns of the public at large (see Bhatti 1994a). Recent evidence suggests that attitudes are changing and people are now not only more aware of local and global problems but demanding action (DoE 1991a, chapter 9; 1992b, chapter 16). This adds a new dimension to housing policy and practice as the environmental impact of housing activities comes under public scrutiny, and management systems designed to minimise these impacts are put into place.

Finally, the rising cost of domestic fuel brings together issues of housing inequality, poverty and environmental concern. V.A.T. on fuel has been imposed to reduce energy use and hence carbon dioxide (CO_2) emissions (and of course bring in extra revenue for Central Government), but will lead to grave social problems. 'Fuel poverty', defined as 'the inability to afford adequate warmth because of the energy inefficiency of the home' (Boardman 1991), is set to become a key housing issue in the 1990s. Over 7 million households are affected, and this number will increase as energy costs rise. If fuel poverty is to be eliminated the emphasis must be on developing targeted energy policies, increasing capital investment, and better housing management in both the private and public sectors.

The implications of these developments are far reaching but have not been subject to critical debate and are under-researched. Nonetheless, there is considerable pressure for the incorporation of green thinking into housing policy and practice, and a growing concern for the environmental impact of housing activities. It is still not clear where this increasing awareness will take us, but we suggest that the speed of change towards a greener housing provision in Britain will have to accelerate if it is to deliver global, as well as local, environmental improvements.

The Environmental Impacts of Housing Activities

The nature of the housing system in Britain arises out of specific sets of relationships of production, management and consumption, with varying levels of state intervention (Ball 1983). This particular 'structure of provision' has major impacts on the environment which operate across space and time and on different scales. These range from the micro-climate of the home which both determines and arises from every day activities of households, to the immediate locality or neighbourhood which is the subject and object of local environmental management, and to the level of the city at the interface of home, work, shopping and leisure. Decisions at all these levels directly affect global environmental change. Thus global warming, ozone depletion, depletion of non-renewable resources, as well as human health and well being are influenced by the particular way in which housing in Britain is provided, managed and used (see Rydin 1992b).

Global warming is caused by the 'greenhouse effect'. In much the same way as the air is heated in a greenhouse, the atmosphere traps some of the sun's long wave radiation of heat as it bounces from the surface of the earth. Carbon dioxide, methane and other lesser gases prevent the warmth from escaping into space too rapidly, keeping the earth warm enough for life to flourish. A change in the balance of the mixture of gases in the atmosphere traps more and more long wave radiation than in the past. Scientists have predicted that the temperature will rise between 1.5° and 4.5°C by 2050, and the effects could be catastrophic. It is feared that the polar ice caps will start to melt, and the oceans will rise and flood many low lying areas. Existing forms of agriculture will not be possible in some regions and weather patterns will become erratic. If, as seems possible, the eco-system cannot adjust quickly enough the earth's capacity to support human societies in their present form may be compromised.

As carbon dioxide is the main greenhouse gas, attention has focused on minimising CO_2 emissions into the atmosphere. The burning of fossil fuels such as coal, oil and gas for power is the major contributor to CO_2 emissions. 28% of UK emissions are from the household sector. These are expected to fall to 19.1% if the energy efficiency measures currently being put into place by Central Government actually work (DoE 1994a). Reduction of household energy consumption is seen to be a key factor in stabilising CO_2 emissions thereby relieving the pressure on global warming. Attention is therefore focused on implementing measures to conserve fuel, and in making dwellings more energy efficient.

Energy use is affected by:

* the design, production, exchange and consumption of housing
* the use of capital intensive construction methods
* the manufacture of high energy building materials such as concrete, steel and plastics, as well as their transportation
* and most importantly, household energy consumption patterns.

Unless this energy comes from renewable sources such as wind, wave or tidal power, it will generate CO_2 and other emissions as fossil fuels are burnt (nuclear power has its own problems). The CO_2 generated in manufacturing building materials, the construction process, and the manufacturing of domestic equipment is not accurately accounted for in our calculations of energy use. Such calculations allow us to think about alternative forms of housing production. For example chapter 11 points out that labour intensive methods, with local materials and community self-management, can radically reduce energy use and therefore CO_2 emissions. Chapter 6 shows how the process of urban regeneration can be made more environmentally sensitive if the issue of carbon dioxide embodied in existing dwellings is taken on board. Space heating counts for nearly half of domestic CO_2 emissions whilst water heating and appliances account for the rest (see Boardman 1990 and chapter 7 of this book). This suggests that increasing the standards for energy efficiency in new dwellings and improving the thermal efficiency of existing homes will have a substantial impact on the UK's contribution to global warming. CO_2 emissions also vary by type of fuel used. There is a major disparity between electricity and gas; electricity produces 45% of emissions, but only 17% of delivered energy; gas on the other hand is more efficient, producing fewer emissions per unit of delivered energy. Thus a shift away from electricity towards more efficient gas central heating and water heating, combined with improvements in the thermal efficiency of the house, can produce quite dramatic results in cutting energy use. In order to meet the targets set by international agreements at The Earth Summit reducing energy demand at the point of consumption, that is, in the home, is a key factor in the response to global warming.

Secondly, ozone is a gas found high in the Earth's atmosphere; it cuts out harmful ultra-violet radiation produced by the sun. However, the ozone layer is beginning to thin due to the release of artificial gases such as chlorofluorocarbons (CFCs). CFCs are used extensively in industrial societies in many products ranging from aerosol cans, insulation, to refrigerators; but they do not break down very easily, and where they reach the higher levels of the atmosphere they react to decompose ozone. Thus increased levels of high energy ultra violet radiation are now reaching the earth's surface; in places where ozone depletion is particularly acute scientists are warning of increases in skin cancers in humans and animals and damage to the food chain. CFCs in the house and home are found mainly in certain insulation products used by the building industry, most models of fridges and freezers and some fire protection products.

The choice of materials for house building and maintenance has significant environmental impacts (see Elkin et al 1991 pp33-38). Land is taken in the extraction of aggregates, stone, iron, clay, and wood. The manufacture and transport of building materials such as bricks, steel, glass, copper, and plastics causes pollution as well as depleting non-renewable resources and the whole process is energy intensive. The resources used are often imported and damage habitats threatening bio-diversity both locally and globally; for example 50% of hardwoods from tropical forests imported into Britain are destined for the building industry. The by-products of the manufacturing processes are also a problem. 90% of the raw material used to produce chemically based paints ends up as waste, much of which is toxic; in contrast when paint is produced from natural oils, resins and dyes, only 10% of the raw material ends up as waste, which is generally harmless. There are often major problems with the disposal of building materials when the dwelling is at the end of its useful life, most is dumped in land-fill sites. If plastics are incinerated under less than ideal conditions, toxic gases may be produced. Finally housing is a major item of land use in the urban areas in the U.K. The form of towns and cities, whether they are compact or dispersed, can have a major impact on the amount of land used for housing development and infrastructure and demand for private cars. Indeed Elkin et al argue that:

> *"The city is being suburbanised by redevelopment and infilling of open space at suburban densities, particularly for housing. The advantages of intensive use of space are being lost. Compactness goes hand-in-hand with the goal of livability"* (1991 p.16).

Post War decentralisation, and in particular the loosening of the planning system over the last 10-15 years, has resulted in more and more dispersed development. In many places land, labour and housing markets have combined to produce severe energy demands and environmental impacts that affect the overall quality of life in the area (Owen 1992).

Turning to the new environmental health aspects of housing; the resources needed for house production and the pollution effects at the internal, local, regional as well as international levels. We can start by looking at the house itself which may be a container for pollution and chemical hazards. Modern dwellings are full of synthetic materials including noxious chemicals often contained within a tightly sealed interior full of mechanical and electrical systems. The building and do-it-yourself industries use chemicals in most products such as paints, varnishes, glues, timber treatments, and plastics (Kruger 1991). Many of these chemicals slowly bio-degrade over time (or outgas) and the long term effects of this on occupants are unknown. 'Sick building syndrome' is now widely recognised as a problem in office buildings, but a similar understanding of effects arising out of daily exposure to small quantities of toxic gases in the home has not so far been developed.

To sum up, there are a range of environmental issues and problems involved in the housing process at several levels. The large number of factors involved makes it difficult to think environmentally about the housing process. Tenure issues add a further complexity and even though analysis of the environmental dimension of housing goes across the tenures, the policy response is often mediated by tenure. For example, in Britain 11 million homes are energy inefficient and the vast majority are in the private sector. This means that policy mechanisms have to enable, facilitate and encourage individual households or private landlords to implement energy efficiency and conservation measures. Where local authorities and housing associations directly manage housing there is greater potential for a speedy comprehensive action. Even so, policy makers and researchers have not yet begun to ask environmentally informed questions about the housing system. It is this sense that we suggest that housing debates about homelessness, tenure, standards and management need to be more closely linked to the debate on sustainability.

Housing and Sustainability: Key Themes

There is no precise definition of 'sustainability' and little agreement as to how it should be pursued (for example Pearce et al 1989 p173-185 list 24 definitions, and see chapter 2 for contrasting approaches). Even so, we want to set a framework which may be helpful in understanding the relationship between housing and environment by putting forward four key principles (Elkin et al 1991).

* Futurity
* Environment
* Equity
* Participation

Futurity
As the Brundtland report suggests sustainable development is,

> *"development that meets the needs of the present without compromising the ability of future generations to meet their own needs"* (WCED, 1987 p.43)

The ideas and practice of sustainable development which have emerged in recent years are a response to global environmental problems and the relief of poverty, but we can see how this approach can be useful in housing. For example, many of the problems being encountered by council tenants living in systems built estates arose out of the failure to think through the needs and demands of future generations. Housing policies and practices must look to the future and consider how the next generation are to meet their housing needs.

Environment
This recognises the effect of human activity on the planet, and the effect of the planet on human activity, and seeks to work within natural limits. Thus we may question the extent to which cities can go on expanding, or highlight the wider impacts of housing building. If we take into account improved knowledge of the capacity of the environment to provide resources and absorb pollution and apply it to operations of the housing market, we will tend to be directed towards rehabilitation rather than new build to solve housing problems, if the appropriate stock is available.

Equity
Whilst the first principle emphasises inter-generational equity, it is also important to consider access to resources within the current generation (intra-generation equity). We argue that the present housing system plays a major part in perpetuating and generating environmental poverty. A central aim of any green housing policy must be to redistribute environmental resources equitably across the population.

Participation
Many of the unsustainable policies and practices identified in this book arise out of failure to actually involve people in decision making. Thus, historically, solutions have been imposed from above so that users remain outside the housing process. Even so, the development of tenant participation in the social housing sector may present some openings for user involvement in local environmental policy.

Sustainability is a contested concept so we offer a framework rather than impose a precise definition. The four principles of futurity, environment, equity, and participation lie at the heart of green housing policy and practice. Each is a necessary condition for pursuing greener housing policies, but not sufficient on its own. Thus participation without equity may mean that certain groups could secure more environmental resources for themselves. If resources are redistributed without considering present and future environmental impacts, or providing environmentally sound alternatives, total consumption would merely increase thereby causing problems for the next generation. All the contributors in the book highlight these principles, even though we may not all agree on how these are to be achieved.

The following chapters offer a critical assessment of current, and rapidly changing, policies and practices, as well as offering ways forward for the development of a green future for housing. **Mark Bhatti** starts by assessing the failure of housing studies to take up the challenge of sustainability. He argues for the need to go beyond the conventional understanding of housing issues, and introduces debates and ideas currently being developed in environmental studies that may be useful in the housing arena. Bhatti shows how modern environmentalism is itself divided, which has major implications for the 'greening of housing'. A model for understanding the environmental dimension of the housing process is proposed, and 'environmental poverty' and 'home ecology' are suggested as key concepts for linking housing and environmental studies.

In chapter 3 **Mike Gibson** outlines the impact of the new environmental agenda on national housing policy. He sets current housing issues within broader debates about planning for sustainable urban development and the greening of cities. Gibson argues that a national policy and programme for energy efficiency led housing and neighbourhood renewal would be an important step in the right direction. A review of recent policy developments demonstrates only limited progress. The chapter concludes by arguing that progress towards sustainable housing requires a re-orientation of housing policy towards a 'social democratic' model, to deliver a planned increase in public sector capital investment in housing renewal, as part of a strengthened national environmental policy.

Janice Morphet then goes on to examine the European context for the development of housing and environmental policy and emphasises the significance of the European Union for the establishment of a wider framework for change. She assesses the importance of key factors such as political union, citizen rights, economic convergence, and regionalisation for the future development of housing and planning systems. Morphet concludes by looking at the implications this emerging framework has for housing in Britain.

The theme of **Tim Brown's** chapter is the relationship between environmental policies and housing strategies at the local level; he briefly outlines the fall and rise of local housing strategies (or plans) and highlights the emergence of 'green charters'. Brown focuses on the 'enabling role' and looks at a number of local authorities that have attempted to link housing and environmental policies using this approach. He argues for a user perspective and assesses the role of Local Agenda 21 as a mechanism for the co-ordination of local housing strategies incorporating environmental themes. Brown illustrates some of these themes by looking at Leicester's experience in this area.

In chapter 6 **Jane Brooke** explores the debates around housing and sustainability by looking at approaches to urban regeneration. She introduces a framework for developing a symbiotic relationship between housing, the city and the environment. Brooke then looks at Glasgow and assesses green policy responses to housing and urban regeneration. She concludes by emphasising an holistic understanding of the processes of urban change and city-wide environmental impacts. A number of 'performance indicators' that may enable local authorities to examine the environmental impact of a range of activities within the city are put forward. **Brenda Boardman** assesses the impact of energy conservation measures on low income households and highlights the growth of fuel poverty. She begins by clarifying key concepts in this debate and then outlines the relationship between energy consumption, fuel prices and environmental pollution. Boardman goes on to consider the factors that have increased fuel poverty in recent years and critically assesses energy efficiency measures. The chapter highlights growing social polarisation whereby the homes of the better off are being improved at a faster rate than that of the poor; proposed Government measures are likely to reinforce this situation.

In chapter 8 **Yvonne Rydin** considers a number of approaches to greening the private housing market. The prevailing (technocentric) approach is examined because it takes current structures of the market as given. The implications of small and modest changes being proposed, both from within the market place and through government regulations are critically assessed. The approach is criticised for failing to take into account the conflicting role of various agents involved in housing provision. Rydin then offers an alternative model for highlighting key structural features of capitalist housing provision that act as barriers to environmental improvements; she concludes by suggesting ways in which these relationships could be reorganised. In contrast to the technocentric approach **Fionn Stevenson** takes an ecocentric perspective and shows how this can be applied in architecture. She starts with a critical review of training, the role of users, team work, and technology in current architectural practice. Using illustrations and examples from practice, Stevenson highlights the role of the architect and barriers to green thinking and green practice. She suggests that user participation, low technology, and a more enabling profession are important vehicles for greening the design process. However, she goes further by proposing a green model for housing design and practice which involves an understanding of housing as a native eco-system. Stevenson explains this model by using the metaphor of a woodland as a living organism. This radical viewpoint incorporates a 'systems' approach to housing and involves the development of new structures of housing design and practice.

Chapter 10 shows how environmental assessment systems can be used for evaluating current development practice, and **Sue Barker-Wolff** illustrates this by looking at opportunities and problems encountered by one development agency in the social housing sector. She begins by reviewing the most widely used system (known as the Building Research Establishment Environmental Assessment Method (BREEAM)) and shows how it has been applied in the housing industry. Barker-Wolff explores the limitations and opportunities of this approach by looking at a housing association development that started with green principles at the outset. She concludes by highlighting barriers to the penetration of green building methods and argues for improved standards, financial incentives, more information, and statutory building regulations relating to energy efficiency. **Jon Broome** focuses on community self-build and emphasises the role of users in greening the building process. He starts by making a case for self-build in the context of current housing provision and then goes on to explore the 'Walter Segal building method'. Broome shows how this approach is environmentally friendly in the way it uses technology, materials, and labour, as well as the simplicity of the construction process itself. He outlines a number of areas where self-build can make positive environmental impacts such as cutting energy consumption in construction, reducing embodied energy of the house, avoiding harmful materials, and enhancing the local environment. Many of these benefits arise from the fact that people are actually involved in the design and building process; they can construct houses co-operatively that meet their long term needs. Broome illustrates the approach by looking at a self-build project completed in 1994. In chapter 12 we return to the main themes in the book and evaluate the implications of the new environmental agenda for future housing policy and practice. We start by highlighting the tensions and barriers to a green approach that currently exist in the housing system and suggest ways in which these could be overcome. We believe that there are many opportunities that currently exist and these need to be taken seriously. Housing is undergoing rapid change and there are indications that given an imaginative approach, housing and environmental issues can be coherently integrated.

Conclusion

The importance of considering environmental issues in the housing process must not be underestimated. The provision of housing is a basic necessity that consumes a vast amount of natural resources. The use of these resources must therefore be a central issue for housing providers, environmentalists and users alike. Global environmental problems now upon us are occurring at a time of major change in the housing system. This may present us with an opportunity for green issues to become an important part of future housing debate. For housing to make a positive contribution towards sustainability we believe that a greener approach to housing policy and practice is required. This is not an optional extra but a way of achieving qualitative improvements in housing provision for the benefit of users, landlords, and the economy. The book attempts to link together issues of sustainability, housing inequality, and global and local environmental change so that co-ordinated policy responses at several levels can be developed. We hope to suggest ways in which a greener approach in the management and development of housing can be introduced. The contributions in the book show how policy makers, users, and practitioners can take up the environmental challenge.

CHAPTER 2: Environmental Futures and the Housing Question

Mark Bhatti

It is a paradox that in recent years more and more housing research is being conducted, housing journals have been established, there has been dramatic growth in housing education, and yet housing debates have retreated from wider issues. Indeed the present period is characterised by a failure to actually pose 'The Housing Question' for the 1990s. This is as much a crisis of housing policy as of housing analysis, and has resulted in some of the major concerns of our time, particularly environmental issues, being neglected. The idea of sustainability has not been critically debated in the housing literature and the environmental dimension of the housing process has yet to be fully explored. Potentially the study of housing has a lot to say about the future of 'spaceship earth', but so far it has failed to address the environmental impact of housing activities. 'The Housing Question' arises out of a political desire to tackle housing problems. Historically concern over housing conditions in the urban arena has led to varying forms of state intervention and housing studies has developed specifically to analyse these policies. At the same time established academic disciplines such as sociology and economics have focused on housing as a means of explaining wider social change. However, housing academics have not drawn attention to the environmental crisis. For example, recent texts on housing policy and theory such as Malpass and Murie (1994), and Kemeny (1992) say very little about the environmental constraints of housing provision, or about the impact of housing activities. Why has this been so? One reason is that housing studies is increasingly orientated towards short term issues. Murie and Williams (1993) argue that during the 1980s successive Conservative governments have set the pace for housing reform, forcing academics to respond in the housing debate rather than explore long term social and economic changes in the housing system. There has also been a shift of emphasis by the funders towards policy research; what the state does and does not do has become the driving force behind what is to be studied. Thus parameters for housing research are taken from state activity rather than from wider debates in society.

Housing studies appears not to be engaging with key analytical debates and is growing apart from theoretical advances in the social sciences. As Murie and Williams suggest this may account for the current weakness in housing studies. If this is the case then housing providers will find it very difficult to talk with environmentalists. The tools, that is, the concepts with which understanding and explanation can be developed for policy development and action, appear to be missing. As currently constituted housing studies is ill-equipped to explore environmental processes. So how can housing studies engage in the environmental debate? The suggestion here is that 'The Housing Question' of the future must embrace environmental concerns. In short the policy solutions to major housing problems need to be sustainable for the planet. This requires the establishment of greener housing policies and practices, as the contributions in this book suggest, but at the same time it is necessary to explain and understand fully the links between housing and the environment.

The main concern of this chapter is to remedy the deficiency of environmental analysis in the housing literature and to establish a two-way dialogue between housing studies and environmentalism. The aim is to show that green policy and practice in housing can be enhanced by engaging in contemporary environmental debates. Housing can make a major contribution to the development of environmental policy. The way in which housing is produced and maintained, and in the way it contributes to social life, has major implications for the environment. Exploring these interactions means looking at the way in which environmental resources enable the housing process to take place, as well as assessing the environmental impact of housing activities. The first section discusses key ideas from the environmental literature; however modern environmentalism is characterised by contrasting approaches which have major implications for the greening of housing. In the second section a socio-ecological model for understanding the relationship between housing and environment is put forward. It is argued that this model must be overlaid by a theoretical account of the capitalist structure of housing provision. The third section evaluates the greening of the 'home'; and finally, 'environmental poverty' and 'home ecology' are proposed as key concepts for introducing a green dimension into contemporary housing studies.

Perspectives on the Environment

Behind policy solutions and daily management practices lie assumptions about the way in which society works, about the nature of individuals and households, and the way they interact within the housing system. Certain concepts can sensitise us to these processes and reveal the underlying mechanisms of resource allocation. However the study of housing is characterised by a diversity of approaches and perspectives. This in many ways reflects that complexity of the subject; for example, Basset and Short (1980) suggest:

> *"Housing is a heterogeneous, durable and essential consumer good; a direct indicator of status and income differences between consumers; a map of social relations within the city; an important facet of residential structure; a source of bargaining and conflict between various power groupings; and a source of profit to different institutions and agents involved in the production, exchange and consumption of housing"* (p.1).

Furthermore, as Saunders and Williams (1988) argue the concept of 'home' is an important theme for future housing research. Given this scope it is useful to see housing as having a substantive focus, which could be the house, home or residence, depending on the questions being asked. Considering the multi-dimensional nature of housing then, it would be surprising if housing studies had nothing to say about environmental issues.

The environmental dimension of housing provision relates to the nature of housing itself, that is, the particular features of the way it is produced, exchanged, managed and used. Housing is a basic necessity. People seek protection from the climate and need shelter with adequate sanitation and appropriate heating and ventilation; in the process of providing such shelter natural resources are consumed. Because the dwelling outlives its occupants, the way in which houses are built and maintained has major implications for the ability of future generations to meet their housing needs. This aspect introduces a long term perspective into the management and maintenance of dwellings. Furthermore, given that houses cannot generally be moved around the country, dwellings must be durable and flexible so that resources to meet new needs are not used up unnecessarily. Therefore they must be flexible enough to meet the needs of a range of households at different stages of the family life cycle, but durable enough to last several generations. Houses are also expensive to build and costly to run. In Britain most households cannot buy outright so they either rent or get a loan; this means that consumers are part of a 'web of relations' making up the housing system. A holistic view of housing shows that key decisions are taken at the highest levels of the system, and permeate down, having a major impact on the environment, economy and society. For example, a failure of mortgage lenders to insist on energy ratings for houses at the time of purchase means that owner occupiers have little information on the energy efficiency of the home they are buying, and may be unable to conserve fuel with perverse social, economic and environmental results. Housing can even act as a barrier to necessary consumption as when households are in 'fuel poverty' or in 'negative equity'. Finally, the supply of housing cannot be turned on or off like a tap to meet changes in demand. This means that future planning for long term replacement, rehabilitation, and maintenance is required. Again this involves thinking about the resources needed in the future for meeting housing needs that can be identified now.

In examining the environmental dimension of the housing process a number of key ideas from the green literature need to be discussed. It is important to note however that there are disagreements over the meanings of these terms, and often quite fierce debates arising from contrasting perspectives on the causes and solutions to environmental problems.

The term **'environment'** causes much confusion. It has several dimensions: the local or built environment, the natural environment, and the social environment. An environment means 'context' or the surroundings within which some form of activity takes place. In the housing literature environment often refers to the neighbourhood or location of dwellings in a particular area. Thus access to amenities such as leisure, shops, schools, health centres, and parks is usually an indication of the 'environmental quality' of a locality. Housing practitioners, and some academics, (for example, Coleman, 1985), see environmental problems as the presence of vandalism, dog mess, derelict ground and litter. The solutions to these are often described as 'environmental improvements'. The housing market reinforces this definition as it works on the basis of residential segregation which generates a differential access to environmental goods. This is a 'localised' meaning of environment, one that we think is important to keep. The green axiom of 'thinking globally and acting locally' assumes that we take account of the character of our local environment and act to improve it.

The second dimension refers to **'natural' or 'ecological'** processes such as occur in a meadow, a forest, the atmoshere, the oceans etc. Ecology is the study of relationships between plants and animals (including humans) and their natural environment (Owen, 1980). Every living organism exists in some form of natural relationship with other living things within a physical world, and this creates a local and global eco-system. The focus is on relationships and not on isolated 'things'; there is a mutual dependence of human and non-human beings and change does not occur in isolation. It has been suggested by some scientists, (for example, Lovelock 1979), that even though the natural environment is complex, it is self regulating and remains in a delicate balance. The earth provides free 'eco-services' to support life on the planet: clean air, water, flora and fauna, energy etc., which, if not destroyed, maintain optimum life supporting systems. An ecological perspective also challenges the idea that humans stand over and above the nature, as they could not survive without other organisms or the physical world.

This leads us on to looking at the third dimension of environment which refers to the social context, or **'socio-economic relations'.** Environmental problems such as global warming and ozone depletion arise out of the interactions between our socially created 'way of life', the 'built environment', and 'natural processes'. It is important to recognise that humans interact with the natural environment and use nature's resources; for example, we turn trees into wood to provide shelter. This helps us to relate our different aspects of the environment: natural resources are used in a particular way arising from the social and economic system to shape the built environment of which housing is a significant part. As Peter Dickens suggests social relations are embedded in natural processes (Dickens 1992), that is, social relations mediate natural relations within a specific geographical context. What is popularly called the 'environment' is a mixture of ecological processes, the built environment, and social and economic relations. A rounded analysis of the interactions between housing and the environment must attempt to relate all three dimensions of 'environment'. In the environmental studies literature the interactions between the natural and economic processes are seen to be very important in generating problems (see Dobson 1990). One major task for us then is to devise concepts in order to understand and explain how these processes inter-relate in housing to generate environmental problems.

Most environmentalists start from the basis that there are 'natural' limits to the earth's capacity to provide resources and absorb pollution; in short there cannot be infinite growth in a finite system. For example, The Limits to Growth report concludes:

> *"If the present growth trends in world population, industrialisation, pollution, food production, and resource depletion continue unchanged, the limits to growth will be reached sometime within the next one hundred years. The most probable result will be a rather sudden and uncontrollable decline in both population and industrial capacity"*
>
> *"It is possible to alter these growth trends and to establish a condition of ecological and economic stability that is sustainable for the future"* (Meadows et al 1983, p.29).

The present environmental crisis is seen to be the result of unprecedented, uncontrollable, and permanent growth in world economies and population. Indeed we have reached a stage where, if we do nothing, then problems will increase until human life itself is threatened. It is increasingly being recognised that cities play a determining role in environmental degradation. Cities make a potentially heavy demand on the natural environment; they require food, fresh water, energy and materials for building, commerce, manufacture, and mobility (Elkin et al 1991, Giradet 1992). Cities produce solid and liquid wastes, as well as CO_2 and other noxious emissions. Indeed the Brundtland report focuses on 'world cities' and argues:

> *"These cities account for a high share of the world's resource use, energy consumption, and environmental pollution. Many have a global reach and draw their resources and energy from distant lands with enormous aggregate impacts on the ecosystems of those lands"* (WCED 1987 p.241).

Agenda 21 also emphasises the significance of cities as a key factor in issues of sustainable development (LGMB 1992 Chapter 7). Urbanism in the developed countries has received considerable attention as the motor for the generation of major environmental problems. Therefore environmental action in cities is increasingly being seen as the key to overcoming these problems. 'Sustainable cities' is now a key concept bringing together issues of transport, energy, housing, employment, food production and supply, waste and pollution, as well as green spaces. These ideas are now at the centre of debates on the way the built environment should be planned and managed (Elkin et al 1991, Breheny 1992a, Agyeman and Evans 1994). In the housing context then it is important to talk about 'sustainable housing development' and emphasise the role that the housing system plays in the promotion of sustainable cities.

Even though there is a shared purpose amongst environmentalists that 'something must be done', there is some disagreement over how problems are to be resolved. **'Environmentalism'** (or **'green'** with a lower case 'g') denotes a concern for the negative impact our 'way of life' has on the local as well as global environment. But 'care for the environment' can take many forms. Modern environmentalism is characterised by contrasting explanations of environmental problems and competing solutions, which have major implications for greening housing policy and practice. Knowledge of underlying assumptions and competing 'green' theories is important if practitioners are not to accept uncritically the conventional environmental agenda. Delving deeper into environmental analyses shows that choices can be made about the direction of green housing policies. Reviewing the various environmental positions in detail is beyond the scope of this chapter (for a discussion see Dobson 1990, Pepper 1984), but by outlining just two, **'Techno-centricism'** and **'Eco-centricism'**, as opposite sides of the continuum, it is possible to see more clearly the alternative perspectives and the radically different solutions being proposed.

'Techno-centrics' accept that there are natural limits and ecological problems, but argue that these can be solved without any fundamental change in society. Some in this camp (the cornucopians) suggest, rather optimistically, that there are plenty of resources for everyone and our society can go beyond the limits and achieve growth through human ingenuity, science and technology. Others however (the accommodators) are more cautious and suggest that sustainable growth can only be achieved through careful management of resources, and the sensitising of markets to environmental problems. What characterises this whole approach is that it is human-centred. Thus environmental problems are only important so far as they impact on the ability of humans to enjoy life on earth. According to O'Riordan this view is underpinned by:

> "*...a sense of* **optimism and faith** *in the ability of man to understand and control physical, biological and social processes for the benefit of present and future generations*" (O'Riordan 1981 original emphasis p.11).

It is argued that, handled with care, the earth can provide resources and absorb pollution and waste. There is confidence that the application of science and technology can be combined with efficient management to overcome environmental problems. There is a firm belief in current institutional arrangements and an assumption that everyone can ultimately accept responsibility for the environment through the market place.

This approach is based on the assumption that markets can take the lead in developing environmentally friendly practices. Pearce et al (1989) suggest that there is no market for environmental goods and services:

> *"The central problem is that many of these services are provided 'free'. They have a zero price simply because no market exists in which their true values can be revealed through the acts of buying and selling"* (p.5)

Pearce argues that degradation results because the environment is treated as a zero-priced resource when in fact it serves economic functions that have a positive value. Because they are 'free', environmental goods are over-consumed and this leads to the incapacity of the natural environment to meet the demand. 'Free' environmental services hide the true cost of goods and services from the consumer, while production costs are kept down for the producer. In short the market does not reflect the full cost of the production of goods. The environment is also treated as a negative 'externality' so that the impact of production is not costed or taken into account in the price of the product. For example, the development of a new housing estate does not include costings for a beautiful view that may be lost forever, or the increase in CO_2 emissions from energy use, or damage caused by the increase in car based traffic in the area. The solution Pearce offers is to make the market place 'value the environment' on the principle that resources and environments serve economic functions and have a positive value. Pearce wishes to attach monetary values to environmental gains and losses, what he refers to as 'monetization'. These act as a measure of the degree of concern that individuals place upon a particular environmental good articulated via the market place. According to this view by attaching monetary values to environmental goods and services, it is possible to measure the willingness of individuals to pay for a given environmental quality and thereby help the market to improve it.

A number of implications follow from placing monetary values on environmental goods. Clearly if such values can be placed then it is likely that a market can be generated, which implies that certain environmental goods can be privatised. It is also possible to establish cost-benefit analysis for any action: the 'environment' becomes a part of the equation, a cost that has to be met. Finally, as the environment becomes a commodity like any other with a supply cost, the true cost of the production of goods and services can be charged, and the market place will signal changes to the process of production for resources to be used more efficiently. In theory this should also cut waste and introduce recycling thereby reducing pollution. The aim of course is to keep production costs down to remain competitive. Where there are finite resources these will have higher prices and be used more efficiently.

It is also argued that the 'green consumer' must lead the way and Pearce suggests:

> *"If consumers change their tastes in favour of less polluting products and against more polluting forces, market forces will lead to a change in the 'pollution content' of the final product and services"* (1989 p.155).

Some have seen the 'green consumer' as the driving force behind saving the planet (Elkington and Hailes 1988). Individual preferences of the purchaser are seen to be the key in forcing producers to 'clean up their act', to produce environmentally friendly products, and for everyone to accept responsibility for the environment. More than this, some capitalists have actively taken advantage of the green consumer as a market niche to be cultivated. The outcome of this approach is the focus on short term solutions with the market as the central mechanism for tackling environmental problems. This may not ensure long term sustainability for the planet. Yvonne Rydin in chapter 8 draws out the implications of greening the housing market using the techno-centric approach.

On the other side the **Eco-centrics** or the Deep Greens (for example Porritt 1986) challenge the view that human wants and desires should dominate the natural world. There is a rejection of the 'technical fix' of the previous approach, thus environmental problems created by advanced industrial technology and growth cannot be solved by that same technology. An eco-centric view goes beyond saving the planet for the sake of human survival. In contrast the natural world must be saved *for its own sake*. There is no hierarchical organisation of the world in which humans stand at the pinnacle, and are at liberty to use the earth as they wish for their own ends. Environmental problems can only be overcome through a radical change in our personal and social relations which means a fundamental rethink of our relationship with nature. This relationship is based around the idea that all life has value, and nature has its own rights and limits which must be respected. For example Naess argues:

> *"For us it is the eco-sphere, the whole planet, Gaia, that is the basic unit, and every living thing had intrinsic value"* (Naess 1990 p.135).

Eco-centrics suggest that humans are subject to the same 'natural laws' as any other natural being and must be seen as one part of the global eco-system. Nature is to be respected with human and non-human nature having equal rights. We are all seen as part of a 'web of relations' whereby each part is essential and makes up the whole. Greens have a holistic view and just as the natural world is complex and diverse, and yet stable, the solution to environmental problems must aim to bring together interacting processes and themes for long term sustainability. The Greens also argue for social justice, freedom, and democracy whereby the liberation of humanity goes hand in hand with the liberation of nature. Thus the exploitation of the developing countries is rejected as well as the domination of women. As Kemp and Wall point out:

> *"The Green Movement is very much a women's movement and eco-feminists.... argue that patriarchy and male domination are the root causes of environmental catastrophe"* (1990 p.19).

There is belief in subsidiarity, i.e. decentralised power structures allow decisions to be made at the lowest level possible. And there is a spiritual side which is based around the rejection of material things and an economic view of humans and nature. Humans will never be happy, even with ample consumer durables, unless there is a spiritual outlet so that we can be close to nature.

The outcome of an eco-centric view is the creation of a more 'sustainable society' through a radical shift in social and political values whereby society is able to produce and consume at a level that conserves the earth's resources, causes the minimum amount of pollution, and produces minimum waste. Exactly *how* this is to be achieved is still a matter of intense debate which reveals a number of tensions within the political ecology movement. For example, Pepper points to the divisions:

> *"If politically to the right they may emphasise the idea of limits, advocating compulsory restraints on human breeding, levels of resource consumption and access to the 'commons'. If to the left, their emphasis may be more on decentralised, democratic, small scale communities using 'soft' technology and renewable energy, 'acting locally and thinking globally' "* (Pepper 1993 p.33).

The discussion above suggests that there are many shades of green. But environmental studies does have something to offer the housing movement, especially if policy makers and practitioners are to develop long term housing strategies. Even so, given the lack of agreement on precisely how environmental problems are to be understood, and quite bitter conflict about what is to be done, it is not surprising that in weighing up both perspectives the techno-centric view is perhaps the convention in Britain today; i.e., most action on environmental issues starts from where we are now and assumes incremental change. As Rydin suggests in chapter 8, many of the measures designed to 'green the housing market' are modest, small adjustments to existing operations of the housing system. However, techno-centric approaches can lead to short term solutions which in the long run become a part of the problem. They may be partial and fragmented, presenting an unco-ordinated approach to solving environmental problems caused by a range of housing activities. Eco-centric solutions on the other hand may open up a range of alternative options that challenge current practice. For example, the self-build approach presented by Jon Broome in chapter 11 can emphasise radically different ways of living and providing housing. Or as Fionn Stevenson shows in chapter 9 an eco-system approach can re-evaluate housing design practice. However these ideas may appear too radical and are often marginalised by policy makers working with conventional ideas of the environment. The dichotomies between eco-centricism and techno-centricism often exist in the realm of philosophical and political debate. Indeed they are ends of a continuum with several positions in between; the positions are less conflicting when practical action is considered. There may even be many shared policy goals, for example, recycling or promoting energy efficient homes. Even so, why certain solutions are being proposed, and the limitations of green housing policy, can only be adequately understood with reference back to the underlying assumptions of the environmental perspectives outlined above.

Housing as a Socio-ecological Process

Traditional housing analyses are rather limited in exploring the environmental dimensions of the housing system. This is in part because of the inadequacy of conceptual tools to explore the environmental impacts of the housing process. Housing is not only an economic good and social service, but it is at the same time a **'Socio-ecological Process'**; i.e. it involves the transformation of natural resources, via labour power into livable spaces. In many ways the house stands at the crossroads of providing shelter, using and reproducing energy, taking resources from the natural environment, delivering waste to the wider community, and perhaps most importantly providing us with social and cultural capital. Once this is recognised the environmental impact of housing activities becomes transparent and the way the natural environment enables, sets limits to, and mediates the housing process can be examined. It may then be possible to develop mechanisms for increasing ecological value rather than economic value.

Figure 1 offers a model for incorporating an ecological dimension to the life cycle of the house(see Rydin 1992a). The diagram illustrates the main phases at which natural resources are used and environmental impacts are activated. At the project conception stage certain choices are made which mean that opportunities for environmental enhancement or conservation are lost. For example, a decision to site housing on a greenfield site as opposed to a brown field site means that a claim is made on new land thereby closing off opportunities for nature conservation. Moreover this stage is crucial in helping to establish sets of spatial relationships which then flow into demands for infrastructure and transport. Given the long term impact of choices at this stage it may be appropriate to ask questions relating to the most environmentally friendly use of the site: can different uses be accommodated in the future? How does the development fit into existing uses for land and infrastructure? Does it increase energy use or reduce it? Land use planners are now beginning to ask these types

Figure 1 Environmental impacts of building production and building use during a full building life-cycle

Project conception and brief	Design	Construction phase	Building use	Refurbishment	Obsolescence, demolition
Is the project the most appropriate use for the resources employed (land, energy, minerals etc.)? Is the project capable of accommodating appropriate uses throughout its life span? Does the project complement existing infrastructure which will permit environment friendly uses?	Is the design drawing on all available experience for resource conservation (energy, water, etc.)? Will the design generate useful new experiences to improve future building projects? Is the design of human scale and conducive to simple life styles, (e.g. use of outdoor spaces, cycling, preparation of food)?	Is disruption (noise, dust, traffic etc.) kept down to the unavoidably necessary? Are toxic substances and hazardous processes handled safely? Does the construction process avoid unnecessary dangerous or noxious site procedures?	Do users accept and understand building facilities which permit more environment friendly life styles? Does the building enhance personal comfort and well-being when the environmental impact is at the intended level? Does the building contribute to a supportive environment for people of all needs (e.g. children and young people)?	Are large-scale replacements of building components necessary, or are small-scale repairs possible? Can refurbishment periods be extended by initial specification and careful maintenance? Can building components be taken from, or returned to a recycling pool?	Can alternative uses be found, when the economic building life expires before the physical life? Can redevelopment make a positive contribution to local environmental impact (see project conception and brief)? Is noxious building waste handled safely?
● foregoing opportunity to conserve resources, use resources elsewhere or for a different purpose ● claim on land ● creation of new spatial and land use relationships ● demands on infrastructure ● changing travel patterns, transport requirements	● claim on stock and live resources as construction material ● claim on stock and live resources for construction process ● impact on flora and fauna during building life ● impact on local environment, microclimate, daylighting ● indoor living/working conditions ● impact on global	● use of stock resources ● construction traffic ● construction noise ● airborne pollution ● construction waste ● water consumption ● energy consumption ● toxic substances ● health and safety of site operatives ● materials	● safety of surroundings ● benefits/disbenefits to users and community ● indoor environment and users' health ● microclimate ● impact of fauna and flora ● waste ● toxic substances ● energy consumption	● write-off of existing building fabric with embodied resources ● construction traffic and noise ● airborne pollution ● construction waste ● water consumption ● energy consumption ● toxic substances	● blight ● waste, release of hazardous substances ● provision of land for new development cycle ● destruction of heritage ● energy consumption

of questions (Blowers 1993a). The next stage is devising the layout of the estate and the design of the house itself. Again this is an important juncture because architects incorporate features which can either have negative impacts or enhance the local and global environment. Thus siting for maximum solar gain; the design of heating and lighting systems; specifications for materials that are to be used for construction; the durability and flexibility of the dwelling; the scale of the buildings; the disposal of the dwelling at the end of its life; the aesthetics that portray a particular life style. All these features have a significance throughout the whole life of the house. Construction itself has major impacts. There is considerable use of energy and disruption to the local environment as well as the release of toxic substances used during this phase. Again it is possible to minimise these or exclude them all together. For example Jon Broome in chapter 11 shows how capital intensive, as opposed to labour intensive methods of construction, are likely to use more energy.

The use of the house is one of the most crucial areas of environmental impact. Heating and lighting, preparation of food, leisure, gardening, working at home, DIY and many more activities of daily living involve consuming goods and services in and around the house, which themselves require natural resources for their production. Thus the house is a container for an infinite number of activities, indeed a major part of life itself. The form of daily life may be shaped by the tenure, standard, design, and condition of the house. Energy use or health of the occupants has a direct relationship to the dwelling. The nature of the house itself, its physical aspects, the size, and location may enhance or inhibit environmentally friendly practices. If 'saving the earth begins at home' then housing studies needs to unpick the interaction of people and their homes, and show how this can be a significant force for sustainability.

Because houses have a long life they have to be repaired and maintained using resources and materials, and again these may be energy intensive depending on how it is done and the scale of the refurbishment. However it is also at this stage that energy inefficient houses can be improved. As only one percent of dwellings are new in any one year the refurbishment of older houses to increase environmental standards is important and should be an expanding activity. Thus not only is the life of the house extended, but houses built without the benefit of environmental considerations can be updated. For example, the incorporation of energy saving features during routine refurbishment can have dramatic affects on fuel costs. As Jane Brooke points out in chapter 6, renewal of older housing has to be energy conscious with an emphasis on capital investment in energy efficiency measures. Finally, as the life of the house comes to an end questions of what to do with the building, the site, and the material are pertinent; can the site be used for new housing? Can the building material be recycled? Where does the waste go? Redevelopment raises many of the issues that we started with in the project conception and design.

It is possible to ask environmentally informed questions using the model above for any system of building. Thus self build, or social sector development and management, or owner occupation can be incorporated into this model. We could add an exchange phase, as well as one for finance. Breaking the housing process down is useful because it helps us to see the multitude of ways in which housing has major implications for the local and global environments. However it is important to overlay this socio-ecological model with the particular 'structure of housing provision' in a capitalist economy (Ball 1986, Ball and Harloe 1992). What does this mean for an environmentally informed analysis of housing? Firstly, the production, exchange and consumption of housing is based on the profit motive and capitalists are concerned to realise surplus value at certain stages. Various forms of capital are involved, in this case industrial capital, commercial capital, landowners, and loan capital, who all want to maximise profits and so tend to be in conflict. This suggests that the system is inherently unstable and fragmented; any long term ecological concerns to conserve resources, reduce energy, or prevent pollution, in short to increase ecological value, are likely to be marginalised. For example, pressure on development on greenfield sites is greatest because it reduces the cost of production, and therefore maximises profits, and yet these developments may cause untold damage to the local environment.

Secondly, as the capitalist system is crisis prone, the peaks and troughs have major effects on the housing process. Harvey (1985) suggests that housing investment represents one part of the overall investment in the urban environment which is linked to various circuits of capital. Thus overproduction (or under consumption) in one sector leads to capital outflows into 'fixed' capital such as land and buildings. In this process many old investments may simply be written off and housing areas can be redeveloped or left redundant (for example areas of Glasgow, see chapter 6). The built environment experiences cycles of building activity but overall expansion and growth is inherent in the housing system as greater surplus value can be extracted from new commodity production. The system writes off housing assets in favour of new developments and in the process takes more land, materials, and energy. Quite simply repair and re-use of housing, designed to be flexible enough for long term household needs is not an objective of the capitalist housing system. Harvey also points to suburbanisation, the spread of home ownership, and consumption based lifestyles, as a way for capitalism to mitigate the effects of over production and create new markets. The argument here is that suburbanisation is an environmentally unsustainable form of housing development as it is associated with the development of greenfield sites, individualised modes of consumption, private transport, single family dwellings, and mass consumption goods.

Thirdly, housing requires natural resources and energy as well as land, labour power, finance and capital. This means that 'free' natural resources required for housing production are over-exploited as they offer a simple means for cutting costs thereby increasing profits. The system is prevented from adopting environmentally friendly practices unless profits can be realised easily. Finally, capitalist uneven development produces a housing system that is based around generating residential segregation. Thus the balance of tenures, location of dwellings, and social status are the outcome of employment opportunities, the local housing market and institutional discrimination which combine to generate inequalities. One major aspect of residential segregation is that it introduces unequal access to environmental goods and services. Thus operation of the housing market works to exclude low income groups from areas with natural amenities and clean local environments. Finally, under capitalism, housing is both a commodity and it has a use value, i.e. it is a 'home' for workers and their families. Housing plays an important part in the overall well being of people and the psychological and social dimensions of home are just as important as the provision of shelter. Households value the use of the house and with it various aspects of living in a particular place. Because housing has a major impact on the environment, it is important to discover the social and cultural conditions under which needs are actualised in and around the home.

The Greening of the Home

There is a tradition of 'consumption as display' in capitalist societies which is concerned with enjoyment, taste, identity, style and status differentiation. In Britain this aspect of consumption has recently emerged as an important dimension in housing analysis (Saunders 1990). The Greens have traditionally emphasised the role of consumption in modern industrial societies for generating environmental problems. For example, Porrit argues:

> *"...in order to achieve growth, more things must be produced. And for more things to be produced, more things must be consumed. The more people consume, the better it is. The shorter the life of a product, the better it is.... Consumption becomes an end in itself"* (1986, p.47).

However environmentalists have not fully considered the significance of the idea of 'home' as a key to understanding and overcoming these problems. If consumption patterns have major impacts on the environment then it is important to discover the social and cultural conditions under which these take place, and to determine what motivates people into a particular 'way of life'. The suggestion here is that the idea of 'home' is important in at least two ways: as a basis for consumption patterns which have a major environmental significance; and as a locus for natural relations. The home is a major factor in shaping people's life styles and consumption patterns and hence their use of resources which have multi-impacts on the environment. This can be seen most clearly in the 'ideal home' project which found expression most vividly in suburban Britain from the inter-war period onwards. As Tomlinson explains:

> *"Suburban consumers wanted, first, a sense of the past built into their homes, whilst craving new labour-saving appliances. Second they aspired to a cosy internal environment, but alongside an expansive outlook towards the great outdoors... ambiguity in their suburban culture was expressed in a thrifty approach to spending and consuming which ran alongside the desire to display affluence. Finally the suburban dweller wanted a practical house, but with a hint of modernity"* (1990, p.64).

In this context the 'ideal home' related specifically to individually owned single family dwellings characterised by the house itself as 'a place' called home. The notion of home that underpins the current period can be summed up as a movement away from 'keeping up with the Joneses' to 'being different from the Joneses'. Who we are becomes associated with the kind of house we have, where we live, and the objects we possess.

The fact that this search for difference through the home causes major environmental problems has not been adequately discussed in the housing literature. There is little doubt that today green consumerism represents an important and growing life style. The 'green consumer' is a growing niche in the market place, now specifically targeted by business. Individual preferences for goods are seen to be the key in forcing producers to 'clean up their act' and to promote environmentally friendly products. In this way everyone accepts responsibility towards the environment through the market place. Indeed some capitalists have actively taken advantage of the green consumer as a particular market to be cultivated. The housing industry is also beginning to respond and a recent report points out that environmental features are increasingly being emphasised:

> *"Any builder who can offer a strong environmental package in terms of the actual building method and in-use performance has an extremely strong selling tool at his (sic) disposal"* (URBED, 1992, p.13).

Today we can all create our own home, as long as it is the one sold to us by Ecover, Habitat or Laura Ashely. This is a process of marketisation, of market penetration into new areas where profits can be very high. The 'way of life' being promoted revolves around the green home, often sold in the 'rustic olde farmhouse' style (closer to nature?), but is associated with increasing consumption of goods. There are numerous guides for would-be green householders, and one of these illustrates the point:

> *"Far from our homes being safe havens, they may be significant contributors to the global problem... So what can you do about it? The answer is a great deal!... Start in simple ways, such as changing your household cleaners... be guided by H is for eco-Home, and make your home a safer healthier and happier place for you and your family"* (Kruger, 1991, p.12-13).

The significance of this is that the 'green home' that is being promoted is based upon *changing* consumption, not necessarily reducing it, and is therefore still environmentally problematic.

However, the promotion and uncritical acceptance of this 'style of life' is coming under increasing attack from environmentalists. The dispersed (suburban) settlement pattern that the 'ideal home' implies means the problem of mobility has to be overcome; the private motor car becomes not just a means of transport but another symbol of stutus and contributes to pollution and congestion. The environmental significance of this has only recently been recognised in urban planning. Historically, estates were built on the false assumption that energy would always be cheap and resources for construction would always be available; this now has to be reassessed. As housing design became standardised the siting and spatial context of the dwellings were not considered to be important. Indeed as Hayden, commenting on the North American experience suggests:

> *"The same house was built facing north, south, east and west because the builders didn't care about the position of the sun so much as the profitability of the tract"* (Hayden, 1984, p.46).

Moreover, developers market their products by appealing to the assumed core feelings of convenience, status and unique style. The 'ideal home' could only function through the unpaid labour of women, and the purchase of a range of consumer appliances. Thus each family acquired its own cooker, washing machine, refrigerator, television etc. for the (re)production of labour, dependent upon specific gender roles. Achieving status through the home meant the house has to be kept at its best; objects for display rather than use, and often they have to be continually changed to confirm status. But to establish status in this way means that households have to engage in consumption patterns that are unsustainable for the environment.

The home is also a key to understanding people's relationship with the natural world. Notions of home range from locale, family, and nation, and must now include the planet earth. It also seems rational to consider the everyday practices of households and the type of natural relations they are involved in. Key processes that involve interactions with the natural world relate to having and bringing up children, keeping pets, gardening (both indoor and outdoor), leisure activities such as walking in woods or parks; all involve some idea of getting 'close to nature'. Most of these activities are centred in and around the home. People like to get closer to nature and yet we have scarcely begun to research what this means and how it may be facilitated through the housing process. Natural relations are mediated by culture and how these interactions are understood in part reflects the role of the 'natural' in the social construction of the home.

New and emerging notions of home must be located within an overall shift towards an environmental culture, that is, green ideas and everyday practices aimed at care for the environment. The idea of 'Home Ecology' (Christensen 1989) may be useful here, for it focuses on the way households understand and engage in natural relations in their local environment. The idea of home ecology helps us to keep in touch with the natural environment that we all depend upon; it focuses on everyday practices that contribute to a sense of home, based around an awareness of the way we live in our local environment, and the natural resources we use and the waste we release. Home ecology can be seen as a mode of daily living with the aim of increasing ecological value, based on the premise that home is a central part of our ecological awareness; it contributes to our sense of being at one with nature.

Towards the Greening of Housing Studies

The discussion above points to the need for a radical rethink of the subject and object of housing studies. The main suggestion here is that a greener housing study can develop within a broader area of social environmentalism (Weston 1984) which has a long history (Engels' The Condition of the Working Class published in 1854 being an early example); it is linked to environmental planning and social justice as well as having close associations with neo-Marxist housing studies. Social environmentalism encapsulates the needs of citizens, consumers and householders for a healthy urban environment which improves their well being and at the same time ensures the survival of the natural world. It recognises the dependence of humans on the non-human world and seeks to sustain natural resources for the equitable reproduction of all. It accepts physical as well as social limits to growth and argues for an environmental culture that incorporates resource conservation, protection of natural areas, healthy cities, and housing needs that go beyond the provision of shelter. Social environmentalism is based around increasing ecological value (as opposed to economic value), for purposes of meeting human needs across the whole population, is concerned with user participation as a method for increasing environmental quality, and demands a safe, clean and green local environment based upon principles of social justice. It starts from the eco-Marxist premise that capitalism generates inequalities as well as environmental problems. To illustrate this approach the concept of 'environmental poverty' may be useful here to help us analyse the way in which environmental resources are unevenly spread through society, with low income households, and those groups who suffer discrimination living in the poorest conditions (Byrne et al 1986, Townsend 1979). It refers to processes that produce a given level of environmental quality, and takes into account the 'unequal exposure' of households to atmospheric pollution, noise, dirt, and traffic congestion. Environmental poverty can also help us to focus on the 'lack of access' to gardens, play spaces, parks, and other facilities. The table below shows that exposure to pollution and access to environmental goods is closely associated with class.

Table 1 Environmental Deprivation by Occupational Class

FORMS OF ENVIRONMENTAL DEPRIVATION	OCCUPATIONAL CLASS %			
	Professional & Managerial	other non manual	skilled manual	unskilled manual
No sole use of garden	11	17	22	31
Garden too small to sit	1	6	9	14
No safe place for children to play	25	27	35	44
No safe place to play near home	35	32	33	34
Air dirty, smokey or foul smelling	17	22	31	34

SOURCE: Townsend 1979 p.532 table 14.1

As can be seen households in the unskilled manual class were three times as likely to have 'no sole use of garden' than professional and managerial households. Similarly 14% of the former group had small gardens, compared to only 1% of the latter. Place of residence has a major effect on access to natural amenities, as well as leisure facilities, health services, and education. It has also been recognised that location of dwellings is an important factor in the household's experience of noise, dirt, atmospheric and lead pollution. For example, Murie reports studies that show high levels of atmospheric pollution are to be found in areas where households of low socio-economic stutus reside (Murie 1983 p.16). This is backed up by recent evidence which suggests that the percentage of dwellings in 'poor' environments varies from 26% in Inner London to 3% in East Anglia (Elkin et al 1991 p.13). Townsend concludes:

> *"the wealthier households were able to halve their chances of living in polluted surroundings"* (1979 p.541).

This is significant and points us towards the importance of looking at who suffers most from environmental problems. In the context of the debate about sustainability the ability of households to participate in a wider environmental culture involving 'care for the environment', and engage in environmental action to 'save the earth', is in large part determined by their experience of the immediate environment and an understanding of how daily actions affect the global commons. Households suffering from environmental poverty, due in part to the operations of the housing system, are likely to have a weak sense of environmental culture (Agyeman and Bhatti 1994); their 'closeness to nature' is marginal and there is less of a concern to save the planet, and more effort to secure daily living conditions. Indeed as Lowe and Goyder (1983) have shown, the modern 'green' movement is characterised by middle class groups who are concerned to protect 'nature' and wild life, and stop any developments in their backyards.

Confronting housing problems and inequality raises the question of how environmental poverty can be tackled. One approach might be to raise people's income so that they can gain access to cleaner and greener environments. For example, low income households in the inner city may benefit from regular trips out into the countryside. Poor households may even be subsidised to move out to the suburbs or new towns, which had indeed been the general approach in the immediate post war period. However, environmental poverty cannot be tackled in this manner for two reasons.

First, as Beck (1992) has shown, environmental risks pervade the whole society; they affect the rich and the poor alike. Thus moving people around simply shifts the problem for a short while, it does not resolve it. It may make matters worse if increasing numbers of people attempt to gain access to environmental resources that are diminishing. Pressure for housing development on greenbelt land, or traffic congestion in Cumbria are good examples.

Second, subsidising access to increased environmental quality means that public money is spent on consumers themselves for their own immediate benefit rather than for future generations. Environmental poverty can only be tackled by environmental protection combined with increased capital investment in specific localities thereby raising environmental quality for all citizens. For environmental action to succeed and be socially just, means empowering precisely those people who do not now benefit from the system (Bhatti 1993).

Conclusion

To sum up, the main argument here is that housing studies can make major contributions to current environmental debates. The way in which housing is produced and maintained, and in the way it contributes to social life has major implications for the environment. Moving housing studies towards a green agenda means building upon previous insights as well as constructing bridges with environmental studies. Exploring the green critique and its implications for housing are useful starting points for housing studies to begin to engage with environmental issues. It is important to examine the environmental poverty generated by the capitalist structure of housing provision, and at the same time to study how people experience the natural world. A key aspect here is the notion of 'home ecology' in shaping day-to-day relations. Finally, the greening of housing studies can only come about if 'The Housing Question' is posed within the context of sustainability, and it responds effectively to environmental problems. This requires the analysis of housing as a socio-ecological process.

CHAPTER 3: The Greening of Housing Policy

Mike Gibson

Housing policy has recently taken on a green hue. History may record 1994 as a watershed in the development of green housing policy. For the first time capital allocations for social housing were linked to energy efficiency performance. Proposals were announced for a new grant regime, funded by a levy on gas and electricity consumers, to augment resources for energy efficiency investment by private householders. Good practice guides documenting demonstration projects were complemented by a second generation of guidance setting out the requirements for a strategic approach to energy efficiency by local housing authorities. These developments were the first major impacts of the new environmental agenda on national housing policy.

If the momentum of policy development is maintained, a substantial increase in energy investment could be the cutting edge of change towards green housing provision, making a 40% contribution towards the government's post-Rio target of a 10 million tonnes of carbon (Mtc) reduction in CO_2 emissions by the year 2000. Energy efficiency measures could widen beyond improving the thermal efficiency with which housing is used, to reduce the (embodied) energy used to build or renovate houses, and to consider the occupiers' use of transport. A widening range of environmental issues, such as the waste and pollution associated with housing production and use, would be given a higher priority. The location and siting of new housing development would be increasingly influenced by environmental concerns, and housing renovation would be part of sustainable urban regeneration programmes. In this evolving scenario the European Union would provide continuing impetus for the evolution of national, regional and local planning for sustainable urban development. An increasingly holistic policy process would gradually integrate the environmental dimension of central and local government action in the sectors of housing, planning, energy, transport, education, water supply, waste and pollution. Environmentally sensitive housing policy and practice would make a significant contribution to local authorities' key role as environmental protection agencies.

But is this really likely? Whilst the changing climate of ideas and some recent government initiatives augur well, powerful forces will constrain progress. 1994 was also the year the government imposed VAT on fuel, allegedly as a contribution towards achieving its target reduction in CO_2 emission, but without earmarking any of the £2.3 billion per annum tax revenues for energy efficiency investment. 1994 also witnessed further drastic cuts of £600m in social housing investment, reducing the expenditure on energy efficiency measures. The credibility of the post-Rio national environmental strategy has been further undermined by the government's intransigence in pressing ahead with its £23 billion road programme.

This chapter explores the potential, current, and prospective impact of the new environmental agenda on national housing policy. It first identifies a new role for housing policy – that of contributing to environmental policy in the context of the 'greening' of cities. Progress towards this vision of housing as component of sustainable urban development is assessed through a review of the reality of environment related policy and action in the housing sector. The chapter concludes by arguing that significant progress requires a major reorientation of housing policy to achieve targeted energy efficiency investment, as part of a reinvigorated programme of housing and neighbourhood renewal.

Housing Policy Analysis and the New Environmental Agenda

An exploration of the potential environmental role of housing policy needs to link housing policy analysis with the concept of sustainable urban development. A major concern of housing policy analysis is the long standing and continuing debate about the appropriate aims, scope, and instruments of policy. Such analysis shows how successive resolutions of this debate have produced periodic shifts in the orientation and roles of housing policy. In a recent contribution, Clapham et al (1990 ch. 2) identify three interrelated roles of housing policy which have had a greater or lesser significance, with the ebb and flow of state intervention in housing.

Housing as local environmental management originated in public health and safety concerns. The earliest role of housing policy was to ensure minimum housing and environmental standards. The policy responses to poor housing environments included the regulation of new development, from the building by-laws of the 1870s through to current building and planning regulations. But this role is most fully expressed in the housing and neighbourhood renewal strand of policy from the earliest slum clearance measures to the Renewal Area, Estate Action and Housing Action Trust programmes of the 1990s.

Housing as social welfare expresses the egalitarian belief that all citizens should have a right to decent housing. As the welfare state evolved in the 1950s this concern led to the direct provision of new housing by local authorities, let at subsidised rents to a wide range of people in need.

Housing as a market commodity is a third perspective emphasising the pre-eminence of the market in meeting housing needs, restricting direct state provision to that of meeting special needs, increasingly by (part privately financed) housing associations. This role focuses on government subsidy of market provision through fiscal instruments, including mortgage interest tax relief and capital gains tax exemption.

The new environmental agenda emphasises further social concerns which housing policy has only recently begun to address and will lead to a new fourth role; **housing provision as a component of sustainable urban development.** This agenda poses questions about the relationship between housing provision and global environmental change – what are the impacts of housing on the natural environment and what can be done to minimise adverse effects? It focuses on: "...the over-arching needs of environmental protection and resource conservation" (Elkin 1991 p.3). But it also stresses intergenerational and intragenerational equity, questioning the social sustainability of contemporary processes of urban growth and decay which produce the deepening contrast between affluent owner-occupied suburbs and impoverished council estates. This points to the need to reduce housing inequality and redefine housing's local environmental management role, to bring the standards of declining neighbourhoods much closer to those of the rest of the city. Moreover, the emphasis on futurity challenges policy makers to think these issues through well into the 21st century, rather than the date of the next General Election.

In their discussion of the three long established roles of housing policy Clapham et al point out that:

> *"...the environmental, social welfare and economic aspects of housing policy have co-existed for much of the present century and it would be erroneous to assume that any one has or is likely to supersede another substantially."* (1991 p.22)

But the view that housing should be regarded primarily as a market commodity has held sway since 1979. In the context of a continuing restructuring of the welfare state, housing provision has moved from a 'social democratic model' towards a 'market model' with a concomitant move towards a minimalist role for the state. This has led to the progressive privatisation of housing provision, involving sustained reductions in public capital investment in both new building and housing renewal, the subsidised promotion of home ownership and the reduction of the local authority role by tenure transfer.

The new environmental agenda has emerged since the late 1980s in parallel with this major and continuing transformation of housing policy. The greening of housing policy will initially focus on improving the energy efficiency of the nation's housing stock, particularly existing housing. Since the 19th century, concerns for 'public health' have continued to prompt housing improvement action. However, if concerns for 21st century 'global health' are to engender the development of a new environmental role for housing policy, a metamorphosis of current housing and neighbourhood renewal programmes will be required. Minimum 'public health' standards – the fitness standard – will need redefining to include 'global health' standards for energy efficiency. In the new environmental management role for housing policy, local renewal action will have a global as well as local purpose. But, can a housing policy which is increasingly reliant on market provision develop a significant contribution to environmental policy? Or does this require a shift towards a reconstituted 'social democratic model', involving the re-emphasis of the social welfare role and direct public sector capital investment in housing and environmental programmes?

Housing and Sustainable Urban Development – the Vision

Sustainable urban development is the link between housing policy and the new environmental agenda. In his foreword to the benchmark text '*Reviving the City: Towards Sustainable Urban Development*' David Gee, then the director of Friends of the Earth, commented:

> *"Whilst concern for environmental issues has increased dramatically since 1988, the environmental movement has paid little attention to cities.... yet cities are where some 90% of our population live, often in unpleasant or degraded environments."* (Elkin et al 1991 p.IX)

However, this text and several other key contributions (notably Breheny 1992b and Blowers 1993a) have begun to analyse the negative long term environmental impacts of urban development and advocate a new form of environmental planning to promote sustainability. Housing is a major component of urban development and the 'greening of housing policy' will be part of the wider process of the 'greening of cities'. The following sections of this chapter first draw from this debate the policy implications of pursuing sustainable urban development, illustrated by an ecosystems analysis of London. The discussion then applies sustainability principles to develop a vision of sustainable housing which embraces an energy efficient housing stock, the eradication of unfit housing and a secure, long term future for neighbourhoods which are currently declining. The chapter ends by returning to the wider debate and linking this housing focused vision to recent proposals for a new form of environmental planning.

Cities and Sustainability

Cities and towns account for a huge proportion of the world's consumption of natural resources and the world's production of pollution and waste. Cities have always had a destructive effect on the natural environment, which is replaced by the built environment as urbanisation has continued (Mumford 1961). Similarly the history of cities is replete with examples of the adverse effects of waste and pollution on their inhabitants. Polluted water supplies caused epidemic disease in early Victorian cities. In the much more populous 20th century conurbations, the use of coal for domestic heating caused 'pea-soupers': smogs which were both a serious health hazard and disrupted the economy of cities by regularly bringing traffic to a standstill. These urban environmental problems were essentially local and controlled by the local implementation of national policies – public health legislation, pollution control and town and country planning's attempt to control urban growth. But the recently identified environmental problems, rooted in cities' consumption of natural resources, are global in their reach. The response requires national governments to meet internationally agreed obligations through new forms of action, such as the reduction of CO_2 emissions, particularly from domestic energy consumption and road traffic. However, much of the implementation is, of necessity, through local government, where the new environmental agenda meets long established environmental action.

Rethinking urban development from a global change perspective not only introduces new policy themes and principles, but it can also bring a new legitimacy to long established concerns. The traditional planning objective of preserving the countryside 'in the interest of amenity' now has added to it 'in the interests of sustaining the biomass of biological diversity'. Similarly the long-standing transport planning debate about 'model split' – the balance between journeys by car, public transport, bicycle and walking – hitherto conducted in terms of the efficiency and equity of the city's transport system, now embraces differences in CO_2 emissions and overall environmental impacts. Public open space, traditionally provided for recreational and amenity purposes is now, in more naturalistic forms, part of the green space which is "a key element in the diversity of the urban ecosystem, as it is often in very short supply" (McLaren 1992 p.62). Energy efficiency investment in housing, first introduced to save money at a time of rising fuel prices, then directed to assist low income families achieve affordable warmth, is now also seen as central to reducing CO_2 emissions and the threat of global warming.

Sustainable London

This reinterpretation of the long established environmental agenda and its integration with the new is illustrated by McLaren's analysis of "London as an Ecosystem" (1992). The discussion of London's 'urban ecosystem' is couched in terms of the degradation of the environment as experienced daily by Londoners: the deteriorating home and street environment, air pollution (the heat-island effect and ground level ozone), water pollution (80% of London's drinking water is below European Community standards), land contamination, unused and

derelict land and buildings, loss of public open space, playing fields, and wildlife habitats, and the absence of greenery in the property-led, large scale, regeneration schemes of Docklands.
The analysis then turns to "London in the Wider Ecosystem" – an examination of the "...more fundamental aspects of the resource demands generated by London: and the crisis of unsustainability" (p.63). London generates huge amounts of waste and will run out of landfill sites by the end of the century. Yet the proportion of recycled waste, highest in the Borough of Richmond at 8% compares unfavourably with Portland, Oregon, USA, which achieved 22% in 1986. But the thrust of this analysis is on London's energy consumption and CO_2 emissions: the energy inefficient housing stock, the virtual absence of district heating based on combined heat and power, and the need to reduce car usage in the city.

McLaren's conclusions provide some indications of a path to a more sustainable future which centre on "...planning policies which will encourage the development of a city which is not only less wasteful of energy resources, but provides a more liveable environment for its inhabitants" (p.66). He recommends urban regeneration which focuses on improving housing, particularly its energy efficiency, and the street environment, through traffic calming. Together with a range of inter-related policies for local economic development, transport, open space, wildlife and flexible long life building around decentralised focal points, neighbourhood regeneration would make London a more desirable place to live and thus reduce 'unsustainable dispersal'. Such policy packages would also make more effective use of the natural resources (materials, embodied energy) already invested in the city's buildings and infrastructure and reduce the city's contribution to global warming.

Sustainable Housing in Sustainable Cities

A central sustainability theme is the relationship between energy consumption and urban development. Households are the source of 28% of CO_2 emissions (by final energy consumer) whereas road transport accounts for 21% and other transport 3% (Webb and Gossop 1993). All new housing development should be energy efficient and located where it contributes most to the sustainability of cities and towns. However, as the production of new housing will add only 3m to the existing 24m dwellings in the next 20 years (DoE 1994a para. 11.13), changes to the energy efficiency of the stock and the broad pattern of residential location through new-build will be marginal. Most of the housing which will be used far into the next century is in place now. Thus improving the energy efficiency and general condition of existing housing is a major sustainability issue.

The principles of sustainability also emphasise intra-generational equity and widespread participation in decision making about urban development. Thus a second theme is housing inequality and the future of deprived areas, which focuses attention on housing and neighbourhood renewal policies. Blowers (1993b) quotes the statement in '*This Common Inheritance*' that "...we have a moral duty to look after our planet and hand it on in good order to future generations" and links it to the Brundtland sustainability criterion of "meeting the basic needs of *all* and extending to *all* the opportunity to satisfy their aspirations for a better life" (my emphasis), to argue that:

> *"...it will not be enough simply to hand on the environment as it is now to the next generation. It behoves the present generation to hand on a better environment in those areas where it is heavily degraded or socially deprived, such as the inner cities"* (p.5).

An Energy Efficient Housing Stock

The potential environmental gains from an energy efficient housing stock are considerable as "...overall we have perhaps the worst insulated housing stock in Northern Europe". (Webb and Gossop 1993 p.64). The '1986 English House Condition Survey' (EHCS) established that 15% of owner occupied, 36% of local authority and 51% of private tenanted property was energy inefficient (DoE 1991b table A5.1). The 1991 EHCS showed that 3.2m dwellings (16%) lacked central heating and a further 16% had only partial central heating. The profile of elements which improve thermal efficiency also demonstrated continuing scope for significant improvement: whilst 91% of houses have some loft insulation, in only 8% is the current standard of 150mm achieved; 74% of houses have no cavity wall insulation; 48% of dwellings have no double glazing and 64% are without stripping (DoE 1993f table 5.10).

But there is also an intra-generational issue of equity. 'Fuel poverty' is the term used to describe the situation where warmth is relatively expensive for the poor, because to achieve a given room temperature they have to use more energy to make up for that lost through inefficient heating appliances and poor insulation. It is a stark illustration of one of the key statements of principle of the Brundtland report: "Poverty reduces people's capacity to use resources in a sustainable manner: it intensifies pressure on the environment" (WCED, 1987 p.49). In equity terms the poor should have the most energy efficient stock, whereas at present their homes are predominantly the least efficient. Giving priority to energy efficiency measures for the poor would both reduce their contribution to global warming and provide healthy homes, which are warm in winter and free from damp, condensation and mould.

As a contribution to a move towards sustainable housing a national strategy and phased programme is needed to systematically improve the energy efficiency of the housing stock, in a way which eliminates fuel poverty within 15 years: see figure 1.1.

Figure 1: Towards a national strategy for energy efficiency led housing and neighbourhood renewal

1.1	Energy efficiency investment for affordable warmth
■	*The aim should be to ensure that by 2010 UK domestic energy efficiency standards are above the European Union average;*
■	*standards should be set using the National Home Energy Rating (NHER);*
■	*national policy should ensure the necessary combination of public and private sector resources for programme implementation, through a combination of grants for low income households and affordable loans for other households;*
■	*the NHER for new build should be increased from its recently established level of 7 (10 is the most efficient and 4.4 the current average) to equal the highest in the EU by 2000;*
■	*priority for public investment in the existing stock should be given to the implementation of the programme advocated by Boardman (in chapter 7 of this book), for eradicating fuel poverty by 2010 - an NHER of 8 would provide affordable warmth for the 8m poor (in both social and private housing) at an average cost of £2,500 - a total public capital investment of some £20b over 15 years at £1,330m per year.*

Eradication of Unfit Housing

The DoE energy efficiency study pointed out that "... the general state of repair and condition of housing appeared to be a major factor affecting its energy efficiency" (DoE 1991b p.5), with 70% of unfit dwellings in 1986 being inefficient. Thus the energy efficiency investment programme would need to be integrated with mainstream housing renewal policies. The 1991 EHCS bore witness to the continuing need for more effective housing and neighbourhood renewal policies. The number of dwellings lacking basic amenities had dropped to 0.2m (1% of the stock), but 1.5m dwellings (7.6% of the stock) were found to be unfit. Allowing for changes in the fitness standard this represents a fall of 11% in unfitness over the five years 1986-91. If this rate of improvement continued and no more houses fell into unfitness, it would take some three decades to eradicate unfit housing.

But unfitness is caused primarily by houses falling into disrepair and this is a dynamic problem. The fact is that the market fails to deliver reinvestment which would prevent decay into unfitness. The number of unfit dwellings has fluctuated around the 1.5 – 1.7m level (using the current fitness standard) for the past twenty years. The 11% improvement "...is probably a reflection of the high levels of activity in the housing market in the late 1980s" (DoE 1993f p.69) when in boom conditions "...pressure of demand encouraged people to take on almost any property that was available, including dwellings that had been vacant for some time" (p.30). The likelihood is that the boom temporarily slowed the rate of decay, but that the 1996 EHCS will reveal an increase in unfitness back up to 1986 levels, if not worse, as a result of the property market slump. In the 1980s it was estimated that properties were falling into unfitness and disrepair at a rate of some 125,000 per annum (Gibson 1986 p.96-97). As the backlog has remained roughly constant, the broad effect of renewal policy has probably been to offset this rate of decay.

However, if the role of housing renewal policy continues to be restricted to this minimalist 'holding operation', some three million people will continue to be consigned to live in unfit housing. This clearly conflicts with the Brundtland sustainability criterion of "meeting the basic needs of all". Moreover this situation may well not be socially sustainable, as housing inequality is a key component of social polarisation which could eventually threaten social stability. Moving beyond a 'holding operation' requires a long term strategy with three components: a **remedial** component to deal with the backlog of unfit housing; a **preventative** component to secure reinvestment in dwellings approaching unfitness; and an **educational and promotional** component to secure continuing repair and maintenance throughout the rest of the stock (Gibson and Groves 1990). This strategy would contribute to sustainability by minimising decay through 'a stitch in time' approach to 'conservative reinvestment': it would concentrate on renovation (unless significant environmental benefits could be demonstrated for redevelopment), incorporate NHER standards, and emphasise resource efficient, comprehensive, long life renovation.

As a contribution to a move towards sustainable housing, a national housing renewal strategy and programme should be developed, with the aim of eradicating unfit housing within 15 years: see figure 1.2.

1.2 Dwellings fit for human habitation

- *The aim should be to achieve an irreducible minimum of unfit dwellings by 2010 – those which are short term voids pending sale, demolition or improvement, at around the 1991 level 145,000 (DoE 1993f table A.7.1);*
- *all renovations undertaken with grant and/or loan assistance should achieve an NHER of 8;*
- *a remedial programme to remove the backlog of unfitness (net of voids) within 15 years, through an annual programme of 90,000 mandatory grant-aided renovations, for a 30 year life, at an average cost of £10,000 per dwelling (the average mandatory grant in 1991 was £8,500 (DoE 1993f p.63) – £900m per year – £740m per year net of 1.1 above;*
- *a preventative programme to secure a 30 year life for 125,000 dwellings per year, on the margins of unfitness, through a combination of grants and affordable loans, at a unit cost to the Exchequer of £3,300 (the average cost of remedying unfitness estimated by the EHCS (DoE 1993f p.63) – £400m per year;*
- *a total programme of £1,140m per year.*

The energy efficiency investment programme and the remedial renovation grant programme would overlap, as at least 70% of the unfit dwellings would need energy efficiency investment, reducing the annual cost of the remedial programme by £160m to £740m. The total cost of this 15 year energy efficiency-led renewal programme would be some £2470m per annum – £37b. But the energy efficiency investment would virtually pay for itself in energy savings, reducing the figure to £17b – substantially less than the cost of the currently proposed roads programme. These targets and investment costs are very rudimentary. However, a recent study for the National Housing Forum calculated that to deal with unfitness and disrepair in social and private sectors would cost the public purse some £44b (Leather et al 1994 table 3.6) – the same order of magnitude. These indicative estimates demonstrate need to develop and cost a housing renewal strategy in order to debate the public sector capital expenditure priorities appropriate for a move towards sustainable urban development.

Liveable Neighbourhoods

A significant proportion of this energy efficiency-led national investment would be directed through neighbourhood programmes. The continuing need for neighbourhood renewal is demonstrated by the EHCS 1991 analysis of the relationship between housing conditions and the quality of the neighbourhood and environment (DoE 1993f ch.9). That survey identified three types of areas:

* **Areas of poor repair** are where "...more than 30% of dwellings in blocks which are neighbourhoods of the block in which the surveyed dwelling was found were assessed by the surveyors as defective". It is estimated that 1.42m dwellings are in these areas.
* **Poor environment areas** are where there is "...at least one significant problem related to unkempt areas or abandonment, *or* the overall impression of the environment is poor". There are 2.2m dwellings in these areas, of which 0.45m are worst condition dwellings.
* **Rundown areas** are "...the areas where poor environments and poor repair overlap", containing 0.5m dwellings of which 0.2 are worst condition dwellings.

As part of a move towards sustainable housing, a national strategy and programme for neighbourhood regeneration should be developed to secure the long term future of neighbourhoods which are currently vulnerable: see figure 1.3.

The focus of this programme would be the 2.2m dwellings in the 'poor environment' category, with priority for the 'rundown areas'. The identification of target neighbourhoods would use indicators of urban deprivation to take account of the wide range of non-housing problems to be addressed in comprehensive and integrated programmes (Thake and Staubach 1993). This programme would need a minimum of £1025m per annum net of the contribution from the energy efficiency investment and remedial renovation programmes, giving a total of £3500m per annum for an energy efficiency led programme of housing and neighbourhood renewal – £53b, or £32b if energy savings are discounted.

1.3 Liveable neighbourhoods

- *The aim should be to significantly improve the neighbourhoods suffering the worst housing, environmental, economic and social deprivation, in order to ensure their continued viability, conserve the large scale resources already invested there and reduce pressure for population decentralisation;*
- *the 2.2m dwellings in the target neighbourhoods should be given priority in the allocation of resources under 1.1 and 1.2 above;*
- *in statutory Renewal Areas there is currently provision for £1,000 per dwelling for central government subsidised environmental work – applied to the 2.2m dwellings in the 'poor environment' areas this would require £2.2b over 15 years – £150m per annum;*
- *the Estate Action and HATS programmes are currently running at £373m and £88m respectively (DoE, 1994e, Figs. 75 and 88) targeted to estates with the most serious problems – this should continue at £500m per annum;*
- *the City Challenge programme is currently allocated £230m per year for 31 projects @ £7.5m per project per year – this should be expanded to 50 projects at £375m per annum;*
- *In total a national commitment of £1,025m per year.*

Planning for Sustainability

A national strategy and programme for improving the energy efficiency of housing stock, eradicating unfit houses and regenerating deprived neighbourhoods is essential if significant progress is to be made towards sustainable urban development. But these programmes will have to be integrated vertically, between levels of government, and horizontally with other sectoral programmes, each developing their 'green dimension'. An integrated and holistic planning process is needed. A practice oriented vision of such a process is the Town and Country Planning Association's (TCPA) report '*Planning for a Sustainable Environment*' (Blowers 1993a).

The report identifies five *goals* of sustainable development to guide policy making:

* resource conservation,
* balanced development to minimise impact of built environment,
* the promotion of environmental quality,
* social equality and,
* political participation.

The *rationale* for environmental planning is the need to deal with environmental problems caused by the market, particularly the exploitation of resources at a rate which exceeds the possibilities of replacement, and 'negative externalities' – the imposition of costs on third parties, such as the industrial pollution of rivers. The report acknowledges that the 'polluter pays' principle could contribute to the resolution of these problems, but argues that even a market modified in such a way would have to operate within a planning framework if the goals of sustainable development are to be achieved. The *principles* for the new environmental planning are that it adopts a precautionary approach and develops as an integrated process operating in a strategic framework, as summarised in figure 2.1. The report first applies these goals and principles to a range of *key sectors* – natural resource planning, energy, pollution, waste, construction, transport and the economy – providing a range of specific recommendations for 'green' policy development in each area. The subsequent discussion of planning for the *sustainable city region* is particularly relevant to the issue of sustainable housing.

Figure 2: Planning for sustainable urban development

2.1	An integrated and strategic approach
■	***Integrated environmental planning*** *should co-ordinate pollution control, waste management and land use planning, promote the horizontal integration of policies by ensuring that all sectors of policy (transport, energy, housing, ...) take environmental issues fully into account, and integrate vertically between different international, national, regional and local levels of government;*
■	***a strategic approach*** *- at each level of government, there should be an environmental plan - a clear statement of policy which specifies objectives, sets targets, identifies delivery mechanisms and monitors progress against performance criteria:* • *the **national plan** would develop policies and set national targets for the implementation of international agreements, and establish the framework for regional and local plans eg. allocating their 'share' of national targets for household waste recycling and monitoring their progress;* • *the **regional plan** would require a regional level of government, for the democratic resolution of strategic and often conflicting pressures for development and environmental conservation; and* • *the **local environmental plans** would be pivotal, not only providing for the implementation of national and regional targets, but also developing an active 'bottom up' role, harnessing a wide range of participants in innovative and community-based environmental initiatives.*

The report addresses the key question of whether some types of urban form are more sustainable than others and, if so, whether urban change can be guided to achieve the most favourable form. The *compact city* proposal is supported by the European Commission on the basis that a mixed use, high density city will be energy efficient, as travel distances are reduced and public transport operating conditions optimised. However, the implementation of the compact city would require the reversal of decentralisation which has been the dominant urban trend since the 1930s – an unrealistic proposition. Others advocate *radical decentralisation* based on telecommunications, in a world where electric cars will eventually solve pollution problems. A further viewpoint is that the evidence on energy and urban form is unclear and technological breakthroughs are uncertain.

The TCPA eschew simple overriding policies and argue that a move towards future sustainability for the 'Social City Region' needs:

> *"...a whole set of distinctive policies, attuned to the varying conditions and environmental potential of the different parts of the region, but complementary and mutually reinforcing"* (Breheny and Rookwood 1993 p.156).

The way forward is to develop a variety of strategies appropriate for different parts of the city region: city centres, inner city areas, city suburbs, small towns and new communities, mixed urban-rural areas and remote rural areas. All these strategies would build on established policies, but link the built environment with issues of natural resources, energy, pollution and waste – issues hitherto not prominent on the policy agenda. Within this environmental planning of the city region there is a key strategic role for the regeneration of inner city neighbourhoods – reducing pressures for decentralisation. Whilst unsustainable dispersal cannot be reversed, it could be slowed by imaginative inner areas action. There can be no blueprint for sustainable neighbourhood regeneration but features which will be increasingly prominent as practice develops, are illustrated in figure 2.2.

2.2 Towards sustainable neighbourhood regeneration

- *Resource conservation through the re-use of land and buildings and the achievement of an energy efficient older housing stock;*
- *priority for traffic calming and investment in public transport (both bus and light rail), and together with provision for safe walking and cycling;*
- *maximising the opportunities for enhancing the mass of trees and other greenery and identifying any opportunities for protecting natural features;*
- *sensitive design of improvements to mixed use areas to ensure continued diversity;*
- *reduction of excessively high residential densities and provision of additional open space where seriously deficient;*
- *enhance provision of community and leisure facilities in local centres;*
- *extend the range of neighbourhood services to include improved facilities for the collection and disposal of waste, to maximise the percentage recycled;*
- *exploit any opportunities in redevelopment schemes for the introduction of combined heat and power;*
- *strengthen local economies, formal and informal, to improve job prospects and quality of life.*

Figures 2.1 & 2.2 adapted from Blowers, A., (ed.), (1993), **Planning for a sustainable environment – a report by the Town and Country Planning Association,** London, Earthscan.

Housing and Environmental Policy: the Reality

So much for the vision. What about the reality of policy and practice? The new environmental agenda has prompted the emergence of environmental planning, interlocking at international, national and local levels. This is a major innovation in public policy, within which an increasingly important focus of concern is the development of policies to chart a path to sustainable urban development. However, parallel changes in housing policy, reinforcing the 'market model' of provision have constrained progress towards more sustainable housing which could be achieved through an energy efficient housing stock, the eradication of unfit housing and securing the future of declining neighbourhoods. Some progress is being made towards the greening of housing policy, but contradictions are apparent, not least in priorities for public expenditure and the continuing withdrawal of public sector investment from housing and the inner cities.

Environmental Planning: Sustainable Development Touchstone

The *'Brundtland Report'* (WECD 1987) was the benchmark for the development of the international environmental policy process. The impact of post-Brundtland global debate and policy making on the UK was influenced by a significant shift in European Community environmental policy to embody the principles of sustainable development in all new programmes, including its developing urban policies. The *'Green Paper on the Urban Environment'* (EC 1990b), was criticised for its myopic advocacy of the 'compact city' (Breheny 1992b), but it certainly stimulated debate around the proposition that as cities of the north were a major component of the environmental crisis, environmentally-led city planning would have to evolve as part of the solution. A related *'Green Paper on Sustainable Mobility'* (EC 1992b) focused attention on the negative impact of transport on the environment and the EC's Fifth Environmental Action programme, titled *'Towards Sustainability'* (EC 1992a) included the urban environment as one of its seven themes. In post-Maastricht Europe, as Morphet emphasises in chapter 4 of this of this book, "EU environmental policy is UK environmental policy". The EU's influence can only increase, by requiring (as a condition of funding) or supporting changes such as the environmental assessment of housing development, a more environmentally efficient relationship between transport and development, the use of 'brown field' rather than 'greenfield' sites and improvements to the energy efficiency of existing housing.

In this context of growing international pressure for environmental protection the Environment White Paper *'This Common Inheritance'* (DoE 1990) was published as the government's response to the Brundtland Report. This first national environmental policy statement established the breadth of the environmental agenda, setting out a commitment to sustainable development, explaining the implications of global warming and reviewing issues and policies in energy use, transport, land use, the countryside, towns and cities, heritage preservation, air and water pollution, waste and recycling.
The White Paper was widely criticised for its timidity and lack of firm policies. The tenor of its proposals was epitomised by the target of reversing the upward

trend in CO_2 emissions and returning them to their 1990 levels by 2005. This was described by the White Paper as challenging, when in fact it was lower than the European target year of 2000, which the government later agreed to. Similarly, the section on transport acknowledged the polluting effect of the private car, but pinned its hopes on reduced travel and improved fuel efficiency of vehicles; accepted the Department of Transport's projected increase in road traffic by 2025 of between 83% and 142% and said nothing of substance about improving public transport. However, the White Paper signalled improved environmental protection legislation, a strengthening of the land use planning system and, importantly for housing policy, a revitalisation of the work of the Energy Efficiency Office to promote energy savings – all of which were counter to the policy directions of 1980s deregulation. Moreover, it established an environmental policy development process, which included a review of all policy sectors to ensure that environmental issues are fully taken into account in decision making, the development of guidance to assist this reappraisal and a system of annual reports to review progress (Blowers 1993c).

The adoption of 'Agenda 21' by the 1992 Earth Summit at Rio launched an international environmental policy process which provides a continuing impetus for the development of national policies. The 40 chapters of 'Agenda 21' set out a comprehensive programme of action needed across the world to reconcile environmental concerns and development. (LGMB 1992). The importance of making cities sustainable is a major theme. Urban environmental planning is needed to secure environmentally sound transport systems, through the integration of land use and transport planning and the promotion of public transport. The adoption of 'Agenda 21' obligates governments to prepare national plans for sustainable development and to submit progress reports to the newly established UN Commission on Sustainable Development. 'Agenda 21' also provides a major stimulus and integrating framework for the development of local environmental plans (Agyeman and Evans 1994). Chapter 28 emphasises the crucial role of local authorities in promoting sustainable development. Their range of functions will involve them in implementing over two thirds of the Agenda's action programme and they are uniquely placed to develop a decentralised, democratic planning process in partnership with their local communities (AMA 1993). Chapter 28 also encourages local authorities to submit their Local 'Agenda 21' Plans by 1996. Local authority associations and the LGMB, back by the government, are supporting local authorities through the production of guides and by networking to exchange experience (Hams 1994). Local practice varies, but its profile is increasing (Gosling 1994) and in chapter 5 of this book Brown examines the housing dimension of this work.

In January 1994 the government published the UK national sustainability plan in four volumes, covering sustainable development, climatic change, sustainable forestry and biodiversity, which reflect the main themes of 'Agenda 21' and the 'EC Fifth Environmental Action Plan'. In the introduction to *Sustainable*

Development: the UK Strategy, (DoE 1994a) John Gummer, Secretary of State for the Environment stated:

> *"The United Kingdom is determined to make sustainable development the touchstone of its policies... Year by year we shall need to revise and refine our policies so that our economy can grow in a way that does not cheat on our children"* (p.5).

The strategy is impressively comprehensive in its scope, very informative about the pervasive nature of environmental issues and the need for policy development in all sectors, and reflects the debate since 1990 about the importance of sustainable urban development – now a significant policy theme. The government's interpretation of the principles of sustainable development emphasises the importance of the 'polluter pays' principle, but acknowledges the difficulty of placing values on the environmental impact of economic development. The need for regulation – the setting of environmental standards which are legally enforceable – is accepted in areas such as pollution control and land use planning. However, the government re-iterates its overall commitment to deregulation, and emphasises the importance of using market mechanisms, such as taxes and prices, to influence consumer behaviour. Yet, apart from VAT on fuel (introduced to assist the Exchequer deficit rather than the environment) and a 5% per annum increase on the cost of petrol, there has been very limited progress in implementing this approach. This reflects the contradictory and overriding concern to avoid adding costs to business. But this is to ignore the wide range of actions which are environmentally positive and virtually cost free, such as the withdrawal of environmentally unsound subsidies. Moreover, the over reliance on market mechanisms reflects the absence of any discussion about equity and the environment – an issue which was brought into sharp focus with the debate about the impact of the introduction of VAT on fuel.

The discussion of sustainable urban development focuses on the need to locate new development, not least housing, where transport needs can be minimised and on the extent to which urban regeneration can recycle land and buildings to provide good quality environments, thus reducing pressure for greenfield development. The intention is to strengthen the regulation of development in the countryside and to check the excessive dispersal and conspicuous environmental consumption which characterised the property boom of the 1980s. Thus, for example, out-of-town regional shopping centres and business parks, being almost entirely car dependent '...are, therefore, unlikely to form part of a sustainable approach (DoE 1994a para 24.19). In a sharp reversal of 1980s deregulation, the land use planning system has been strengthened to enable it to function as '...a key instrument for helping to deliver sustainable development objectives' (para. 35.14).

The Planning and Compensation Act 1991 requires country-wide coverage of detailed development plans. The government has issued a revised series of Planning Policy Guidance (PPG) notes, setting out the environmental considerations which local authorities have to take into account in preparing development plans. For example, research sponsored by the DoE, as part of the follow up to *'This Common Inheritance'*, indicates that planning policies to reduce demand for travel (such as locating housing development where it is accessible to public transport) combined with related transport policies (parking restrictions, park and ride, traffic calming, better provision for pedestrians and cyclists) could reduce CO_2 emissions from transport by 10–15% over the next 20 years (Owens and Cope 1992; Ecotech Research 1993). PPG 13 on transport endorses this approach in combination with 'polluter pays' measures of increased fuel taxes and the prospect of motorway charges (DoE 1994b). But there are no plans to increase investment in public transport, whilst the £23b road programme has recently been re-affirmed. There have already been 250 anti-roads campaigns and the pressure for change is growing (Whitelegg 1994).

The recent publication of *'Environment Appraisal of Development Plans: A Good Practice Guide'* (DoE 1993b) will assist planning authorities to make explicit the way in which the environment has been taken into account in the formulation of the plan and the likely impact of the plan's preparation. As this system evolves, the location and siting of major new housing development will be subjected to increasingly sophisticated environmental impact analysis. The extent to which this reconstituted land use planning system can guide development in ways which minimise environmental impact will only be fully tested when the property market moves out of recession and pressures for development mount. However, this strengthened regulation has clear potential for contributing to the greening of housing policy.

The housing development section of the national sustainability strategy (DoE 1994a) is brief – four paragraphs. The aim of a "decent home to be within reach of every household" is stated along with the key policies of promoting home ownership and expanding the availability and choice of rented housing, and the comment that "...to achieve Government housing policy objectives is clearly a key component of sustainable development" (para. 24.8). But the continued existence of 1.5m unfit homes does not intrude into the discussion of sustainable housing. Yet failure to deal with this problem means failure to achieve the aim of a decent home for everyone and thus, on the government's own definition, failure to achieve a key component of sustainable development. It is stated that "...an important element of government housing policy of relevance to sustainable development is the regeneration of run down areas" (para. 24.9) but only in the context of providing sites for new development. Whilst housing renewal policies are not specifically discussed, the strategy does emphasise the importance of the neighbourhood dimension of urban regeneration policies:

> *"sustainable development in run down city areas entails making a concerted attack on the range of problems which affect such areas... to provide the basis*

for long term revival in the chosen areas and decrease pressure for greenfield development." (para. 24.29)

It endorses the example of City Challenge projects and the partnership regeneration of peripheral estates in Scottish cities. But there is no national strategy for housing and neighbourhood renewal; no discussion of the scale of renewal problems, of resources, priorities, programmes or targets. It is a failing common to most areas of the national sustainable development strategy.

An exception to this general weakness is the commitment to return emissions of CO_2 to 1990 levels by the year 2000. This requires a saving of 10 million tonnes of carbon (MtC) of which 4 MtC is to be achieved by reducing domestic energy consumption. A programme for achieving this target is set out in *'Climate Change: the UK Programme'* (DoE 1994c). This means that the rapid improvement of the energy efficiency of the housing stock is a key component in achieving one of the most important short term objectives of the national sustainability plan, and this will require a major improvement on performance during the 1980s.

Towards Energy Efficient Housing

The development of national environmental policy has prompted the rescue of energy efficiency programmes from the near terminal decline they had reached in the late 1980s. The greening of housing policy is currently energy efficiency driven, building on experience of 'pre-sustainability' programmes. These programmes initially focused on the economic objective of reducing energy consumption to save money after the 'oil price hike' of 1973. But recognition of the growing incidence of fuel poverty in the early 1980s led to the introduction of the social objective of providing affordable warmth for low income households. At the time of the publication of the Brundtland report, energy efficiency programmes pursuing these objectives were being run down and faced an uncertain future. However, in 1988 Mrs Thatcher's Royal Society speech acknowledged the threat of global warming and signalled a shift in energy policy to emphasise the environmental objective of energy efficiency savings (Anderson 1993). By 1994 policies for a more energy efficient housing stock were fully incorporated in mainstream housing policy.

But these developments have evolved in the context of major reforms of housing finance, housing and neighbourhood renewal and urban regeneration programmes. This wider context is important, not least because since the 1970s there have been three main components of policies to improve the energy efficiency of the housing stock:

* Specific energy efficiency programmes – national initiatives to promote basic retrofitting (mainly loft insulation and draught proofing) and targeted, to varying degrees, to low income households.
* The significant energy measures content of mainstream housing rehabilitation programmes, in part determined at local authority level, usually involving more costly work, very often central heating The EHCS 1986 (DoE 1991b ch.9) found that in the "public sector... three quarters of

all local authority energy work was done in conjunction with other repair and improvement work" (p.70). DoE has also calculated that some 25% of local authority housing spending on improvement and repair work is on energy measures (DoE 1994d para.6.52). In the private sector the EHCS found that over 40% of grant-aided improvement schemes included some energy work.

* Publicity, promotion and advice work to stimulate non grant aided energy investment by private owners, which the 1986 EHCS found to be accounting for over 90% of major jobs.

How far have interrelated changes in national environmental, housing and urban policies taken us towards sustainable housing and neighbourhood renewal?

Declining Programmes in the Late 1980s

Specific energy efficiency programmes were introduced in 1978 by the last Labour government in a two pronged strategy. The first prong was the **local authority energy conservation programme**, aimed at installing loft insulation and draught proofing in all local authority housing within 10 years. By 1987 some 2.3m homes had been insulated – well short of the target. The annual programme was running at 66,000 dwellings compared with 630,000 in 1979 – a decline attributed by the AMA to competing priorities in the face of a 75% cut in HIP allocations during the 1980s (AMA 1991). However, mainstream refurbishment programmes were partially offsetting the decline. The Estate Action programme was renovating some 60,000 dwellings a year (DoE 1994d fig.85), as part of the local authority renovation programme which expanded rapidly, but temporarily, from 150,000 dwellings per annum in 1987 to 230,000 in 1990, in a short lived municipal investment boom, prior to the long expected clamp down on capital receipts expenditure in 1990. The second prong was the **Homes Insulation Scheme** (HIS), a successful, local authority administered, programme, providing 350,000 – 450,000 grants per annum from 1979 for loft insulation in private houses. It was a mandatory (as of right) grant available to all households at 66% of the cost of the work (90% for elderly and severely disabled people on low incomes), and it has been estimated that a third of these grants went to low income families (Owen 1989a). In 1988 HIS grants were restricted to households claiming income support and take up plummeted (AMA 1991).

Through the 1980s these local authority led programmes were supplemented by the work of **Community Insulation Projects** (CIPs) committed to reducing fuel poverty. Developing from a Friends of the Earth initiative, **Neighbourhood Energy Action** (NEA) was formed in 1981 and combined Supplementary Benefits single payments for draught proofing with labour for installation from job training schemes. At its peak in 1987, 400 NEA projects undertook work on nearly 160,000 houses (Owen 1989a). In 1988, the abolition of single payments and changes in training programmes brought the scheme to an end. A stop gap replacement, the Energy Grant, was introduced but the CIP network was decimated by the end of 1989 (NEA 1991). At this stage mainstream private sector renovation programmes were running at about 100,000 grants per year, immediately prior to the introduction of the new renovation grant regime in

1990, having fallen from a peak of 229,000 in 1984 (Wilcox 1993).

The outcome of these programmes and non-grant-aided investment was a slow improvement in the energy efficiency of the housing stock. The EHCS 1986 and 1991 showed that loft insulation had increased from 62% of all households in 1981 to 91% in 1991, wall insulation increased from 7% to 26%, and central heating from 60% to 84%. Moreover, it was demonstrated that "...in the main improvements in both heating facilities and thermal insulation had been targeted towards the least energy efficient properties and the lowest income groups". (DoE 1991b p.76). However, the standards achieved were often only very modest, particularly in loft insulation. Draught proofing materials last for only five years and there were more people in fuel poverty at the end of the 1980s than at the beginning (Owen 1989 a & b; Boardman 1990).

Policy Reviews and Programmes for the 1990s

Cuts in HIS grants and CIP's work derived from a sharp shift in energy policy in 1987 to secure the privatisation of the electricity industry. Energy Efficiency Year 1986 was succeeded by a 40% cut in the EEO budget, marking the return to a 'market forces' approach, rooted in the belief that if energy efficiency is cost effective, businesses and households will invest in it (Anderson 1993). But with privatisation secured in 1989, the advent of the green agenda prompted a reappraisal, as the development and presentation of *'This Common Inheritance'* emphasised the importance of energy efficiency, especially in housing. The new environmental objective implied a restoration of specific energy efficiency programmes and introduced an energy efficiency dimension into the final stages of the reform of mainstream rehabilitation programmes, underway as part of the continuing privatisation of housing.

For both energy specific and mainstream rehabilitation programmes policy, questions were raised and answered within the parameters of the 'market model', which placed inevitable constraints on the development of policy.

- Should grant aid to private house owners be primarily viewed as a 'welfare benefit', restricted to the poorest households in the worst condition properties, or as an 'investment incentive' to encourage a wider range of households to install energy efficiency measures and improve their homes? Or should grants fulfil both functions? The position adopted was to restrict mandatory grants to the welfare role, and to rely mainly on publicity and improved advice (and in the case of energy investment the possibility of energy industry funded incentives) to stimulate more owners to invest.
- Should minimum energy efficiency standards be specified and included in the housing fitness standard, thus integrating 'global health' standards and 'public health' standards? This suggestion did not find favour as it would have substantially increased the number of unfit dwellings eligible for renovation grant aid.
- Should a time scale be set for the achievement of minimum energy efficiency and fitness standards, with resources committed to achieve the resultant programme? This was not appropriate when the overriding priority was to secure continuing reductions in public expenditure rather

than create an investment programme to meet improvement targets.

The general thrust of the review of housing renewal policies in the late 1980s was to reduce the local environmental management role of housing policy to a minimum – at best 'a holding operation' – the logical corollary of which is a limited government role in direct capital investment in energy efficiency measures in older housing. Nonetheless policy development in the 1990s can be interpreted as providing foundations for a move towards an energy efficiency-led housing renewal policy, foundations which could be built on if there was the political will to remove current constraints.

The **Homes Energy Efficiency Scheme** (HEES) was introduced in January 1991. This ended years of uncertainty about specific energy efficiency programmes addressing fuel poverty by replacing the HIS and Energy Grant with a single funding regime. The Energy Action Grants Agency (EAGA) administers the scheme on behalf of the EEO which is now, appropriately, part of the DoE. The grants are intended to cover advice and the costs of loft insulation and draught proofing in the homes of people eligible for income related benefits, and, (since the introduction of VAT on fuel), to people over 60, in both public and private sectors. The grant (maximum £315) can be paid for work done by EAGA's accredited Network Installers (some of whom have evolved from NEA type projects into 'community businesses'), or by commercial contractors or on a DIY basis. NEA monitoring of the scheme indicates that most teething troubles have been overcome, including the scepticism of some local authorities as landlords, which constrained initial take up (NEA 1992 & 1993). The estimated out-turn expenditure of over £40m in 1993 will have resulted in work in over 240,000 homes and, in the context of the imposition of VAT on fuel, the budget has been nearly doubled for the next three years to £75m, with a target of 440,000 homes per year (DoE 1994e fig. 21). Should this be achieved it will constitute the long overdue rebuilding of a large proportion of the capacity lost by the cuts of the late 1980s. But it remains a very basic retrofitting scheme. The NEA and others are currently lobbying for the abolition of the clients contribution and increased grants to fund cavity wall insulation, low energy lighting and new heating and hot water systems (NEA 1994).

The **local authority renovation programme** is becoming increasingly energy efficiency-led. Moreover, with privatisation and unemployment increasing the proportion of tenants claiming benefits, it is increasingly contributing to affordable warmth. The immediate effect of restrictions on capital receipts expenditure introduced in 1990 was to reduce local authority renovation activity from an annual programme of 230,000 to 175,000 in 1992 (Wilcox 1993 table 2.3). Within this the Estates Action programmes maintained an output of 60,000 – 70,000 dwellings improved per annum. The 1991 'House Condition Survey' showed that local authorities were investing some 25% of their renovation work in energy efficiency measures and in 1992–93 this accounted for £370m. This trend has been stimulated by the **Green House Demonstration Programme**, launched in December 1990 following the commitment in *'This Common*

Inheritance' to improve the energy efficiency of council housing. This highly effective programme allocated some £60m of top sliced Estate Action funding to a national network of 180 schemes from 130 authorities over three years. These schemes demonstrated that it is possible to achieve CO_2 savings of 50% over current levels, with a 40% reduction in energy consumption, in addition to reducing future management and maintenance costs and tenants' fuel bills. The project demonstrated the substantial scope for energy efficiency improvement and the need for a systematic and strategic approach, the importance of which was underlined by the introduction of VAT on fuel. Interim Guidelines were issued in 1993 and a comprehensive manual was published in 1994, with accompanying technical guides which show how energy efficiency can be made a more integral part of council programmes, often at little extra cost (DoE 1994d). Much of this work is relevant to *housing associations*, although their rehabilitation programme fell from 11,000 dwellings in 1990 to 7,000 in 1992. (Wilcox 1993 table 23)

The private sector renovation programme is in serious decline. The 1989 Local Government and Housing Act introduced a new system for the subsidised improvement of private housing which came into operation in 1990. There are three main types of grant:

* **Renovation grants** are mandatory, available as of right to owner occupiers to bring dwellings up to the fitness standard. Discretionary renovation grants are also available to achieve higher standards. The grant is means tested and can vary from 0% to 100% of the qualifying costs of work up to a limit of £20,000.
* **Disabled facilities grants** cover adaptations to enable a disabled person to live in a dwelling – grant for some types of this work is mandatory and all these grants are means tested.
* **Minor works assistance** is available to those on certain means tested benefits up to a limit of £1080 per grant and is mainly used for work to enable people over 60 to stay put in their own home.

The number of grants under the old system was running at about 100,000 per annum in 1990. The number of renovation grants under the new regime in 1992 and 1993 was 50,000 together with some 30,000 minor works assistance grants. This programme is expected to fall to 35,000 renovation grants and 29,000 minor works grants during the current year. Whilst some 40% of the grant-aided schemes under the old system included energy work, very little is being carried out under the new regime because the vast majority of grants being awarded are mandatory and the work is confined to that necessary to meet the fitness standard, which does not include insulation or heating standards (Leather et al 1994). Most local authorities do not have the resources to make discretionary renovation grants available, which could fund energy efficiency measures as part of a higher standard scheme. Similarly, although Minor Works Assistance grants could potentially supplement HEES grants, as they can be used for cavity wall insulation, limited budgets are giving priority to staying put work. Thus, whilst the new system targets resources to low income groups its potential contribution to affordable warmth is not being realised. Moreover, the decline in this programme also means that the number of unfit houses is probably increasing and the prospect of sustainable renewal of private housing is receding.

In this context a great deal hangs on the effectiveness of the Energy Savings Trust, (EST) an independent organisation established by the government, British Gas and the Regional Electricity companies, to initiate and implement programmes to promote energy efficiency in the domestic and small business sectors. Direct government funding supports the EST pilot network of 30 Local Energy Advice Centres, but other programmes are to be funded by the utilities through a small levy on consumers. Consultation papers at the end of 1993 outlined proposed grant schemes for social housing and for private owners (EST 1993), suggesting a £10b investment by the year 2000. But this major initiative is now in doubt as the gas industry regulator is opposed to the levy, arguing that energy efficiency investment should be funded through taxation (Tieman 1994).

From 1994 local authorities are required to take a strategic approach to energy efficiency across tenures and demonstrate progress in their HIP submissions. The DoE have made it clear that performance in this area will be taken into account in the annual allocation of funds. Energy efficiency is thus in the mainstream and the housing sector has the basis for participating in the development of Local Agenda 21 plans, as discussed by Brown in chapter 5. However, there are continuing contradictions in national policy. A private member's *Energy Conservation Bill* was killed by the government – if passed into law it would have required local authorities to do sample audits to draw up conservation plans. But the major issue is that the inadequate level of funds is more likely to be exacerbated than alleviated. In the local authority sector a temporary 'capital receipts holiday', which boosted expenditure in 1993, is coming to an end and a £200m cut was imposed for 1994-95. Moreover, the Estate Action programme ends in its present form this year, having been subsumed in the Single Regeneration Budget (SRB) (DoE 1994e A.5). The SRB is economic development led and there is concern that the £370m Estate Action programme is at risk. There are no plans to restore the cuts in the private sector improvement programme. Overall the developments in the 1990s have strengthened the affordable warmth programme but not provided an effective mechanism for energy efficiency investment on a wider scale in the private sector – the CO_2 emission targets are increasingly vulnerable.

The development of neighbourhood renewal in the 1990s is a similar story of improving capability but inadequate resources in relation to needs. In the private sector, Renewal Areas have replaced General Improvement Areas and Housing Action Areas and are larger in scale, and more comprehensive in scope – integrating housing and environmental renewal with action on the local economy and jobs, and the provision of neighbourhood services. Some seventy of these 10 year public-private investment projects have been established, but the further development of the programme is being slowed by resource constraints. Similarly, and in parallel, the Estate Action programme evolved in the 1990s from relatively narrowly based estate improvement schemes into Comprehensive Regeneration Schemes, with an increased emphasis on environmental and employment initiatives. The City Challenge projects were launched in 1991 for comprehensive regeneration of disadvantaged areas through integrated development strategies, but there are no plans to increase the programme beyond the thirty-one in place. The impact of the SRB on neighbourhood regeneration has yet to emerge.

Housing and Environment: the Challenge of Change

The short term prospects for the development of programmes to achieve sustainable housing and neighbourhood renewal are at best, uncertain and at worst, bleak. The key issue is the continued downward pressure on public sector capital expenditure. However, some developments in recent years indicate a basis on which to build towards the kind of programmes outlined earlier that would provide (adapting from Elkin 1991 p.9) a major plank in our bridge to an environmentally sustainable housing and urban future. The development of environmental planning, the major advance in planning and delivering energy efficiency programmes for housing, the capacity of the renovation grant system to target expenditure, the more integrated approach to neighbourhood renewal developing in Renewal Areas and Estate Action type programmes, increasing tenants' and residents' involvement, and the potential of the Single Regeneration Budget to provide an appropriate funding system – all are positive developments.

But, progress towards sustainable housing requires a re-orientation of housing policy towards a 'social democratic' model, which would include a carefully planned increase in public sector housing capital investment, as part of a strengthened national environmental policy. As Blowers points out:

> "*...sustainable development will require substantial changes in behaviour at every level, giving priority to such unfashionable ideas as planning, community and greater equality*" (1993b p.18).

The essence of planning for sustainability is a perspective rooted in long term time horizons. The earliest role of housing policy – local environmental management – established byelaws which prevented houses being built to such low standards that they very quickly became slums. But because the local environmental management role was restricted to minimalist intervention by the prevailing 'market model' of housing policy, it was not until the social welfare role evolved in the post-war period, as part of a 'social democratic model' of housing policy, that comprehensive redevelopment was possible through the replacement provision of council housing. Thus, the expansion of the traditional local environmental management role, with its emphasis of securing minimum housing standards, was dependent on the development of the social welfare role, with its egalitarian concern for decent standards for all. Since the turning of the social democratic tide in the 1980s, the re-emphasising of the market role has resulted in the withdrawal of much of the direct public investment in housing and neighbourhood renewal, resulting in increasing urban inequality.

As we move into the 21st century, the new concerns for global environmental health may well ensure increasingly environment-friendly provision of new houses, through imaginative planning and design, combined with eco-labelling and other adjustments to the operation of the housing market. However, as long established concerns for the impact of poor housing on the health of its occupiers are joined by global health concerns for the impact of an old, energy-inefficient, housing stock on the health of the planet, there are some three million poor tenants and owners living in unfit dwellings. There is no credible body of evidence from history, or from the analysis of contemporary conditions, to support the case that an increasingly market-led structure of housing provision can change this situation for the better.

A Vigorous Enabling Role

If we are to meet the housing needs of all the people in ways which do not damage the planet, an effective energy efficiency-led programme of housing and neighbourhood renewal must be developed and put in place during the next five years. This would lay the foundations for the longer term evolution of an increasingly sophisticated process of sustainable housing and neighbourhood regeneration. Such a shift in the early 21st century would be analogous to the move from the ineffective reconditioning of the slums in the 1920s to large scale comprehensive redevelopment which, for a time, weakened the link between poverty and bad housing. But, by definition, sustainable housing and neighbourhood regeneration would have none of the negative consequences of the paternalistic and sometimes coercive characteristics of comprehensive redevelopment. It would be local authority-led, in an enabling sense, but a decentralised style of working with local communities as equal partners, would ensure a sharp contrast with post-war programmes. However, in three ways these early 21st century programmes would echo their mid 20th century antecedents:

* whilst many individual schemes would be small in scale, the aggregate scale of investment would be congruent with the substantial needs for housing and neighbourhood renewal;
* they would share the concern of the post-war programmes for the reduction of urban inequality; and
* their implementation would require a metamorphosis of existing neighbourhood programmes, radically expanding the local environmental management role of housing policy, as did the advent of comprehensive redevelopment.

Together with environment friendly new housing provision, these programmes for the improvement, repair and maintenance of housing, as part of a local community-led regeneration process, would constitute the evolving housing dimension of sustainable urban development, and the new environmental role of housing policy. The housing and neighbourhood renewal strategy, as a key component of the local authority's housing plan, would have a strong corporately defined environmental rationale and content, derived from the authority's local environmental plan. This would strengthen the enabling role of local housing authorities, by allowing a higher volume of direct targeted public investment to both lever in private resources and encourage community involvement in neighbourhood renewal, and would be a key part of the developing environmental protection role of local authorities.

Finally, an inter-generational perspective focuses on the consequences in 20 years time of failure to act during the next five years. If the current withdrawal of public funds from housing and neighbourhood renewal continues, the rate of physical deterioration will increase, accompanied by growing social polarisation, with the danger of a return of the riot-torn bitterness of the early and mid 1980s. The next twenty years would be analogous to the first twenty years of this century, when ineffective reconditioning policies failed to prevent the deterioration of large numbers of houses into slums, which eventually had to be dealt with by large scale and resource expensive clearance. Failure to halt the emergence of conditions in our cities similar to those evident in the downtown neighbourhoods of many US cities would be to grossly 'cheat on our children'.

CHAPTER 4: The European Dimension of Housing and Environmental Policy

Janice Morphet

Within the European Union (EU) there are a number of trends which will have a major impact on the practice and operation of housing systems within the Member States. As indicated in chapter 3 a number of structural changes will have a major impact on the ways in which housing and planning systems evolve in relation to environmental pressures. At the international level these trends are apparent from directions within EU policy on a number of fronts relating to political union, citizen rights, economic convergence, regionalisation and plans for sustainable development. There is very little discussion at present on the potential implications of current trends at national or European level for housing. Indeed the European Commission has not signalled its intent to develop an EU wide housing policy, as this is seen to be an issue of domestic policy. However, this may only be a matter of time for a number of reasons. The EU has become involved in the production of housing through the Single European Market (SEM) which has led to an increased standardisation of products and regulations that will become evident in the supply of housing. The SEM may also lead to the creation of a single planning system across Europe. Finally there are major influences from the SEM in respect of the introduction of competition, particularly as it influences the implementation of Compulsory Competitive Tendering (CCT). In a number of ways then housing in the UK will be subject to pressures from Europe, requiring specific policy responses and adaptation in the market place, as well as improvements in housing practice (see Drake 1992).

This chapter sets out the European context for the development of housing and environmental policy in the UK The first section briefly introduces a number of key developments and then explores these trends in detail. The second section focuses on the implications of this emerging framework for housing in the UK

The European Context

In the UK, some 60-70% of our legislation is derived directly from the EC. In the past, particularly when Mrs Thatcher was Prime Minister, there was a tendency to mask the EU provenance of much of our domestic legislation. This was achieved primarily by transferring the European legislation into UK law without any reference to Europe. The 1990 Environment Protection Act is a good example of this. The second approach was to introduce the measures required by Europe but to put a specific domestic political spin on them. The introduction of compulsory competitive tendering is derived from the General Agreement on Tariffs and Trade (GATT) via the EU Services Directive 92/50 (Financial Times 19/4/94 p1, Boris 1993).
The moves towards competition in Europe came in the mid 1970s with the introduction of the Works Directive which required all major construction contracts to be advertised. The move to competition which was already foreshadowed was incorporated within the 1980 Local Government Planning and Land Act. The 'Next Steps Agencies' in Government are introducing the concept in central government. The most recent round of CCT seems to be the result of an agreement in Europe reached around 1988, at the start of the current GATT round and when the Single European Market began in earnest. In the UK, local authorities have always been direct providers of services in a way in which local authorities in other Member States have not. This is why UK local authorities are being compelled to privatise through CCT (Council of Europe 1993). In other Member States other areas of public ownership are passing through the same process e.g. the privatisation of the railway in Germany.

Turning more widely, the EU is concerned with the implementation of environmental policy as it meets its commitments made at the Earth Summit in Rio in 1992 (European Commission 1993a, b). This will include consideration of energy usage, land use planning, environmental assessment and transport issues. The Union has also specifically addressed both urban and rural policies in the round. All these issues will be considered in this chapter. Perhaps the most important point to consider at the outset, is that EU environmental policy is UK environmental policy. EU law, made through regulations must be applied in the UK within a strict time frame and in the manner required from Brussels. The EU also issues Directives which member state countries are required to implement through domestic legislation. However, recent case law on Directives (Frankowich and Pandolfi) suggests that Member States cannot take an unreasonable time to implement Directives and further, citizens of the European Community can expect the rights conferred on them through Directives to be available almost immediately. Hence there may be little practical difference between a Regulation and a Directive.

There are a number of key developments within the European Union that will have far reaching consequences for the housing system in Britain. Five areas are identified and explored in more detail below. These are:

* Influence of the Maastricht Treaty
* The Development of Equal Citizen Rights
* The Role of the Single European Market
* The New 'Europe of the Regions'
* The New Environmental Agenda

The Influence of the Maastricht Treaty

The Maastricht Treaty is a key document which amends the Treaty of Rome, the foundation of the EU. The European Economic Community is now the European Union as all the member states have ratified Maastricht which takes on the integration of Europe into a potential federation including a common Foreign policy. It also incorporates areas which have long been seen as the province of domestic policy such as health and social issues. One of the key debates in the preparation of Maastricht was the concept of subsidiarity. How far should the EU be involved in specific policy areas? What are the appropriate levels of intervention? In many ways these are the transitional pains of member state governments ceding powers to Brussels. One of the areas where there was particular discussion on this issue was on the environment. Debates within the European Commission and Member States were held, with some of the Member States arguing that this was clearly a local issue. However, the Commission responded that the environment was an area which, more than any other, was no respecter of political boundaries. Environmental regulation was also seen to be an issue which had implications across the Community both in application and monitoring. It was therefore held that the Community was the appropriate level for consideration of environmental matters. The Maastricht Treaty in sections 130 [r] and [s] confirms this point and includes planning specifically.

The Development of Equal Citizen Rights

As part of Maastricht and the promotion of European integration, the European Union has been developing a programme to ensure equal citizen's rights. The main thrust of development hitherto has been in rights at work, an area which has always been subject to domestic legislation. This includes health and safety, maternity provisions and rights of individuals when services are transferred from the public to the private sectors. These have now been extended to the consideration of health and education and more recently to consumer rights and the provision for local access to justice. The consumer rights Directive has taken many years to develop and is still to appear in its final form before agreement by the Council of Ministers. However, when adopted it will provide citizens with equal rights in respect of goods and services provided by the public and private sectors. In the UK this has spawned a variety of responses. In the private sector a number of sectoral ombudsmen have been appointed for banking, insurance, building societies etc. In the public sector the Government has pushed forward the principle of the Citizen's Charter and performance indicators for statutory bodies, including the delivery of local authority services. The rights of the individual at the local level are likely to be extended through the inclusion of provisions on local access to justice, although this appears to be bogged down at present. If implemented, it will provide all citizens with third party rights in respect of planning and environmental issues. In itself, this could have a fundamental effect on the operation of any planning or housing system.

The Role of the Single European Market

The SEM was finally brought into effect at the end of 1992. Its function is to create a major internal trading area which will take forward the EU's aims of economic integration. The internal market in the EU, which now also has an arrangement with the EFTA states (Norway, Sweden, Finland, Iceland, and Austria) creates the largest potential market in the world. Its development has been part of the creation of new major markets in North America through NAFTA (US, Canada and Mexico) and in the Pacific Rim, for example. These internal markets have also been a key element in the Uruguay Round of the GATT. Within the EU, the development of the SEM has had many implications. Perhaps the most obvious one is of the removal of cross border control which has been one of the most difficult, not least in the light of recent developments in Eastern Europe and the subsequent population movements.

If the SEM is to work it also has to deal with a number of other practical issues, including the establishment of common standards and legislative frameworks for processes. There is no point in having an SEM if the non-tariff barriers to trade remain in place. In the initial stages of the development of the SEM, much of this standardisation of regulation has concentrated on the products directly, e.g. developing standard brick size and quality. However, the SEM is now moving on to higher order issues such as qualifications of staff, consumer rights and the application of local taxation policies as a means of conferring unfair price advantage. As part of this process of developing the SEM, the legal framework governing the means of achieving development has attracted some attention. In the UK, for example, the development industry is far more mature than in other member states and is a critical element of the national economy. At present, the operation of twelve different planning systems across the EU could be seen to be a barrier to entry to these development companies (Cox 1993). With the implementation of the European Economic Area, then this will extend to 17 systems. Research on the barriers to integration has been commissioned by the Commission and will feed in directly to the preparations for a new regionalised EU.

The New 'Europe of the Regions'

A growing element of EU activity over the last decade has been regional policy. Initially, and still primarily, this was an economic planning policy geared towards meeting the needs of those regions which were weaker than the rest. It also included within it a means of providing positive financial support to the economically weaker peripheral member states viz Ireland, Portugal, Spain and Greece and as a means of returning contributions to countries such as the UK which do not benefit from other major European funds. More recently, the regional dimension of the Community's role has been enhanced. Although the economic regional strategy has been reviewed it is still largely in place. However, the need to provide financial support to the peripheral states has been formalised into the 'Cohesion Strategy' agreed in 1992. This scheme is primarily aimed at improving infrastructure links between the periphery and the heart of the Community for economic reasons. It also has the additional benefit that much of the infrastructure investment is in net contrbutor states. This infrastructure or 'super highways' are seen to be critical to the development of the EU economy; they could also have a substantial influence on settlement patterns in the future as they are essentially major transport corridors.

The Commission has also undertaken a review of all the regions in the Community, under the banner of Europe 2000 (European Commission 1990a), work which is being continued through Europe 2000+. Europe 2000 establishes the role of ten supra regions within the EC which are primarily based on geographical rather than political boundaries. They include the Atlantic Arc, the Western Mediterranean and the Centre Capitals region. These supra-regions are made up of smaller regional units. Each large Member State may be represented in three to five of these supra-regions. Now regions are becoming an important focus for Community policy. They will be supported by the Committee of the Regions which will be made up of locally elected political representatives from each of the Member States. The Committee of the Regions is seen to be a transitional body which will be reviewed by the EU intergovernmental conference in 1996. It is possible that after this there will be a directly elected regionally representative upper chamber of the European Parliament. Meanwhile the Committee of the Regions will oversee much of the regionally based expenditure derived from the EU. They will also require this to be set within a regional framework and to be environmentally assessed.

In financial terms much of the Community's funding is also moving towards a regional structure. In future it is possible that funding will be based on regional bids rather than on the current basis of Member State bids. This approach will further downgrade the role of Member State governments and will bring serious disadvantages to the UK which at present has only a regional tier of administration but not of government. The new Integrated Regional Offices (IROs) of government with control over a growing amount of regional spending will be critical in developing this emerging EU regional structure in the UK. Already, the EU has required that local central government make joint submissions of regional plans to the EU which should also now be accompanied by transport infrastructure proposals on the same basis. In the UK this may be having a fundamental influence on the structure of the state (Morran 1993).

Already local authorities are being reviewed with a view to creating a single tier of local government. Central Government is also reorganising itself in order to establish a regional tier of administration without an elected steer. These implications are important but at present are not being discussed (Morphet 1993). It is also possible that this process will accelerate the merging of member/officer roles in local authorities as decisions are taken increasingly at the European level.

The New Environmental Agenda

In 1992, at the Earth Summit in Rio, the United Nations Commission on Environment and Development produced a number of outcomes which now require governments to translate internationally negotiated policies and commitments into actions that are relevant at the national and local levels (see chapters 3 & 5 in this volume). The EU response to the new environmental agenda is contained in the Fifth Environmental Action Programme (5AP) entitled 'Towards Sustainability' (European Commission, 1992a, b; LGMB 1993a). The 5AP reviews key themes and targets for the Community's action until the end of the decade but more particularly in the period until 1996. The key themes include those of highest importance in Rio, climate change and air quality, but also they focus on waste management, coastal zones and the urban environment. The EC is concerned that a sectoral or problem-solving approach will be too fragmented. Recent statements by the EU's Environment Commissioner have suggested a much more generic approach to issues such as pollution than an approach which concentrates on specific media (European Commission 1993b).

The potential conflict between economic growth and economic decline is also recognised by the EU (European Commission 1990b, 1992c). There are always problems of demand – too much or too little. The EU is proposing that economic growth should be the engine of environmental change. In addition to these themes, the 5AP considers both the 'key actors' involved in developing sustainable policies and broadening the range of instruments which are to be used. The key actors include the public and private sectors and the general public. Changing public behaviour is seen to be fundamental to all of this. The range of instruments to be considered will also have a key effect on what many of us do and how we live. In some areas, the Commission is looking to provide better comparative data. Most of the world now seems to be currently involved in the search for sustainable indicators and the EU is no exception to this.

There are other tools which the EU wishes to explore which may lead the way. There is a recognition that land use planning systems may be a major means of implementation of sustainable policies. Within organisations there will be campaigns to introduce Environmental Management and Audit Systems (EMAS). In the UK a pilot project to extend this to local authorities has been undertaken and the new scheme was launched in 1993 (LGMB 1991,

DoE/LGMB 1992, DoE 1993c). The European Commission also appreciates that the environmental costs have to be appropriately apportioned to ensure that life cycles and ecological footprints are transparent throughout the process and not passed onto the purchasers or users. This part of the 5AP will concentrate on GNP tables, the introduction of green accounting mechanisms and full environmental disclosure of enterprises. The introduction of a system of civil liability for environmental damage, with perhaps the equivalent of a US super fund, may bring much abandoned urban land into the reckoning again. Finally, the commission will be seeking to fully integrate the environment into its other programmes particularly as a means of evaluation of any project or initiative, including economic projects funded under the 'structural funds' to the poorer areas of the Community. If the EU is willing to apply this level of appraisal to this and its other projects it demonstrates a considerable level of environmental commitment.

What are the Implications for Housing?

As yet, the real implications of Maastricht for the UK have yet to be fully understood. The European Union now has competence over many areas of UK policy. Housing is one area where there is no direct competence but, as this review has shown, the indirect influences are considerable, whether this be in respect of production of housing or through converging financial rules and products. One of the main difficulties for those wanting to consider the relationship between the EU and the UK, housing and sustainability, either to understand or to promote policy change, is the diversity of interests in Brussels. In respect of changing building standards, planning or energy initiatives, then the Environmental Directorate General [DG] is the main focus. However, others will be involved such as the Competition, Social Affairs and Energy DGs. One of the main reasons for this confusion is that housing provision is seen as a matter primarily to be dealt with at local level. However, drawing upon the model of the housing production life cycle outlined in chapter 2, page 24, the EU's impact on housing can be summarised as follows:–

Project Conception and Brief

In the future, the nature of project development and evaluation will be changed to ensure that environmental considerations are taken into account. In order to implement this, the EU will be introducing Strategic Environmental Assessment (SEA) which will require all plans, policies and programmes to be environmentally evaluated. This will apply to public and private sector projects but there is no formally agreed and accepted methodology. The SEA will extend to include issues such as siting, materials and location. As the EU is also proposing that much closer scrutiny be placed on the relationship between development and transport with an emphasis on public transport modes, some sites may no longer be acceptable for development. It is anticipated that the EU will be supporting a far greater use of land within existing built up areas. It may be that far less green field land is available for development, which will be regulated through the use of planning controls and the application of legislation such as the Habitats Directive.

Design

The design of the dwelling will be expected to meet far higher energy conservation ratings than is currently the case. The external design will be expected to take into account site features and local climate. In some German cities, for example, the effect of wind direction on air temperature is taken into account in both the location of development and the roofing materials required. This concern will also extend to materials used and the way in which the fittings in the interior of the dwelling are conceived. The introduction of the Packaging Directive will probably mean that households will be required to sort and recycle their waste on a far greater scale than hitherto. Separated waste may require greater space requirements for bottles, paper, cans, plastics and toxins (such as paints, medicines, garden chemicals etc.). Gardens will need to have sufficient space for composting and communal developments will need to take this issue into account in their design.

Energy and water reducing systems will be favoured. On housing sites, there will be greater emphasis on car free areas and the use of surface drainage for landscape maintenance rather than encouraging run off. It is likely that roads will be constructed from recycled materials. Landscaping is to be used to positively support heat retention and to support local bio-diversity. A design guide embodying sustainable principles will be published by the Local Government Management Board in 1995. In respect of energy, there are already a number of schemes to support improved energy efficiency in housing available from the EU. SAVE, for example, supports pilot projects and has funded Heatwise, a specially created company in Glasgow. There are also proposals for a Directive on the installation of new gas and oil-powered hot water boilers which will shortly come into effect. The UK government has its own scheme of grant aid to promote the installation of condensing boilers. The EU THERMIE Programme supports projects to develop new technologies for energy conservation in buildings and the use of renewable energy sources including wind and solar power.

Construction

The selection of construction method will be critical in the move towards sustainability. The selection of companies to undertake work may be on the basis that they have an Environmental Management and Audit System (EMAS) in place, which is externally verified. The company's green credentials will also be displayed with increasing frequency in their company report and accounts. The selection of a contractor may not be only on the matter of price. Methods of tender evaluation which include life cycle analysis in respect of durability and maintenance costs will increasingly be taken into account. For example, there should be no need to replace a roof two or three times during a building's life. During construction, contractors will be subject to all EU law on safety, noise and pollution. Construction materials should be recycled products where possible and much of the technical product development has occurred in other countries such as Canada. Some practical examples have been developed in the UK by Robert and Brenda Vale of Nottingham University (see Vale and Vale 1991a, b). Construction waste, particularly arising as a result of redevelopment will be expected to be recycled rather than sent to landfill.

Building Use

Given the increase in tele-working and working from home, homes may need to be more adaptable. They may need to be more self sufficient in all respects. However, this may be one of the most difficult areas to anticipate. In practical ways, it is possible to design buildings so that inner space can be more readily divided, whilst they can also be constructed in a way which is more conducive to extensions. On more major developments, it has also been shown that existing buildings are capable of re-use, whether this be housing to offices or the reverse.

Refurbishment

It is in the retrofitting of homes that one of the most major contributions to CO_2 reduction can be achieved. Given that 90% of our current building stock will still be available in 2020 this is an area which should receive major support. This can be done in two ways. The first is by improving the energy performance of the stock to meet levels comparable with other EU members such as the Netherlands and Denmark. Even in winter many of these homes do not require significant additional heating. Such heating which is provided is often from local 'waste into energy' schemes. Major initiatives of these kinds will also help to reduce domestic consumption bills in addition to being a major component of sustainability. The second major initiative is through schemes such as eco-feedback which have been initiated in the Netherlands. Eco-feedback encourages individual householders to monitor their consumption of energy, waste output and fuel/car use and to reduce their consumption in comparison with the previous year; this can be done through the application of energy-saving measures including turning down the thermostat or through the use of thermostatic valves on radiators. Waste production can be also weighed each week whilst car journeys can be logged. Furthermore the development and support of a major retrofitting industry will be dependent on Government support through leadership, grant aid and individual fiscal incentives, perhaps going back to tax breaks for householders who improve their property. The retrofitting industry will be critical as part of the strategy for reducing development on green field sites. As the potential for new development reduces, the construction industry can use its capacity in major retrofitting programmes, although the shift to owner occupation since the last great push in this area in the

1960s/1970s suggests that this might carry higher overheads.

Obsolescence and Demolition

Once homes have come to the end of their useful life, then the existing buildings can be demolished with materials being recycled and the land reused for housing or other uses. The introduction of EU civil liability regulations and rules of company disclosure of the quality of land owned will mean that there will be far more effort put into re-using existing sites and leaving them in a reasonable state after they have become redundant.

Conclusions

The EU already has a major significance in the operation of environmental standards within the UK. At present this is little recognised or understood. The European Commission understands this point and is currently reviewing its approach to the public sector. Although the private sector is more focused towards Brussels, the Commission is considering undertaking direct training programmes in the EU public sector. The purposes of these programmes will be to advise existing professionals of the role and purpose of EU law and the way it is intended to be applied. It is also true that the rate of progress towards the application of better environmental standards has been laid partly at the feet of professionals of the EU Court of Auditors. This will be particularly important as the environmental agenda turns to consider the implications of moving towards more sustainable goals. It is clear that the production of housing in the UK is fundamentally affected by EU environmental standards and they are set to play a further role; there is already a strong view that the next round of the GATT will be about establishing a level playing field on sustainable principles (Financial Times 9/2/94). If the discussions which have taken place in the current round provide a model then much of the new legislation will be developed in parallel to the GATT process. To some extent this was foreshadowed in the Delors White Paper on Europe's economy which was issued at the end of 1993 (EC 1993c). The main issue for those concerned with housing is the way in which they can be involved in the development of the policy as well as the implementation. This issue will be difficult to locate given the lack of EU housing policy. However, a demonstration of the principle areas of influence of the EU on housing matters may be enough to demonstrate to the EU, including the Commission, the Committee of the Regions and the Parliament that housing is an issue with an important contribution to make to the achievement of strategy for sustainability.

CHAPTER 5: Local Housing Strategies and Environmental Policy

Tim Brown

In recent years local authorities have been required by central government to reduce their role in the direct provision of social housing and housing policies now involve a strategic enabling function. Local environmental policies on the other hand have developed in an incremental and ad hoc manner, and it is only recently that issues of co-ordination have surfaced. It is particularly significant that while there is a statutory requirement to produce a local housing strategy, there is no duty to prepare a local environment plan. The relationship between local housing strategies and local environmental policies has to be located within this wider context. Underlying both of these themes, is the future relationship between central and local government; indeed the chairperson of the 'Local Agenda 21' steering group has commented that local government can only successfully work towards a vision for a fair, prosperous and sustainable future if empowered to do so by central government (Harman, 1993). The theme of this chapter is the relationship between environmental policies and housing strategies at the local level. The first section outlines the development of local housing plans, and the more recent upsurge in interest in local environmental strategies is documented; in both cases wider contextual issues will be stressed. Attention is drawn to a user perspective on local housing and environmental strategies with specific reference to council housing. The second section focuses on Leicester as a case study where some of the strategies outlined in section one are being implemented. The conclusion looks at some of the tensions that are emerging and discusses future prospects.

Development of Local Housing and Environmental Policies

The co-ordination of different local authority policy systems has a chequered history. In the late 1960s and early 1970s, corporate planning was high on the agenda as it attempted to bring together a diverse range of policy statements (such as structure and local plans, transport policies and programmes, and housing plans). In the case of Coventry, for example, as early as 1972 a comprehensive annual plan was produced incorporating all policy statements including housing. During the 1980s corporate planning became less influential due to increasing central control of local policy and public expenditure; penetration of market forces into the public sector; and a general disillusionment with policy planning. In the 1990s, however, there has been renewed interest in co-ordination and corporate planning at the local level. A number of factors have contributed to this development including:

* the acceptance by local authorities of their role as strategic enablers (Brooke, 1989)
* concerns over the lack of co-ordination in policy-making and public sector management (Webb, 1991)
* emergence of environmental issues that require a strategic approach (Elkin et al 1991, Agyeman and Evans 1994)
* problems over the implementation of public policies especially housing (Malpass and Means, 1993)
* and a growing debate about the future of local government generally (Stewart and Stoker, 1989)

An important element within all of these factors has been the issue of public involvement and user participation.

Local Housing Strategies

There is a considerable literature on the development of local housing policies as part of planning policy systems since the late 1960s (see Carter, Brown & Abbott, 1993). The key points are that a variety of factors contributed to the demise of policy planning in general and housing investment programmes in particular in the 1980s, in contrast with the optimism of the mid 1970s. There was at that time a consensus that these systems would help solve local housing problems through the advent of a more rational decision making process involving the allocation of resources to a range of spatial scales to meet identified needs. Indeed, a number of pioneering local authorities, such as Coventry, were developing local housing plans well in advance of the introduction of the formal HIPs system in 1977/78. However by the end of the 1980s, there was a growing pessimism about local housing plans which was summed up by Maclennan who asked:

> *"...how many authorities would now bother to prepare a local housing plan if it was not a statutory obligation?"* (1991 p.191).

The Housing Investment Programme (HIP), established as a rational system for long term planning and investment, had by 1986 suffered cuts in spending, moratoria, and the abandonment of forward planning structures in both bids and allocations. Moreover it was becoming clear that HIPs were being used to control local housing policies which represented a significant shift by central government, having a major impact on the role of local authorities in housing provision (Malpass and Murie 1994). HIPs continued to be prepared but there was a considerable scepticism as to their usefulness. A survey carried out by Carter, Brown & Abbott (1993) found that local authority officers felt that the HIPs exercise had become a mundane bidding exercise between central and local government. The policy dimension had been relegated to a marginal activity.

During the early 1990s there is evidence of a significant revival of interest in local housing policies and strategies. This has taken the form of a consensus that, as part of a strategic enabling role for local government, local housing strategies should be produced which go beyond the narrow confines of the format for HIPs. A particularly useful and relevant example is the incorporation of energy efficiency measures adopted by some local authorities as shown below. The irony is that this call for a wider co-ordinated perspective for housing investment programmes merely repeats 'good practice' advice from the mid 1970s! Nevertheless, there is a wide spectrum of opinion which has promoted the concept of local housing plans.

The Duke of Edinburgh's Inquiry into British Housing (NFHA 1985), suggested that local authorities should prepare comprehensive housing strategies.

The Inner City Commission (1987) report for the House Builders' Federation argued the need for local policy statements which should be developed from existing housing investment strategies.

The Association of Metropolitan Authorities (1987) emphasised the advantages of producing a comprehensive medium term local housing strategy.

This consensus was summed up by the chairperson of the Housing Corporation who stated that

> *"There is no substitute for the local authority's own strategic role in collecting information on local needs, defining priorities, and setting a framework in which housing associations and other agencies can operate effectively"* (Corporation News 1991 p.1).

It is therefore not surprising to find that a number of innovative local authorities have been developing these broader local housing strategies. As early as 1990, 40% of local authorities indicated that they had or were likely to produce such a document (Carter, Brown & Abbott, 1993). Furthermore in recent years, publicity has been given to the 'good practice' of certain pioneering authorities in producing these strategies. Coventry City Council, for example, set up nine liaison groups starting in 1990 to help prepare, implement and monitor its housing strategy (Dunmore, 1992).

Further support for the adoption of more systematic and broader local housing strategies has come from the Audit Commission. They argue that local authorities must develop a housing strategy which recognises the changed legislative and financial environment as well as ensuring that satisfactory relationships are established between local government departments and external agencies (Audit Commission, 1992). They nevertheless have also pointed out that many local authorities still lack a strategic overview especially in relation to the improvement of private sector housing (Audit Commission, 1991). The view of central government on local housing strategies has also changed. In May 1992, a consultation document was published (Department of the Environment 1992a) suggesting, amongst other items, that a greater degree of co-ordination was needed between local authority HIPs and the Housing Corporation's Approved Development Programme (ADP). It implied that this would necessitate a more comprehensive medium term local authority housing statement. This approach was reinforced in February 1993 when it was announced that local authorities should formulate medium term housing strategies within which annual HIPs submissions should fit (Department of the Environment 1993a). Moreover, the strategy should firstly be developed in consultation with other organisations (e.g. housing associations) and secondly adopt a corporate approach so as to ensure close liaison over, for example, community care policies and town planning strategies.

Local Environmental Strategies

The concept of local environmental strategies is a much more recent phenomenon compared to local housing strategies; there has thus been relatively little research on the subject. An important exception to this is Raemaekers (1993), who has charted four phases in the development of local corporate environmental management culminating in the recent interest in 'Local Agenda 21' (see below). Furthermore, Stoker and Young (1993) have claimed that local authorities during the 1980s gradually adopted an environmental perspective leading in some cases to ambitious plans for:

* renewable energy initiatives (Lancashire County Council)
* combined heat and power schemes (Leicester City Council), and
* environmental charters (Kirklees Borough Council).

The major impetus comes from the British Government's signing of the 'Agenda 21' Treaty at the Earth Summit in 1992; chapter 28 emphasises the crucial role local authorities will play in the implementation of the Treaty. By 1996 all local authorities should produce a 'Local Agenda 21' document through public consultation and community involvement, and the Local Government Management Board has given subsequent advice to local authorities to develop this concept (LGMB 1992). The early 1990s then represents a watershed for the linking of housing and environmental policies, with local authorities developing their own individual 'Local Agenda 21s'. The development of local environmental policy is also the result of pioneering local authorities gradually progressing their own environmental programmes. Indeed many local authorities are now moving on from charters and action programmes through to environmental audits, comprehensive strategies and eventually to 'Local Agenda 21s'. In addition, there have been a number of important publications produced by a wide range of organisations especially pressure groups on good practice, for example, Friends of the Earth advice (1989) on environmental charters for local government. Furthermore local authority associations have been active in promoting good environmental practice (Association of County Councils et al, 1992).

It would, however, be misleading to suggest that the majority of local authorities have developed local environmental strategies. Innovative approaches adopted by a few local councils are significant. Birmingham City Council's Green Action Plan (1993) is aimed at providing a comprehensive corporate approach to help protect and improve the environment. It is supported by a Corporate Action Programme (1993) which outlines on an annual basis how the strategy is to be implemented. Similarly Coventry City Council (1992) has produced a Draft Environmental Strategy which aims to bring together policy and action by involving the whole community. But it should be noted that these pioneering authorities are in a minority. There is no statutory requirement for local authorities to produce an environmental strategy unlike other areas of activity such as housing, economic development or community care. Many local authorities have, in fact, adopted an incremental and ad hoc approach to environmental issues by adding environmental policy proposals to existing planning policy systems such as structure and local plans.

Indeed, many local authorities are being 'greened' in this manner. A lengthy 'shopping list' of this type of approach could be identified (see Raemaekers, 1993), but for the purposes of this chapter a more selective but detailed approach has been adopted which highlights the diversity of initiatives. In the town planning arena, an increasing number of district-wide local plans include policies on sustainable development. Many of these pre-date central government support for the inclusion of such policies. There is usually no environmental theme running throughout the plan; they generally take the form of a specific set of policies within a section on the environment. The most significant initiative for the greening of local housing strategies is likely to be the development of 'Local Agenda 21s' (Aygeman and Evans 1994).

Linking Environmental Policy and Local Housing Strategies

The emerging link between local housing strategies and environmental policy can be most clearly seen in the field of energy efficiency. There have been a wide range of initiatives including considerable work on energy efficient homes and energy plans and audits. Local authorities such as Newcastle-upon-Tyne have made use of European Commission funding to develop energy action plans. In relation to energy efficient homes, a wide range of initiatives have been taken at the local level (Taylor, 1993). Newark and Sherwood District Council, for example, developed a 'condensation containment package' in 1988 to tackle problems on their council estates. It involved four elements:

- full heating
- adequate ventilation
- insulation to give affordable heating and
- tenant advice

This scheme along with a number of flagship projects has been monitored through the Department of Environment's Green House Action Programme (DoE 1993d).

Many of these types of initiatives are embedded in local housing strategies and annual HIPs. In many cases, however, there is a lack of an authority-wide perspective on energy policy as well as an overall environmental strategy incorporating an energy efficiency plan. Nevertheless energy efficiency is an important and useful example of where housing strategies and environmental policies meet. Many local authorities have developed energy audit approaches for their own housing stocks and these have been welcomed by the Department of the Environment. Indeed during the early part of 1994 the Department held a series of regional seminars on incorporating energy efficiency within annual HIPs submissions. It is of course ironic that the 'backbench' Energy Conservation Bill which would have made it a statutory duty on local authorities to carry out an energy audit on the housing stock as a whole, has now fallen because of government opposition to the proposals. Even so, a positive relationship has been developing between energy efficiency measures and local housing strategies although there are serious factors which have prevented or hindered progress on this linkage. These include the lack of resources from the government for energy efficiency measures through the housing investment programme system, and the competing pressures on policy-making and resource allocation engendered by, for example, compulsory competitive tendering and increasing levels of homelessness. These problems have been well-summed up by Singh who argues that the competitive nature of the annual HIPs system relegates many issues, such as energy efficiency and sustainability, to a game of second guessing what is likely to please government ministers (Singh, 1994).

Good practice guides emphasising specific initiatives but more importantly comprehensive environmental policy statements are likely to be more significant in the medium term in highlighting future directions for local authorities. A wide range of organisations have produced guides including pressure groups such as Friends of the Earth (1989), 'Environmental Practice in Local Government' (Association of County Councils et al. 1992) and the Socialist Environment and Resources Association (1993). The latter, for example, emphasises the need for an environmental charter whose principles are prominent in all council policy statements. Local authority associations have also been active in campaigning for more effective and wide-ranging environmental strategies. They have, for example, stressed the importance of linking housing, energy and the environment (Association of Metropolitan Authorities 1991). In many respects, these publications parallel developments outlined in the previous section in the late 1980s on local housing plans. In both cases, innovative action by local authorities has resulted in a growing interest and consensus in the wider application of these approaches. Again, in the local environmental policy field as with local housing plans, central government has belatedly shown a degree of interest. They have, for example, published a guide on environmental management and audits for local government (Department of the Environment, 1993c); an optimistic perspective for local policy-making in the 1990s is therefore possible.

But there are still problems to overcome and the example of 'green housing strategies' for housing associations usefully illustrates this. A number of housing associations, including those in Leicester, are keen to develop and implement environmental strategies. But there is a potential conflict between a 'green' strategy and the competitive bidding process for housing development. The Housing Corporation has suggested that it is interested in promoting energy efficiency in housing schemes (Housing Corporation, 1993a); on the other hand it does not favour setting minimum energy efficiency standards or giving favourable treatment to schemes which are more energy efficient at the competitive bid stage in the development process. It is difficult to envisage in practice housing associations putting forward schemes which are likely to give less value for money in terms of Housing Corporation criteria although they may well meet energy efficiency criteria set by a local authority. In such a situation, the Housing Corporation is likely to favour bids from other housing associations which undercut the more energy efficient scheme. Indeed the more recent publication of scheme development standards (Housing Corporation 1993b), further reflects this philosophy, noting that the consideration of energy efficiency is an essential item in terms of compliance with the standards, but fails to provide detailed criteria which associations must adhere to in their development projects.

User Perspectives

There is however a major problem with this policy-making orientation. It focuses on a 'top-down' approach for the development of local policy and ignores a 'bottom-up' perspective starting with users. There is a grave danger that the environmental policy-making arena at local government level will be dominated by the more powerful organisations. A number of studies on urban policy have suggested that growth coalitions consisting of local authorities and powerful business interests may be starting to dominate the policy process at the local level (Imrie & Thomas, 1993). In relation to housing and the environment, this could include key local authority departments (e.g. housing and planning),

major housing associations, volume house builders and infrastructure agencies. It might well exclude smaller housing associations, environmental pressure groups, and users. The difficulties for local authorities of co-ordinating individual complex local policy planning systems, especially in conjunction with irregular and ad hoc funding competitions run by central government (e.g. City Challenge, Estate Action and now Single Regeneration Budgets) further favour the marginalisation of less powerful interest groups.
Yet a strong theme underpinning much of the literature on good practice for local environmental strategies emphasises the empowerment of users. Such a strategy needs to pay particular attention to certain fundamental issues on housing and the environment, particularly what constitutes an environmental problem! It can be argued, for example, that council tenants have for many years campaigned on environmental problems such as damp and condensation. But much of this work has been ignored in mainstream studies of environmental issues and policy-making.

At the national scale, the work of the People's Asbestos Action Campaign (PAAC, 1988) during the 1980s is a useful example of this type of issue. At the local scale, in many towns and cities campaigns have been long-running struggles over damp and condensation. In Coventry, for instance, there have been serious problems faced by tenants since the 1960s (Shelter, undated); while the action taken by Newark and Sherwood District Council arose partly through concerted action by tenants who threatened the council with legal action under the public health legislation (Taylor, 1993). In many cases, however, tenants' campaigns have met with relatively little success because of their powerlessness in the face of local authority domination of the policy agenda. A focus on local housing and environmental strategies from a top-down perspective is thus inadequate. A users' perspective is essential in developing and implementing a co-ordinated housing and environmental strategy. But a critical question for the successful linking of housing and environmental strategies is whether users are going to be empowered through the process of policy-making or whether they will continue to be marginalised?

The Experience from Leicester

So far this chapter has focused on local housing and environmental policies in general with brief illustrations from a number of towns and cities. The aim of this section is to illustrate how local housing and environmental policies can be linked in a specific city. Leicester has been chosen mainly because it is acknowledged to be at the forefront of environmental and housing policies. In relation to the latter, Leicester City Council is often quoted as an example of good practice in many fields. These include the funding of tenants' organisations (Dean, 1992) and working with housing associations (Fraser, 1991). In relation to the former, it was selected as Britain's first 'Environment City' in 1990 and was subsequently chosen as one of twelve local projects world-wide to participate in the Earth

Summit in Rio de Janiero in summer 1992. Previously, during the 1980s, the City Council had attracted attention through a number of earlier environmental initiatives including the preparation of one of the first ecological strategies for nature conservation, the development of an energy strategy, and the establishment of a local ecology trust.

In relation to local housing and environmental policies there has been a shift away from innovative but ad hoc initiatives to a more comprehensive and co-ordinated approach. This (unlike Birmingham and Coventry as mentioned previously) has not involved the preparation of a detailed environmental plan linked to an annual action programme. Instead the City Council has produced a general environmental protection strategy (Leicester City Council, 1992a). The change of emphasis is particularly evident from comparing housing strategy documents from the late 1980s and early 1990s with current statements. Housing investment strategy statements for 1989/90 through to 1992/93 make little formal reference to environmental issues apart from highlighting the need for extra resources to implement small-scale environmental improvements in urban renewal areas and on council estates. The City Council's housing strategy for 1993/94 represents a major change in direction emphasising the key theme of integration of local policy planning systems. The strategy states:

> *"It is vital that an integrated approach is taken to all our work as the strategic housing authority. We will ensure that we take full account of the Council's Planning, Community Care, Economic Regeneration, and Environmental Strategies in all housing initiatives"* (Leicester City Council, 1992b p.1).

It further points out that in all improvement and development work it will adhere to 'the principles of Leicester as Environment City'. These strategic themes are reflected in a more detailed action programme for housing in Leicester. It includes, for example, a policy that no use should be made of imported hardwoods and CFCs in building contract work, and recommends paying discretionary grants for roof insulation and central heating in renewal areas. It should be noted that this action programme includes not just substantive statements on housing policies but also identifies relevant action within the housing department including, for instance, the carrying out of energy audits for all housing offices, and encouraging staff to use bikes and public transport to carry out their duties. These policies and themes are reiterated within the housing strategy statement for 1994/95 (Leicester City Council, 1993). This highlights the twin principles of energy efficiency and environmental soundness. It is reflected in the five key areas identified in the section on 'environment city':

* Ensuring that building work is environmentally sound;
* Undertaking further environmental initiatives as part of City Challenge;
* Greening housing association development;
* Staff and buildings;
* Tenants and estates.

The Housing Department of the City Council has subsequently begun work on a medium term housing needs strategy. It is intended that this will form a major input into the housing strategy statement for 1995/96 and will incorporate environmental issues as a continuing theme. Green issues therefore are no longer a separate isolated policy area but are an integral part of mainstream activities. Indeed the commitment of all staff to the values and goals of these initiatives is seen as essential (Beckett, 1993). A similar change in emphasis can be found in the strategic policy plan documents of other City Council departments. The district-wide local plan for Leicester prepared by the Planning Department, for example, incorporates a strong environmental theme with an emphasis on protecting and improving the environment of the city (Leicester City Council 1992c). This is reflected in the overall strategic policies which include the environment as a key objective. This, of course, is a major change from the local plans prepared in the early 1980s which adopted a narrow environmental perspective by limiting themselves to a single set of policies on such issues, as well as identifying the environment as a relatively low priority.

At the same time as this reorientation of local policy planning towards an environmental theme, there has been a continuing stream of more specific initiatives. Since 1992, for example, the City Council has been working with its twinned cities of Strasbourg and Krefeld on the transfer of good practice on environmental policies. This has resulted, for instance, in Leicester considering the installation of sophisticated air pollution monitoring equipment following a visit by officers to Strasbourg. A further example is the strategy of Leicester City Challenge (1992); the successful submission document included as one of its key strategic objectives:

> *"to create a better environment for people living in, working in and visiting the area, to increase the awareness of the environment and to ensure that all developments are environmentally sound"* (p.2)

To this end, all projects within the bid document were subject to an environmental assessment undertaken by Environment City. Indeed the area chosen for the City Challenge bid was selected partly on the basis of environmental and housing concerns. These included areas of contaminated land, older housing areas requiring refurbishment, and a poor physical environment. The 'code of practice' for ensuring that redevelopment is carried out successfully puts significant emphasis on the environment (Leicester City Challenge, 1993). The 'code' not only highlights the key environmental issues but also illustrates the strong links between Leicester City Challenge Ltd., City Council departments, and the local community. Indeed, there are strong similarities between themes in the 'code' and the environmental strategy within the City Council's comprehensive housing statement (Leicester City Council 1993).

Of equal relevance to local housing policy has been the joint work by the City Council, local housing associations and the Housing Corporation on the most appropriate mechanisms for providing housing with improved environmental performance. A Leicester Housing Associations' Green Forum was established in 1992 and commissioned a study on 'affordable options for green housing' by Environ Advisory Services (1993). It is important to note that this initiative partly stemmed from a desire by local housing associations to respond positively to Environment City and the environmental policies of the City Council. In addition, it is significant that the consultants, Environ Advisory Services, is part of the local environment trust which is concerned with pioneering practical initiatives to improve the environment.

A number of factors have also contributed to this reorientation in favour of the environment in local authority policy planning. Of particular significance in Leicester has been its designation as Environment City in 1990, and its active participation in the Earth Summit. Recent housing strategy statements, for example, make explicit reference to both of these factors. This suggests that these factors are of more than symbolic importance. They have helped to create a situation in which a wide range of local organisations, including residents and tenants' groups as well as environmental pressure groups, are working together in partnership to develop and implement an environmental strategy. Moreover this strategy is gradually being integrated within other local policy planning systems such as housing investment programmes. A complex network of committed organisations has thus been created which appears to meet some of the criteria suggested by Webb (1991), which may help to overcome one of the perennial problems in public sector policy-making and implementation – the lack of co-ordination. 'Capacity building' is a key concept of 'Agenda 21'; it is seen as an important means of implementing environmental goals. Thus chapter 37 of the Treaty (LGMB 1992 p.33) talks about developing capacities, that is, the resources and abilities of individuals and organisations to manage the changes that are necessary. These include a participatory approach, identifying skills gaps, technological and scientific requirements, and improving knowledge and targeting of resources. Thus recent specific initiatives in Leicester form part of this process with a more coherent set of detailed policies located within the broader context of a commitment to an environmental strategy.

Conclusion: the Future of Housing and Environmental Strategies

There is a growing emphasis on the enabling role of local authorities in the housing arena (see Goodlad 1993). The more general analysis of policy making indicates that the development and implementation of an environmental strategy requires local authorities also to act as enablers in the housing sphere of activity. This enabling role involves a number of activities including:

* the establishment of a strong commitment to an environmental strategy – this could take the form of an environmental plan and action programme but it could also be a more general commitment to the environment engendered by a particular event such as Environment City designation;
* the development of detailed environmental strategies within the local authority and their incorporation into other policy planning systems such as housing investment programmes;
* encouraging other organisations to contribute to and to develop appropriate policies through the creation of a network of contacts and links.

Nevertheless, there are dangers and difficulties associated with a strategic enabling approach. Much of the literature on public policy-making and strategic enabling tends towards a top-down approach. In other words, policy is developed and implementation takes place as a matter of course. As Robin Means shows (1993) this is a simplistic and misleading stance. A further difficulty associated with the strategic enabling role for local authorities in housing and environmental policy is the relationship with users. Chapter 2 indicated that in relation to council housing there has been a general failure to take account of users' perceptions of the environment. The development of local environmental policies could well continue this problem by failing to involve users in the policy-making process. So far, there have been relatively few examples of user involvement in the drawing up of local environmental strategies; indeed a 'top-down' approach has generally been adopted. If housing and environmental policies are really going to address the needs of users and achieve a community commitment to 'Agenda 21', then a 'bottom-up' approach to policy-making is also required.

CHAPTER 6: Towards an Ecological City? Poverty and Urban Regeneration in Glasgow[1]

Jane Brooke

Many environmentalists are profoundly worried about the impact of rapidly growing cities on the planet. As these cities have an insatiable demand for energy, food, land and building materials, they generate enormous amounts of waste and pollution; frequently they fail to provide the poorer citizens with safe, sanitary housing or long term employment opportunities. The problem posed by the old industrial cities of 'high income' countries in Britain, northern Europe, and parts of the USA is different. Here, the largest cities are losing population as people move to suburbs, smaller towns and rural areas, often following jobs as old manufacturing industries are replaced by other forms of employment. As population falls, the demands made by the city on the wider economy and society change. As the proportion of the city's population who are ill, old or suffering the effects of long-term unemployment rises, the city is increasingly seen as a bottomless pit demanding subsidies for health care, policing, public housing and welfare: a social and economic problem rather than an obvious environmental problem (Giradet 1992, Widner et al 1993).

Adding environmental concerns to the practical problems of city regeneration looks as if it would turn a difficult task into an impossible one. The city is a complex creature and unless adequate funding is available, the attempt to sort out any one problem characteristically makes things worse elsewhere. A classic example of this is the decision to concentrate scarce public resources in the most problematic neighbourhoods, thereby allowing marginal areas to decline to the point where they too need rescue remedies. Indeed Friends of the Earth have been extremely critical of governmental inner city policy, singling out 'Action For Cities' and the Urban Programme for causing direct environmental damage while failing to make a net improvement in housing conditions or provide jobs for local people (McLaren 1989). The attempt to cope with this complexity however may generate lasting solutions to city problems while lightening the burden of the city on the natural environment.

This chapter explores some aspects of city development and renewal, concentrating particularly on the implications for CO_2 emissions as there is an emerging consensus that global warming is the most urgent and serious problem facing the future of the planet. The chapter also highlights important strands in the debate around cities and sustainability by specifically looking at approaches to urban regeneration. The ways in which various approaches contribute to, or detract from, progress towards global sustainability is assessed. Section one briefly introduces the wider debate on sustainable cities and economic development and a policy framework is outlined. The problems and opportunities for developing a symbiotic relationship between the city and the environment are examined. The second section focuses on a real city, Glasgow, and assesses specific policy responses as well as tensions within the housing aspects of urban regeneration, and the problems of developing an energy policy for council housing. Finally the chapter attempts to contribute to a holistic understanding of the processes of urban change and city wide environmental impacts. Though there are some successful solutions, there are many where social and economic gains for the city will continue to pose environmental problems. Some 'performance indicators' are suggested which may enable local authorities to explore the environmental impact of development activities, while being aware of the need to ameliorate poverty.

City Regeneration Versus the Environment

Chapter 1 has already emphasised that dramatic cuts in carbon dioxide outputs are needed in most high income countries which are directly related to reductions in energy use. Existing housing and infrastructure represents enormous amounts of 'embodied' energy through the creation of building materials, their fabrication into buildings and subsequent maintenance, which is written off if they are replaced before the end of their natural life. Newer domestic buildings often represent larger amounts of energy than older buildings as metal, plastic and concrete replace slate, wood and plaster (Connaughton, 1993). For example certain types of new housing may represent nearly 40% more embodied CO_2, and 30% more embodied energy per square metre than older traditional dwellings.
As chapter 3 has made clear, urban development decisions both through the planning system and the market, have a major impact on where housing is located. They also influence the style of industrial development which keeps people in jobs, so could make major indirect as well as direct impacts on CO_2 reduction targets. Moreover, where there is a stock of buildings which are in reasonable condition and well located for public transport, rehabilitation would generally have a lower environmental impact than new build, as it can produce levels of energy efficiency in use as good as new build but with less energy embodied in building materials.

From this it may follow that strategies to promote the re-use of land and buildings will make a powerful contribution towards sustainability. However, people need income, and economic regeneration strategies may demand greater diversity in the housing stock. For example, attempts to create jobs through investing in conference and exhibition centres, or visitor attractions which capitalise on the 'Heritage of the Industrial Revolution' are designed to encourage yet more travel and tourism. Boyle (1990) suggests that 10 mid-range cars each travelling 10,000 miles per year at 35 miles per gallon would generate around 33 tons of CO_2 in the year. Similarly, greenfield development of new housing for owner-occupation in the suburbs to improve the 'balance' of the urban area will in most cases produce a bewildering array of toxins from building materials (Pearson 1989), and probably increase the number of cars on the road. The process of mining and fabricating construction materials for new homes and the building process itself produce at least 30 tons of CO_2 per 2 bedroom semi-detached house.

FIGURE 1: Some levels at which the relationship between declining industrial cities and sustainability can be addressed

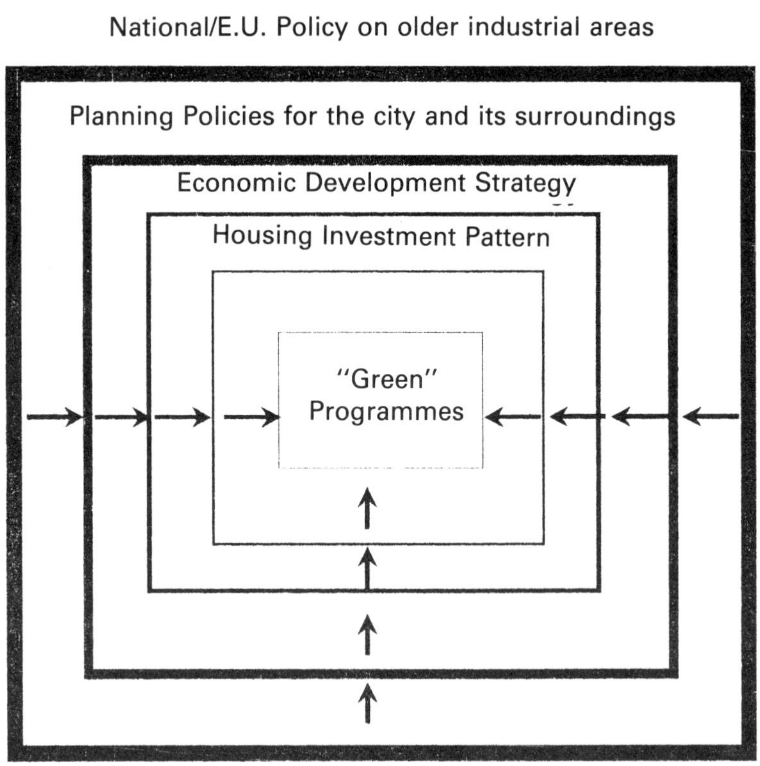

Cities are difficult to manage, and progress in one area of activity almost inevitably causes problems in another. Dedicated 'green' projects such as recycling, protection of wildlife habitats, and environmentally friendly purchasing policies, are only a small part of what is happening. The examination of some aspects of a major city in transition may identify some issues and problems for further study.

A Policy Framework

There are at least five different levels on which the relationship between the city and environment can be tackled. These are:

* regional economic development policies;
* the shape and size of the city;
* economic development policies within the city;
* housing strategies in urban renewal;
* 'green' initiatives.

Figure 1 shows the way different approaches to the problem of city change fit into one another like a set of Russian dolls, with the 'macro' solutions of economic and planning policy operating at governmental or regional level having a greater effect than the 'micro' solutions like neighbourhood improvement schemes.

Regional Economic Development Policies

The continuous pressure for change and innovation in industry means that business decision-makers constantly wish to improve products and modernise processes. This leads to constantly increasing space requirements, which in the absence of special policy measures, are often more easily met by moving to greenfield sites and hiring new workers rather than by retooling and retraining at the existing site. However, if firms move to sites which they consider more advantageous, housing and infrastructure must follow jobs. Buildings which originally housed a thriving community are abandoned or demolished, and houses, schools and shops must be constructed in the new favoured location, which becomes increasingly congested until it too is abandoned.

Any action which challenges this accelerating cycle of construction and abandonment must be a strong movement towards sustainability, no matter what might be the immediate reason of the actors. On this basis, any 'regional policy' which directs investment to existing (older) urban areas is potentially a powerful tool for increasing sustainability. Both the EU's structural funds and the British Government's Development Assistance programmes should tend to steer new development into the older urban areas, but the Glasgow case study highlights the powerful tides of decentralization flowing from other forces and policies.

The Shape and Size of the City

The history of city planning is dominated by an argument between those who place a high value on the compact, high density city, and those who see the city as the source of problems both for humans and the natural world. Both centralization and decentralization are claimed to be necessary for increasing sustainability. The European Commission (and Friends of the Earth) argue in favour of the 'Compact City': a high density, mixed use city which is energy efficient because it reduces travel distances, maximises the effectiveness of public transport provision and offers a high quality of life within the city. In contrast low density alternatives are seen as offering a high quality of life through tele-commuting, access to land and 'a return to rural values'. Breheny (1992b) argues that urban decentralization, which has been a dominant trend in western countries since 1945, cannot be reversed. Similarly, recentralization would be self-defeating, and that any attempt to prescribe a simple, single policy, (such as the high density compact city) is unrealistic and incapable of successful implementation. Sustainable urban development, in Breheny's view, can only be achieved through planning for the broader 'Social City Region' of the city and its hinterland. But this does not negate the idea of the compact city. As our understanding of the energy implications of building and construction become better, the balance of advantage will probably tip towards compact city ideas.

Economic Development Policies Within the City

There are three economic strategies for urban regeneration, two well known and one emerging, and they all have differing environmental impacts for the city. The first strategy gives priority to re-creation of the manufacturing base, both through stimulating and supporting indigenous business, and attracting inward investment. It attempts to generate employment both directly and indirectly. Employers can be encouraged to locate in areas of high housing stress. This may require demolition of housing to create opportunities for industry. Similarly poorly located industrial sites can be made over to housing. The role of housing providers is to supply or encourage the provision of a wide range of housing types and opportunities, with general improvement in housing standards to parallel other changes. This approach may promote global sustainability if manufacturers adopt green technologies, and specifications for house improvements are 'green'. But this does not necessarily happen, and hard won employment gains may be lost overnight if a multinational pulls out.

The second strategy, which was prominent in the 1980s, could be described as 'post industrial service-led regeneration'. It accepts the decline of manufacturing and endeavours to replace it by jobs in service industries, arts, tourism, financial services, head office functions and conference centres. This requires substantial investment in city centre amenities and upper income housing with the risk of gentrification distorting local housing markets. In housing terms this approach may emphasise cosmetic work rather than improving the living conditions of the worst housed. It does not necessarily provide jobs or enhanced income for poorer local residents other than in fast food outlets and warehousing, which have their own limitations. There is an argument that service-led regeneration provides 'clean' growth, but in this context the city consumes the products of polluting manufacturing areas, possibly on another continent, but takes no responsibility for them.

A third strategy emphasises closing the loops of the city's economy. It attempts to keep money and the benefits from this circulation in the local economy by domestic energy policies which increase household purchasing power and encouragement of locally and community owned businesses rather than multiple stores which shift profits elsewhere. It may also encourage non-cash, barter-type transactions between households and local businesses (Ballie 1994), and support local sourcing, including recycling, architectural salvage and urban horticulture (Nozick 1992). This approach is low cost and low risk; it uses local people and their ingenuity rather than inward investment. It also emphasises complex positive feedbacks within the city so many people get some benefit. For example, though savings by tenants after the installation of energy efficiency measures cannot be directly recouped by landlords as higher rents, energy efficiency reduces maintenance costs, reduces rent arrears and makes properties more lettable, so both landlord and tenant gain. Similarly, recycling of goods and materials and local trading increase real incomes within the city while they reduce the impact of city consumption both on the planetary eco-system and other communities (Dobson 1993). It is, however, unclear whether this approach would make enough difference to real income to lift poverty as it could simply mean recycling welfare benefits within a poor community. There are also concerns that this somehow keeps participants on the margins of the 'real world', and by increasing the self sufficiency of local areas, excludes people from the wider society.

Housing Strategies in Urban Renewal

Public investment in housing can attempt to target areas at risk, while maintaining a balance across the city. Public sector investment has increasingly been supplemented (or replaced) by private sector and enterprise company investment, which will operate on more strictly market-led criteria. 'City-wide investment programmes' look at the whole city, but may prioritize houses which are:

- oldest
- in worst condition
- occupied by poorest residents
- most potential for energy efficiency
- most potential for 30 year life.

Energy efficiency and long useful life options are potentially the most environmentally friendly, but they may not concur with residents' aspirations. For example, Figure 2 suggests that an energy efficiency led strategy would give priority to investment in small flatted dwellings, when many households may aspire to terraced and semi-detached homes with private gardens.

FIGURE 2: Energy Consumption and Building Form

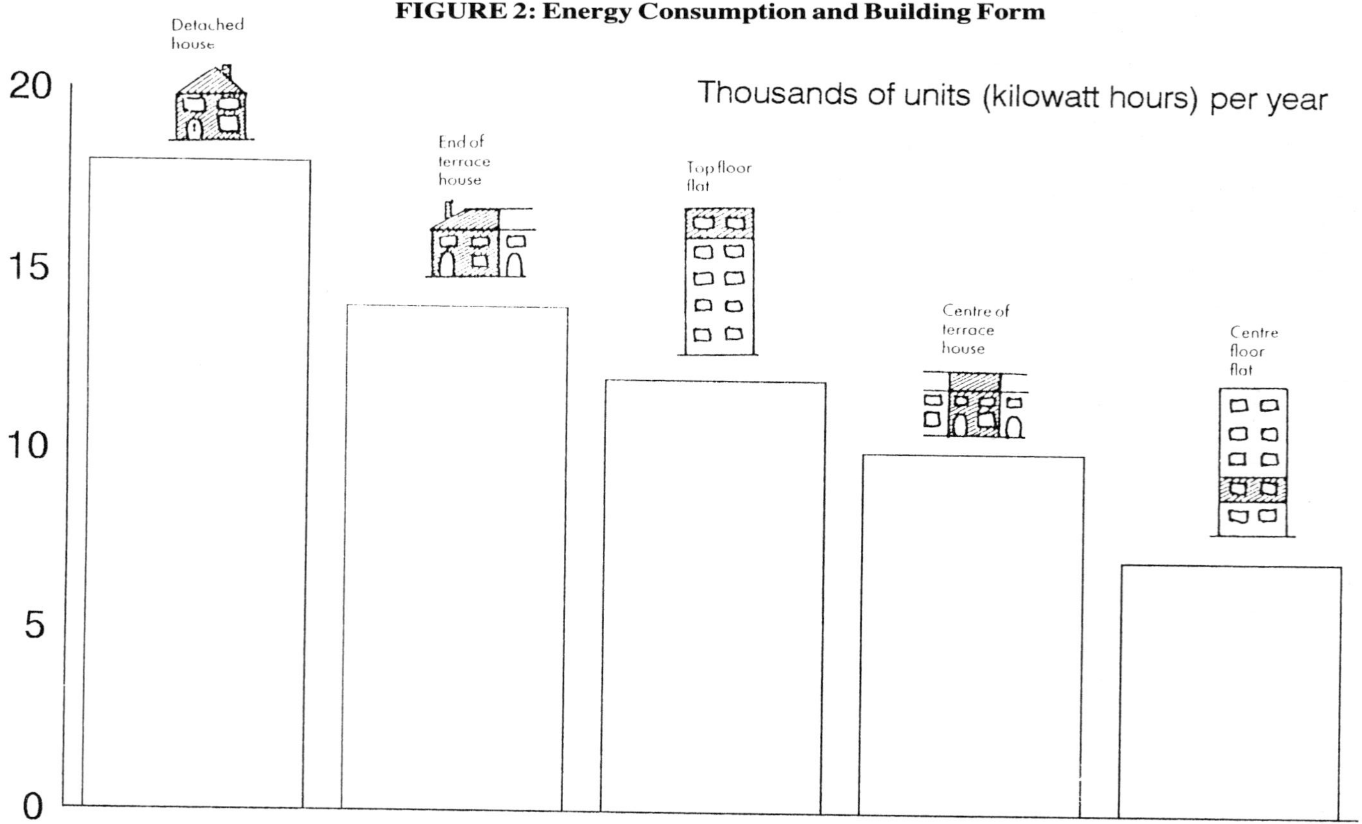

All the houses and flats in the diagram are the same size and have the same proportion of window to outside wall

Source: G.L.C. Reproduced in Edwards 1991

'Area based renewal' concentrates on particularly problematic areas of public or private sector housing, giving high priority to a range of solutions varying between dwelling repair, modernization and neighbourhood improvements – fences, bin stores and public open space – comprehensive restructuring demolition and public/private new build. This approach is environmentally friendly where it invests in dwellings with a potentially long life, both in technical terms and from the residents' point of view. However, unless this is linked to local and city wide economic development initiatives, people may remain poor in nicer houses, deterioration starts again and more investment is required. Moreover, high cost improvements may be necessary to make the area attractive for future residents while tenure diversification, bringing in owner-occupiers may be deemed necessary to save housing areas on the edge of the city.

Housing and economic development strategies are cross-cut by anti-poverty and health promotion programmes, and by community led approaches. 'Anti-poverty' strategies tend to be narrowly based and therefore usually prioritize children, elderly at risk, lone parents, women, and service users. They tend to emphasise access to training, welfare rights, services and child care rather than broader social/economic action, though anti-poverty objectives may prioritize fuel poverty, and may benefit from 'closed loop local economy' approaches. 'Community led bottom up approaches' emphasise closed loop economic development and self build strategies, though self build is probably of limited value in areas where there is excess stock. In Britain community led approaches may arise from pressure to improve the physical environment and develop sophisticated and effective organisational networks starting from an initial 'environmental' problem. Difficulties may arise from this approach when a group or groups' level of organisation and political influence is such that it can demand a high specification improvement, effectively reducing the ability of a housing provider to fund cheaper remedies for the rest.

'Green' Initiatives

Sitting inside these are conventionally 'green' programmes such as tree planting, natural landscaping and wildlife protection, schemes to encourage the use of bikes or make streets safer for pedestrians, better sewerage treatment, environmentally friendly purchasing by public authorities, recycling projects and energy efficiency schemes, particularly those which use urban wastes as fuel (Gordon 1990). 'Green' approaches in most professional disciplines are apparently more likely to be associated with projects which are sensitive to the needs and wishes of local residents, but tend to need more time to work things through with users. The main difficulty is that decisions on purchasing or the design of play areas can be just a drop in the ocean. Governmental decisions on national economic and industrial policy or product changes by major companies will have a much greater effect on the global environment than the decision of an architect to use eco-friendly paints when refurbishing a tower block.

In conclusion, it is difficult in practice to evaluate the environmental impact of these approaches, as there are a multiplicity of deliberate initiatives going on at any one time which complement one another or compete; often aided by, or conflicting with, market forces or other public policies. It is difficult to tease out the major strands, particularly as there is little data available. Measures of costs and benefits are very crude, even if they can be measured on a city scale. For some items it would be more appropriate to measure at a sub-regional scale, but that would complicate the task enormously. In the next section some of the issues highlighted above are explored through a case study of Glasgow.

Glasgow as an 'Ecological City': Problems and Opportunities

Glasgow is a classic northern industrial city, rich in heritage, but now suffering the effects of long term unemployment and poverty, looking for ways to ensure its future. Its experience both of urban regeneration programmes and energy policies may illuminate both problems and potentials for alleviating poverty while limiting environmental impact by utilizing existing resources. In 1900, Glasgow considered itself to be the 'Second City of the Empire', with heavy industries which supplied markets across the globe, and enviable civic amenities; a suburban rail network to rival London, an underground system, theatres, parks, museums and libraries. The urban form was compact, based on 3 or 4 storey walk-up flats ('tenements'), and the railways gave most people easy access to both work and the countryside. Some homes were elaborate and spacious, others were not, and living conditions of the poorest households were among the worst in Europe.

Slum clearance progressed through the interwar years, but the most important recent influence on the pattern of housing in Glasgow was the Scottish Office's Clyde Valley plan of 1946 which attempted to reduce very high population densities in the inner city, 400 people per acre in some parts, by developing New Towns beyond the built-up area. Two New Towns, Cumbernauld and East Kilbride, were built. At the same time Glasgow Corporation built four peripheral estates within the City boundary to provide safe, sanitary housing for people from the cleared slums. Both population and employment of the entire Clydeside conurbation began to fall after 1951, but there was also a considerable suburbanization of employment, which has left the City of Glasgow with a smaller proportion of the stock of jobs, and the surrounding ring of towns with an increasing proportion (Lever and Moore, 1985).

The key problems Glasgow faces now are that the city's population has collapsed from 1.2 million in 1951 to 688,600 in 1991. It is projected to fall to 610,7000 in 2005. Glasgow also has the highest levels of unemployment of any Scottish municipality. At the 1991 Census, only 56% of working age men were in full time or self employment compared with 73% in the rest of Scotland. 42% of primary

FIGURE 3: Effect of inadequate real incomes on housing, economy & community

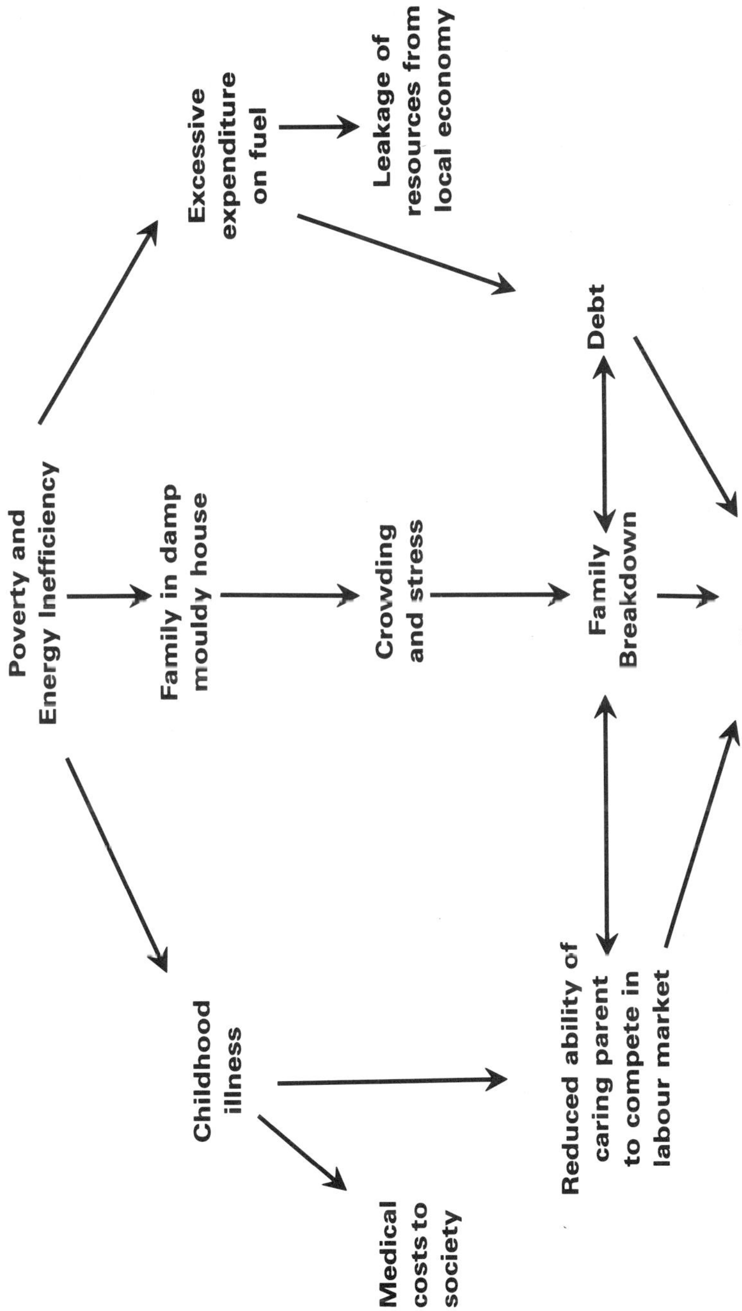

school children received free school meals in 1991/92. Glasgow has the highest proportion of one parent families in Scotland. Furthermore the 1991 Scottish House condition survey found condensation, dampness or mould affected 104,000 dwellings in Glasgow, 36% of the stock, compared with 28% in the rest of Scotland. Almost one-fifth of Glasgow householders (18%) said they were 'bothered a lot' by condensation or dampness compared to 13% in the rest of Scotland. Condensation was particularly bad in the Council sector where 34% of dwellings were affected, compared to 26% for local authority dwellings in the rest of Scotland. Early post-war dwellings were particularly badly affected both in absolute terms and by comparison with local authority dwellings in the rest of Scotland. Poor health is now recognised as central to the City's problems; one third of households in Glasgow had someone with a limiting long term illness compared to one quarter in the rest of Scotland.

From being the second City of the Empire, Glasgow now has many parallels with low income countries. The city's major positive contributions to global sustainability are unfortunately due to poverty, namely the under consumption of fuel and low car availability – two thirds of households had no car in 1991, compared with under two fifths in the rest of Scotland. People are too poor to move to the suburbs so the city stays compact, with a high ratio of flats to single-storey dwellings. But nevertheless Glasgow still has a skilled workforce, a stock of metropolitan amenities, high quality older housing, a compact city form and opportunities for development on brown field sites.

Falling population did not immediately translate into higher housing vacancies as changing family patterns, such as divorce and children leaving home earlier, absorbed potential surplus stock. Now population loss and large scale industrial closures provide opportunities for innovation within the city boundaries re-using land and buildings, potentially countering suburbanization and marginalization of poor communities. However, the particular pattern of population loss raises difficult questions about the role and future of the city's peripheral estates, and the process of suburbanization causes tension between Glasgow and the suburban boroughs. The problem facing Glasgow, and other central urban areas in the same position, is how to escape from unemployment, population loss, poverty and poor housing. The question of whether the actions necessary to reverse urban decline will incur uncompensated environmental costs has yet to be adequately addressed, but pressure both from the European Union and commitments made by the British Government at Rio suggest that local policy makers will have to deal with this problem in the near future.

The rest of the chapter focuses on two of Glasgow's policy responses to urban decline, the housing regeneration programme and Glasgow City Council's energy strategy 'Glasgow Action for Warm Homes'. The two streams of policy response are closely related, as are Glasgow's housing difficulties. Figure 3 suggests the linkages through which poverty and energy inefficient housing can have detrimental effects on health, family stability and local economic

Figure 4: Effect of adequate real incomes on housing, economy and community

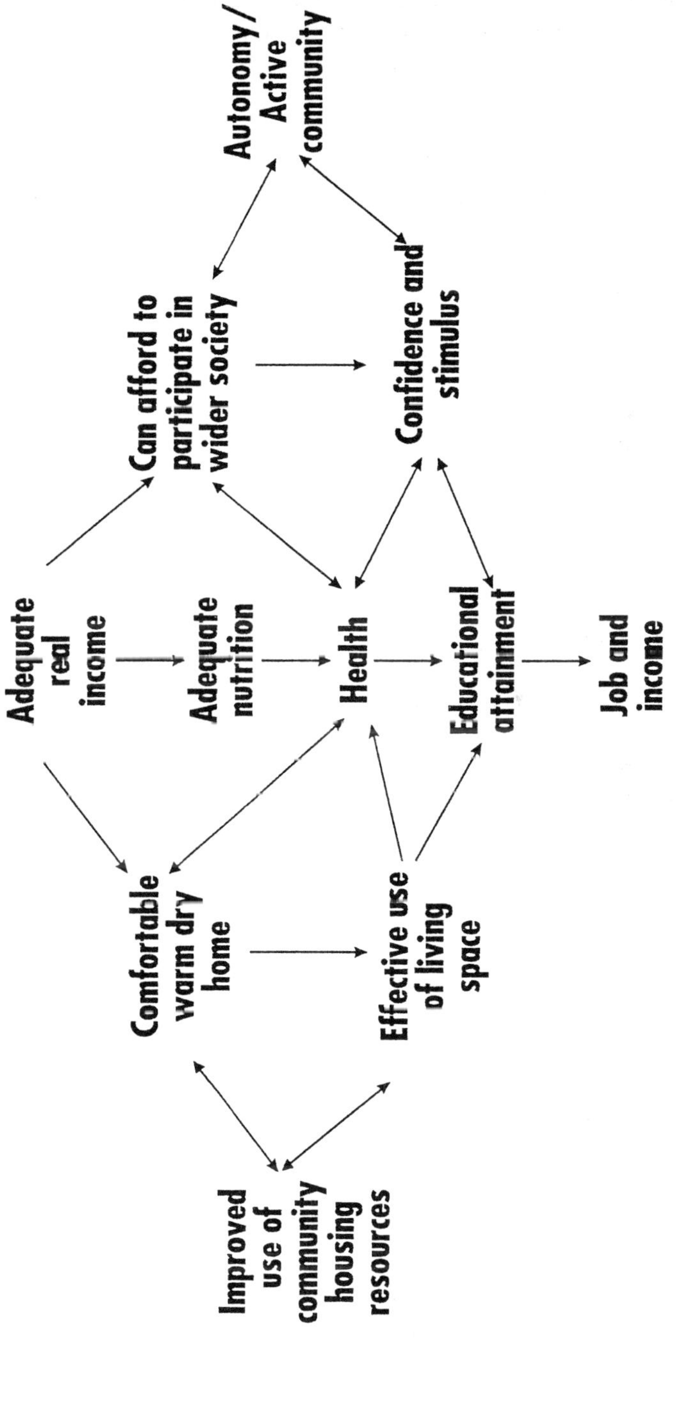

development. Figure 4 describes the other side of the same story, one where adequate real incomes enable households to keep their homes warm and dry. Both landlord and community benefit; good health, confidence and a comfortable home support effective participation in the labour force, thus forming a virtuous cycle.

Glasgow's Policy Response 1: Housing Re-development

Over the past 20 years, Glasgow City Council (GCC) has used a range of programmes to improve the quality of the city's housing stock. It is necessary to try to look at them together rather than analyse a single one in isolation, as it is the totality of programmes which determine change.

Inner City Tenement Rehabilitation

In the 1950s and 60s, there were major slum clearance programmes in most of the inner city areas, often to facilitate road building. In 1969 after a major storm, which left 16,000 inner city tenement flats uninhabitable, the tide turned in favour of rehabilitating those areas which could be saved. Local community based housing associations were used as the main vehicle in areas where conditions were the worst, supplemented by a GCC stone cleaning and back court improvement programme, and grants to owner-occupiers and private landlords for internal and external work. (GCC, 1982).

By 1993, Housing Associations had carried out comprehensive rehabilitation of 17,000 dwellings with less than 1,000 still to complete. These are stone built medium density 3 or 4 storey walk up flats, with potentially high levels of energy efficiency, and easily served by public transport. The rehabilitation of the inner city's older homes makes a strong contribution to sustainability, but there is an argument that these properties are unattractive to young families, who will move to the suburbs unless street level access houses with gardens can be provided in the city.

The Problem of the Peripheral Estates

Throughout the 1970s, population loss continued, though initially masked by high rates of household formation. However in 1978 the Council's Planning Department predicted that up to 40% of dwellings in some parts of the peripheral estates would become vacant, with a net housing surplus of 20,000 dwellings (GCC, 1984). The Grieve Inquiry into Housing in Glasgow (GCC 1986) sharpened the focus of concern, highlighting disrepair, lack of choice and under investment in the Council's stock, arguing that if present arrangements continued, at least 40,000 houses, mostly in the public sector, would require demolition. It recommended that joint planning arrangements, already established in Easterhouse and Drumchapel be extended to the other 2 peripheral estates of Castlemilk and Pollok. Castlemilk was designated a 'partnership' area by The Scottish Office under the 'New Life for Urban Scotland' programme in 1989.

Throughout the late 1980s, there also were over 150 small renewal projects targeted at areas of high housing stress, both within and outside the main initiative areas. In the renewal areas the housing investment strategy has utilized a mixture of private sector new build, tenure change, improvements to former GCC stock by Housing Associations or Scottish Homes, and high specification improvements to GCC's stock using the Council's capital resources. Height reduction and strategic demolition of postwar GCC tenemental properties has been a feature of many projects. There has been considerable emphasis on tenant involvement in the re-design of local areas. Renewal programmes in the peripheral estates effectively re-use existing properties, and increased opportunities for owner-occupation may reduce pressure for greenfield new build. However, the high levels of specification which have been considered necessary to turn the area round represent substantial opportunity costs for other work. There are unresolved questions about the role and nature of some peripheral areas. Continuing (though reduced) population loss re-opens arguments whether they should be re-launched as self-contained suburbs within the city boundary, or whether the city should accept further demolitions and concentrate its population nearer the city centre.

Are People Still Poor in More Attractive Houses?

Much of the economic regeneration activity in Glasgow in the 1980s concentrated on city centre, service led development. These strategies have been widely criticised for failing to deliver jobs to poor communities (Thompson, 1990). A census based evaluation of the Community Renewal Schemes in Glasgow by Fitzpatrick (1993) suggested that high levels of investment in housing were not matched by economic improvement, unless there had been an influx of owner-occupiers to the area. In a broader study, McGregor et al (1992), concluded that housing led initiatives, not solely in Glasgow, had been much more successful in achieving physical regeneration than wider social and economic change. Some initiative areas were stronger in some aspects than others. Despite some good local examples, McGregor identified major weaknesses across projects in their failure to link housing investment to local employment and training, and a failure to build business development around the environmental and housing investment programmes in initiative areas. There is anecdotal evidence that successful participants in employment and training schemes may leave the initiative areas because of limited housing choice and several recent migration studies have shown that Glasgow continues to lose more mature and affluent households to the suburbs, while gaining younger, less affluent households. (GCC 1994a).

Squaring the Circle: the Regeneration Alliance

In response to these continuing problems the Glasgow Regeneration Alliance (GRA) was launched in 1993 as the union of four organisations, Glasgow City Council, Strathclyde Regional Council, Glasgow Development Agency and Scottish Homes, to regenerate eight areas which suffer from strongly marked disadvantage. It covers all four peripheral estates and four areas in the old industrial core of the city. The objectives of the Alliance are to promote Glasgow as a great European city by improving the city's environment and its physical, social and economic infrastructure, including housing, service and industrial facilities; and enhance Glasgow's competitiveness while meeting the needs and aspirations of its citizens. It seeks to develop a dynamic business culture, modernize manufacturing and service industries, and attract inward investment. One aim is to attract and retain population, making full use of sites and buildings, and regenerate run down areas and develop peoples' skills. Finally, the GRA seeks to tackle deprivation and poverty and improve the quality of life for everyone who lives in Glasgow. A prosperous and attractive city centre and maintaining competitiveness is seen as essential to meet these objectives. It is innovative because it provides a balanced, city-wide programme, addressing the particular difficulties of these areas and capitalizing on their strengths, particularly the availability of industrial land and premises, and skilled workforces, to promote the regeneration of the city as a whole (GCC et al 1993).

Though the pursuit of global sustainability as is understood in this book is not an explicit objective of the Regeneration Alliance, the scope of the project offers considerable potential in that direction. For example, 10% of the city's land is presently vacant or derelict offering opportunities to promote high quality housing and employment within the city to counter suburbanisation. There is a substantial role for urban fringe tree planting, countryside management and environmental education. More specifically a focus on manufacturing rather than service industries is emphasised and a light rail/new tram system is being developed. Finally, community empowerment is considered essential; in Drumchapel and Easterhouse communities themselves are starting local exchange trading scheme (LETS) projects. But the completion of motorway links is considered a priority to ensure the development of key industrial sites, which some local organisations consider to outweigh the positive steps being taken towards sustainability (Glasgow for People 1994).

Countervailing Trends

Urban decline is due to many things. There are market and social forces which cannot easily be contained, such as the development of transport and telecommunications, and the decline of economic sectors particularly associated with cities, especially manufacturing. However, in its 1993 Housing Plan, Glasgow City Council highlighted government policies which are supporting decentralisation.

These are:

* Labour market deregulation, which has widened the distribution of pre-tax incomes (the lowest decile of wage earners in Strathclyde in 1990 earned 34% of the top decile, compared with 41% in the early 1980s – (Scottish Homes, 1993))
* Changes in taxation and social security policies which have widened the distribution of final incomes and made the poor poorer
* Planned and assisted decentralisation of both business and better-off people to the New Towns, accompanied in Glasgow's case by a lack of promotion of the city as a location for economic activity other than services
* High, albeit now rapidly declining, subsidies to owner occupation, which have gone disproportionately to support private housing investment outside the city. Moreover the Right to Buy public sector housing, which while not creating social deprivation, has concentrated households in the less popular housing stock
* The imposition of VAT on private housing repair and improvement work has had a disproportionate effect on Glasgow's housing stock as it is older than that elsewhere.

A comprehensive assessment by the Policy Studies Institute of the position in all the most deprived British urban areas concluded that the gap between conditions and opportunities in deprived areas and other kinds of places remains as wide as it was a decade and a half ago, and indeed has widened (Wilmot and Hutchieson 1992).

Three key issues emerge from this exploration:

* If urban regeneration strategies are to be effective in countering suburbanization and the concomitant loss of greenfield sites, additional commuting and new build, they must somehow accommodate the aspirations of young families within the built up area but without losing the advantages of compact city form;
* The concentration of poverty in the city is the consequence of a multitude of governmental policies running counter to the city's regeneration programme. There is an urgent need for consistency across policy areas and policy integration;
* Efforts to lift poverty must be in a framework where increased income does not automatically result in environmental damage. This must include energy efficiency systems which will allow people to enjoy adequate warmth without necessarily increasing CO_2 emissions, and good public transport systems.

The question of poverty, energy use and affordable warmth is developed in the second case study.

Glasgow's Policy Response 2: an Energy Policy for the Real World

The public sector housing built in the peripheral estates of Glasgow largely recreated the tenemental form of the nineteenth century inner city, but postwar material shortages meant that metal window frames and concrete blocks were used in construction. In the 1950s, the concept of energy efficiency was unknown to most professionals, and irrelevant because fuel was cheap and most households had income to afford it. In the 1960s, the focus of redevelopment shifted to create tower and deck access blocks in more central locations, but the problem was still how to rehouse as many people as possible from the inner city slums as quickly as possible at lowest cost. Once again, they were built to acceptable standards at the time, but cost pressure often meant short cuts on heating systems.

The pursuit of what seemed to be an unproblematic environmental objective, of improving air quality, without thinking through the social implications has caused serious problems for the city. In the 1960s the city eliminated smogs by imposing clean air zones and replacing many open fires with gas or electric heating. The mid 1970s saw the collapse of the local economy with massive job losses in shipyards, railways, engineering, and manufacturing. High levels of unemployment and poverty among those who remained and rising fuel prices meant that housing which had been warm and dry when adequately heated became subject to condensation, while the historic concentration on new build combined with the weakness of maintenance systems led to cumulative disrepair in the local authority stock, and a problem of penetrating damp. Resources were lost to the city as families paid up to 30% of their net income on fuel and the housing stock deteriorated. Fuel poverty contributed to the city's health problem with overcrowding caused by rooms becoming unusable. Figure 3 showed how these may lock together into a cycle of poverty, poor housing, overcrowding, ill health and lost economic opportunities. Community led anti-dampness campaigns attracted academics and professional lobbyists. Case material was built up and campaigners gained some ground (Bryant 1979). At the same time, technical analyses of the problem were being developed, often in the voluntary sector and universities. But the broad environmental impacts of energy inefficient housing were not given a high priority.

However attempts were made to deal with the problem in Glasgow District Council dwellings. In 1981 the Council established a 'Dampness Control Unit', appointed local inspectors within District Offices to supervise a repairs programme and introduced a 'Dampness Compensation Scheme'. The Council was aware that these measures represented short term palliative treatments and began a number of projects to tackle the root causes. These included recladding of multi-storey flats, modernisation of non-traditional housing, introduction of collective heating arrangements, including Heat With Rent, together with window replacement but the problems of dampness seemed to be getting worse. The Grieve Inquiry (GCC 1986) put the issues of dampness, heating and insulation first among its proposals. It criticised the Council for continuing with wasteful compensation payments and recommended that the Council should develop design proposals for adequate insulation and whole house heating for each house type and, in addition, assess costs and benefits of upgrading against replacement costs for all house types requiring extensive treatment. It also recommended developing a city-wide ten year programme for heating and insulation for all stock and phase out wasteful compensation payments and superficial treatments.

The Grieve Inquiry, and follow up discussions with Inquiry participants across the statutory and voluntary sector, made it clear that the existence of condensation dampness, mould growth, cold and damp related illnesses and families effectively overcrowding in one room could be traced back to one single common denominator, that is poverty. This examination also showed that much of the economic and environmental gain from previous investment was being seriously eroded by:

* fuel tariff adjustment by Scottish Power and British Gas;
* the Social Security Review of 1988 which meant that 50% of benefit claimants were losing income and 5% gaining;
* the increasing gradient of the Housing Benefit taper resulting in a greater number of families in the poverty trap;
* the reduction in size of the average household, which together with the Social Security Review led to serious reductions in average household income.

This evidence confirmed the need for a strategy not for energy efficiency but one to eradicate poverty – as it was the inability to afford adequate warmth which was the root cause of dampness, condensation, mould growth and cold related illnesses. Such a strategy had to be linked to investment measures and the City's housing management services which would generate and secure economic and environmental benefits for council tenants.

Glasgow 'Action for Warm Homes'

An energy policy framework 'Glasgow Action for Warm Homes' (GAWH) was adopted in 1990, built around the establishment of affordable fuel costs for different types of low income households and the delivery of heating and appliance costs which these households can afford to pay. The main elements in the programme are:

* To redirect existing resources towards addressing the problems of condensation, dampness, thermal inefficiency of stock and assisting the alleviation of poverty.
* Housing management support services, including energy advice, debt counselling to tenants groups and individual householders, and project appraisal and evaluation assistance to local office project managers, plus support to campaign organizations such as Heatwise and Right to Warmth.
* To develop a range of energy demonstration projects from the £17,000 per unit Cardow Road project which combines high efficiency gas fired condensing boilers to GCC Housing's own design with super insulation and double glazing, to a single remedy of the condensing boilers alone at a cost of £3,000 per unit.
* A mass energy audit using the National Homes Energy Rating (NHER) scheme and pre-improvement project surveys to identify levels of energy efficiency and household incomes profiles. These are brought together in packages tailored to achieve post-improvement fuel costs of 10% of net household income.

By 1993 GAWH targets dominated the City's Housing Revenue Account capital expenditure. Between 1994/5 and 1996/7 Glasgow City Council plans to devote £96.5 million to condensation and energy efficiency works, and £61.0 million on works to rectify severe penetrating damp, out of a planned programme of £222 million (Glasgow City Housing 1993a). In pilot projects, fuel costs to the user have been reduced by up to 90%, while achieving whole house heating for 16 hours per day to 21°C in the living room and 18°C in the rest of the house. Pilot projects indicate that substantial CO_2 savings and comfort improvement can be made with advanced heating only. A typical 3 bedroomed ground floor interwar flat, with brick cavity walls, without insulation with a NHER rating of 0.0 and using electric fixed room heaters on normal domestic tariff is currently producing 8.1 tons of CO_2 per year if fully heated. An advanced heating system, but no other work, reduces the CO_2 output to 2.9 tons per year, and increases the NHER rating to 4.8.

A number of difficulties have been experienced in implementation, as might be expected. Two of the most significant demonstration projects, the Easthall Jobs and Energy pilot, and the Easthall European Energy model were tenant-led and many other community groups have been actively involved in the process, but individual users have had difficulty believing that they can heat their whole house for 16 hours per day for less than one room for 9 hours a day. GCC Housing is tackling this through energy advice. But some householders still need to be convinced that their fuel costs will be lower if they resist the temptation to interfere with control systems. Building designers have been reluctant to apply the principles of Action For Warm Homes and have defended inappropriate designs on the basis of alterations not being technically feasible. Demonstration projects have proved these arguments to be false and that the Affordable Fuel Costs can be achieved within reasonable budgets. However not all in the building industry have applied the results; in the City Housing's view designers and industry seem content to specify items readily available on the market in preference to commissioning new designs despite the fact that support for new technology is being encouraged. City Housing is now carrying out a detailed evaluation both of new designs and the processes involved in implementing them.

Fuel price adjustments by Fuel Boards are required, particularly on the issues of standing charges and day rate electricity. City Housing has resorted to fuel switching in an attempt to resolve this. The Fuel Boards do not seem to have sufficient confidence to demand tariff structures which allow lower fuel costs for the poor where the state pays for both accommodation and disposable income alongside higher fuel bills for individuals who can afford to invest in energy efficiency from their own resources. GCC Housing will continue to lobby for such changes. Lack of understanding among regulators, civil service and government of opportunities offered has been a particular problem. The Gas Regulator has taken a keen interest in Glasgow Action For Warm Homes but since September 1992 has been deflected from this interest by the issue of competition. The Electricity Regulator would appear to have failed almost entirely to represent the views of the poor in its dealings with Scottish Power. The Civil Service has been responding, but is slow in recognising the significant savings available to the landlords from eradicating fuel poverty. While the imposition of VAT on fuel by central government may encourage middle and upper income groups to invest in energy efficiency, low income groups will simply be exposed to much more severe levels of poverty. Benefits would have to increase in some cases by 34% for single people simply to maintain their purchasing power. In November 1992 the Treasury launched the Private Finance Initiative, with the object of promoting a general increase in private finance for projects which would normally be entirely or mainly financed by the public sector. The Scottish Office has now indicated a willingness to help facilitate access to private finance for energy efficiency measures in public housing. A variety of projects are possible, including heating and heating control equipment and combined Heat and Power Projects. This is important because previously governments have refused to allow local authorities this facility.

The key issue which arises from this case study is that there is substantial resistance from large utilities and suppliers to local solutions which threaten their profit margins. It is difficult to deliver the best outcomes for poor householders where technical solutions are market-driven. New relationships between tenants and landlords are needed which would enable gains to be captured for the community.

'Trade-offs' and the Problem of Making Decisions

The case study suggests that urban regeneration activities can support progress towards global sustainability while addressing local poverty. There are many activities some of which older cities such as Glasgow are already engaged in, which simultaneously maintain the population and revenue base of the city while reducing environmental damage. These 'win-win' activities would include rehabilitation of older housing areas, 'closed loop' local economic development strategies and programmes to achieve affordable warmth. Rehabilitation of older housing areas preserves communities and protects the city's revenue base, while utilising embodied energy in existing dwellings and increasing the efficiency of public transport. Programmes to achieve affordable warmth protect the physical fabric of the housing stock, and increase disposable income in poor communities without increasing CO_2 emissions. However, with present technologies, some development options may be problematic, possibly contributing more to urban regeneration than they do to the achievement of global sustainability. These may include:

* high specification retrofit or refurbishment which incurs very high embodied energy/embodied CO_2 costs, though this may well be what local tenants' groups want and feel they need;
* low density infill, which may be necessary to meet the aspirations of more affluent households, and may well avoid greenfield new build, but may represent more embodied CO_2 than refurbished older dwellings;
* refurbishment for sale at the edge of the build-up area, which re-uses existing stock and increases tenure diversity, but at the expense of increased car use unless appropriate mass transport systems are available.

It is difficult to make choices as information is often lacking and outcomes are often invisible. Programme beneficiaries may be vocal local residents, while those who suffer most quickly from global warming may be on another continent. Moreover, as Figure 1 and the case studies have illustrated, action at a local level which potentially supports progress towards sustainability is easily counteracted by wider public policies. There is a need for better management tools which will build in good practice, seeking out successful solutions and consciously checking the needs of the city against the demand for global sustainability.

Achieving Sustainability: Management Approaches and Problems

Many organizations, businesses, local authorities, Housing Associations and the voluntary sector are adopting quality assurance techniques, modified to meet environmental ends as a means of understanding or reducing the impact of their activities. These include Eco-audit, BS7750 and environmental charters; existing techniques tend to be bureaucratic, relying heavily on blueprints and checklists and demand extensive documentation. These techniques are unhelpful as they squander opportunities which could encourage people to develop their own paths to good practice. Experience with 'managing change' projects in many disciplines demonstrates that to achieve lasting improvements the people who have responsibility for carrying out day to day tasks need to own the assumptions on which the projects are founded. Good training in (say) equal opportunities or race equality encourages participants to clarify values and assess existing practice against those values. This makes it possible for participants to develop their own models of good practice without recourse to detailed checklists, though obviously good practice must be supported by some form of sanction if behaviour falls below some published threshold.

Ideas for the Future

A new approach is required which, while it understands the need for jobs and incomes, insists on seeing things in context and tries to identify the outcomes of activity to support jobs. Glasgow's problems of poverty, unemployment and population loss suggest it would be helpful to focus attention on incomes, unemployment, amount of empty property and vacant land and changes in the amount of green space/agricultural land in the travel to work area. However, conventional approaches to economic development often fail to recognize both basic social needs and fail to identify ecological consequences. In particular conventional measures focus strongly on changes in cash incomes, but higher incomes may translate directly into higher CO_2 emissions unless other options are available.

Similarly low levels of vacant land and empty properties which the Glasgow example suggests may be desirable might be the result of in-migration and abandonment of useful infrastructure elsewhere, rather than the consistent re-use of land and buildings among a stable population. Moreover, one person's 'vacant site' may be another person's 'urban wildlife habitat'. There will be circumstances when the existing density of city buildings will be unacceptable. Some loss of green space may be necessary to relieve congestion, or locally meet a demand for family housing with gardens which would otherwise have expressed itself as suburbanization. It all depends on context, and the options which are available. Policy development needs to focus on actions which address social, economic and environmental problems in a holistic way and emerge from models of interactions of real problems and local experience.

There is a need for clearly stated values which will enable decision-makers, practitioners and communities to identify whether activities move towards, or away from, a goal. The question of values is explored in more detail in Porritt (1986). If values are clarified, policies, programmes and measures of progress can be developed which attempt to meet social, economic and environmental objectives in a holistic way. The following themes appear to be central in a value-system which could move us towards a more sustainable society:

- recognition that humans are part of nature
- sustainability including equity and participation
- health
- valuing the positive role cities can have in human society

Figure 5 shows how explicit values inform policy, and ultimately determine how that policy is monitored.

Figure 5

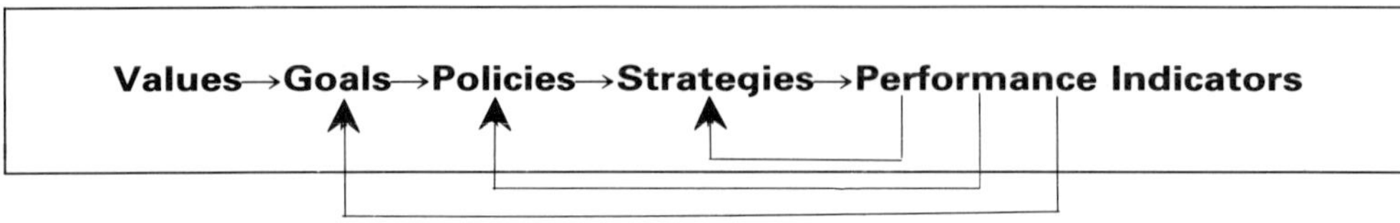

It may be helpful to concentrate on policies which can be implemented at the municipal level, which may coincide with the level at which progress can be most effectively monitored. However, poverty cannot easily be managed at the level of the municipality. Where, as in Glasgow, 30% of the population is dependent on Income Support, the influence of local housing action will be limited. But some policy strands offer real hope. Figure 3 offered a model of how, in Glasgow's case, poverty has combined with energy inefficiency and inappropriate heating systems to reinforce cycles of poor housing, ill health, lost economic opportunities, and further poverty. Figure 4 proposes a mirror image of this cycle of problems, where adequate real incomes allow people to meet basic needs. The conundrum of how to alleviate poverty without incurring long term environmental damage, it seems, can be solved by careful design and implementation of policies such as domestic energy efficiency programmes which meet social, economic and environmental objectives, and the development of sensitive monitoring systems which emerge from models of the interactions of real problems, such as the example of Figure 3.

Table 1 suggests some measures which could be of particular value in a city like Glasgow. These either measure important outputs from the urban system, such as CO_2 emissions, or take soundings at key points in the model of the city's problems. This list is far from exhaustive; many other indicators could be used such as bio-diversity, production of solid waste, or take-up of allotments. Analysis of the first case study in this chapter would probably lead to transport CO_2 in the travel to work area and embodied CO_2 in buildings, both existing and new stock, being given priority as indicators of urban sustainability. Work by Doyal and Gough (1991), Percy-Smith and Sanderson (1992) identify autonomy as well as physical health as universal pre-requisites for successful participation in a social form of life. Autonomy, the capacity to make informed choices about what should be done and how to set about doing it, is not easily measured, but it would be helpful if indicators suggested include those in which local communities can play a key role in collection, and become directly involved in the process of making those informed choices. In Glasgow, the Healthy Cities programme provides a model of how this can work.

TABLE 1: SOME INDICATORS FOR MEASURING PROGRESS TOWARDS SUSTAINABILITY IN A PLACE LIKE GLASGOW

TYPE OF INDICATOR	MEASURE	WHO COLLECTS COULD COLLECT	HOW	HOW USED
Condition	Poverty	National government Local Authorities	Unemployment, housing benefit, Social Security statistics, free school meals returns	Focus attention on poverty
Stress	Domestic CO_2 in use.	Local Authorities, National Government, Voluntary Sector	Energy audit and household survey.	Focus attention on domestic energy consumption.
Stress	Hospital admissions in first year of life	Health Boards	Routine admissions statistics.	Focus attention on social conditions and high priority preventative health intervention.
Stress	Access to a healthy diet	Community Groups, Local Authority	Budget/household surveys	Focus attention on poverty and deficiencies in existing supply network
Response	"Affordable Warmth" % dwellings which can be heated to GAWH standards for less than 10% of household income.	Local Authorities/ Voluntary Sector	Energy audit and household survey.	Focus on fit between energy demand of house and household ability to pay for fuel.
Response	Satisfaction with house and neighbourhood.	Community Groups, LA, National Government	Routine resident surveys	Focus attention on mismatch between needs and available housing stock.

Sensitive indicators of progress towards (or away from) sustainability can be measures of the condition of that society or eco-system, the stresses which it has to face, and the policy responses to those stresses. Condition indicators generally describe the resilience or fragility of a system. For example, if there is a high level of species diversity in an area, the local eco-system can more easily respond to change than an area where species diversity is more limited. In the Glasgow case study, poverty could be the key condition indicator. Where people have low incomes, they are unable to buy themselves out of difficulties. Few low income households are able to purchase efficient central heating systems without assistance. However, for reasons previously discussed, a direct focus on poverty may be unhelpful unless there is a realistic framework wherein higher incomes do not automatically lead to environmental damage. 'Stress' indicators can be social or economic as well as environmental. In the Glasgow case it seems helpful to focus on childhood illness and diet, poor performance in each being the result of poverty. The 'environmental' arm to this Glasgow model prioritises CO_2 emissions as a key environmental stress, potentially producing a family of potential indicators which explore different aspects of CO_2 production in urban development considered earlier in this chapter.

The main 'response' measure in this model is the proportion of dwellings which can be heated to Glasgow Action for Warm Homes standards for less than 10% of household income – a policy response which reduces domestic CO_2 output, while supporting household income and hopefully improving health and diet. 'Satisfaction with home and neighbourhood' is also listed. It is complicated by cultural factors, but significant improvements on this measure, in the Glasgow case, could suggest that the 'Action for Warm Homes' programme was taking effect. The models developed in this chapter show how closely social, economic and environmental problems are linked. But with a little imagination, this closeness and complexity can be used to develop policy solutions which address all three problems, rather than single vision approaches which cause further difficulties. Glasgow City Council has begun to carry out detailed research, both quantitative and qualitative, on the effectiveness of Glasgow Action for Warm Homes in securing environmental, economic and social benefits for the city. This research will also explore some of the issues around 'indicators' which this chapter has raised.

Conclusion

The case studies in this chapter show that in some situations successful solutions to the environmental problems posed by urban regeneration can be found. Without an ambitious 'sustainability' agenda Glasgow has made progress because of the way local circumstances and policy responses have combined together. However, there remain difficult trade-offs, where the balance of advantage is unquantified and outcomes uncertain. There is a consistent problem which echoes the 'Russian dolls' of Figure 1. Though it makes sense to try to measure the environmental impacts of regeneration and energy efficiency programmes at a local level, local authorities' ability to achieve the scale of change which is required is constrained by broader government policy and economic strategies. The crucial direction appears to be an approach which emphasises social, economic and ecological values as being central to achieving sustainability, and a system of measuring progress which reflects these values. This value-system must be widely owned; peoples' participation in the process of measuring progress will determine their ownership of these values.

Notes

(1) The views expressed in this chapter are solely of the author and are not necessarily of Glasgow City Council.

(2) The author is indebted to Lesley Rowan of Stirling University Department of Management and Organisation for assistance with this section and Wendy Simpson-Lewis of the Canadian State of the Environment Reporting Unit for the 'Condition/Stress/Response' framework.

CHAPTER 7: Energy Efficiency Measures and Social Inequality

Brenda Boardman

This chapter explores the theme of growing energy efficiency variations in the housing stock to the detriment of the poorest families. Instead of being able to buy the cheapest warmth, those on the lowest incomes are forced to purchase expensive warmth as a result of energy inefficient homes and heating systems, and are increasingly suffering from 'fuel poverty'. This divergence of housing standards means that the poor are now worse off than they were 10 or 20 years ago, relative to better off families. One reason for this divergence is that low-income households cannot invest in their properties to the extent that better-off families can. Government policies towards energy efficiency have not assisted in redressing this balance and have at times aided social polarisation. Indeed new energy policies, with a green tinge, may continue to benefit the rich more than the poor. For example, the imposition of VAT on domestic fuel (despite Government proposals to compensate the worst hit households) and the programmes financed through the Energy Saving Trust are likely to have a negative impact on those suffering from fuel poverty relative to better-off households. This chapter is written in the belief that the benefits of a cleaner environment should be achieved without adding to the hardship experienced by poorer groups in the present population.

A major cause of this worsening situation is the Government's failure to recognize that capital investment is the key to reducing fuel poverty. The first section introduces the main concepts and issues in this discussion. The second section examines the role of fuel prices over a 20 year period and the implications of a concern for carbon dioxide emissions. In the third section, the effects of income and poverty issues are described, followed by an analysis of the energy efficiency of low-income homes. The final section assesses recent government policies and their effects on low-income households and offers critical analysis of new initiatives in this area.

Fuel Poverty: Key Concepts and Issues

As mentioned in chapter 1, fuel poverty is the inability to achieve affordable warmth because of the energy inefficiency of the home. Households purchase electricity, gas or other fuels not because they want them, but because they want warmth, hot water or light; these energy 'services' are provided after the energy is transformed through a piece of capital equipment. Thus, energy is a derived demand: the quantity households purchase depends both on the level of the final energy service they require and, crucially, on the efficiency of the capital equipment being used. It follows therefore that levels of energy efficiency are inextricably linked to levels of capital expenditure and changes in capital stocks. Fuel poverty is different from ordinary poverty: poverty can be affected by extra income; the solution to fuel poverty depends upon capital investment programmes.

As energy is a derived demand, levels of expenditure cannot be equated with levels of service: it is perfectly possible to have a super efficient home, which provides high standards of service for low levels of energy costs. And, more importantly, it is frequently true that people have high levels of expenditure on fuel, but poor standards of warmth and other energy services. This is what living in an energy inefficient home means: they are paying a lot to be cold. This is somewhat counter-intuitive, but high expenditure on energy conveys no status or benefit; quite the opposite, for instance, from expenditure on housing generally. The difference between the demand for energy and the demand for warmth demonstrates the importance of low levels of capital investment in creating fuel poverty. The fuel poor suffer from both a shortage of income and a shortage of capital investment.

If the poor are to be able to afford adequate warmth on their existing incomes there needs to be capital investment in their favour so that they can buy the cheapest warmth. The relationship between affordable warmth (and other energy services) and energy efficiency is indicated in Figure 1. Based on present expenditure it is possible to define 10% of the weekly budget spent on all fuel as 'affordable' – see Table 4 below. Over quite long time-scales, this is a fixed sum. The temperature of the house that provides 'warmth' can also be predicted, for the majority of the population, as we all have similar physiologies. This would probably be 19°C, 24 hour whole house temperature (Boardman 1991, p.125). The only way that a fixed standard can be provided for a fixed sum of money is through the energy efficiency of the property (Figure 1). If poor households with limited money available for fuel are to have affordable warmth then their properties must be the most energy efficient, not the least.

Figure 1: Relationship between income, energy efficiency and warmth, if affordable warmth is to be obtained

Affordable Warmth

10% of income for all energy services	energy efficiency of the dwelling	24 hour mean internal temperature of 18°C

The above diagram confirms the importance of the price of fuel, in order to assess 'affordability'. Some measures of energy efficiency are based solely on technical efficiency – the amount of useful energy, such as warmth, that is delivered for any given input. The definition of energy efficiency used here includes economic efficiency. This is particularly important in the domestic sector, where the price of a unit of fuel, at the meter, during the day, can vary by a factor of four: 7.5p/kWh for electricity to 1.5p/kWh for gas.

Cold homes are unhealthy and result in an increase both of illness and death. There is strong evidence (Boardman 1991, Burridge and Ormandy 1993, Hunt and Boardman) but the causality is contested by Government, particularly in relation to extra winter deaths. Since the split of the Department of Health from the Department of Social Security, the debate is becoming more open as the DoH is responsible for expenditure that results from limited incomes and restricted capital expenditure. Research sponsored by the Medical Research Council questioned: 'might warmer living rooms decrease the number of winter deaths?' (Woodhouse, et al. 1993). The Secretary of State of Health has, for the first time, conceded that there could be a link between ill-health and poor housing, when announcing a new inquiry (The Guardian 4.5.94).

The energy efficiency of the house can be assessed by an energy audit, for instance the National Home Energy Rating (NHER). This rating reflects the total cost of providing a set of energy standards in the dwelling, normalised by floor area. A code of 0 is the least and 10 the most energy efficient. The average British house is around 4.4 and a new home built to comply with the present Building Regulations would be about 7. A rating of 8 would provide affordable warmth for most low-income households in receipt of benefits.
Figure 2 gives a schematic representation of the spread of ratings across the housing stock (though it is not known in practice) and indicates the position of the average levels for both the whole housing stock and for affordable warmth. From this it can be established that:

* the vast majority of properties do not provide affordable warmth for low-income households;
* if fuel prices rise faster than benefits, the affordable warmth line will shift further to the right and bring even more low-income families into fuel poverty;
* if claimants receive increases in benefit that more than compensate for fuel price rises, then the affordable warmth line shifts slightly to the left and means that more people are living in homes that provide them with affordable warmth;
* every low-income house that is improved to obtain a higher energy rating has lessened the fuel poverty of the occupants, but it is only when the rating is above 8 that the household has the opportunity to afford adequate warmth.

Figure 2: Schematic representation of the energy coding of the UK housing stock

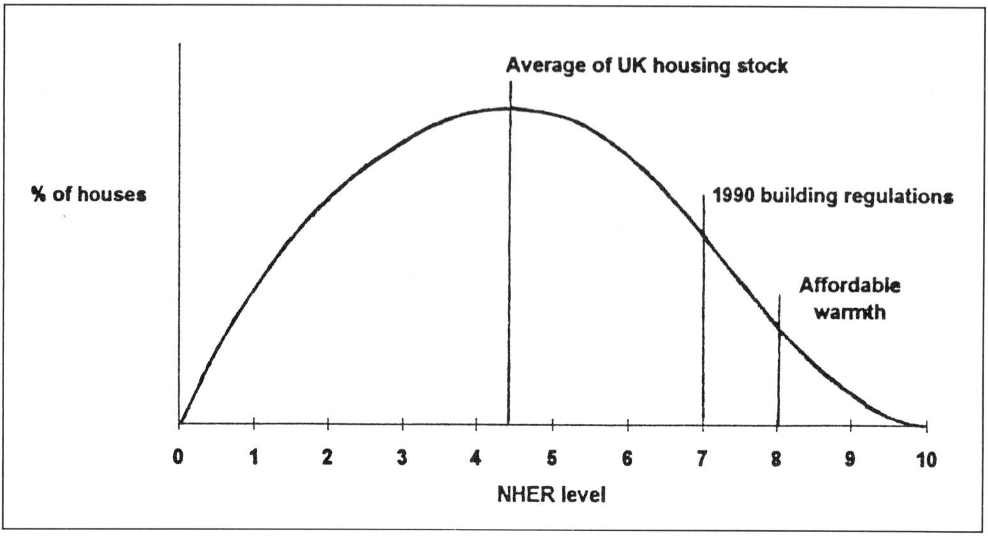

Energy Consumption and Fuel Prices

When the period 1974-1993 is divided into two blocks, there have been considerable differences in the behaviour of gas and electricity in each period. The real price of electricity rose sharply initially and was then static (Table 1), whereas the price of gas rose slightly in real terms during the first seven years but fell substantially in the second period. The net effect is, as the bottom line indicates, that gas in 1993 was 16% cheaper in real terms than in 1974, whereas electricity was 33% more expensive. This demonstrates the financial advantages that have accrued to gas users, particularly those with gas central heating, in comparison with households more dependent upon electricity. Gas usage and central heating ownership is concentrated in higher income homes (Boardman 1991, pp.94-6).

Table 1: Price indices for domestic electricity, gas and all goods, UK, 1974-1993

	Electricity	Gas	Retail Price Index
15.1.74	100	100	100
13.1.87	523	414	395
13.1.87	100	100	100
20.4.93	142	113	141
15.1.74 to 20.4.93	743	468	557

Source: DUKES 1993, P.106

Note the index for electricity and gas is compared to the RPI, to assess whether there has been a change in 'real' price of the fuel.

There is a concentration in poorer homes of:

- electric central heating as the main form of heating;
- electric non-central heating as the main form of heating;
- supplementary electric heating for use in cold weather;
- all-electric homes;
- electric immersion heaters as the main form of water heating, all year round.
  (Boardman and Houghton 1991, p.87).

Thus, fuel price changes over the last 20 years have been more detrimental to low-income households than to better-off families.

One of the reasons for lower price rises recently is the effect of privatisation of gas (1986) and electricity (1990). A major Governmental objective was to increase the opportunities for competition and thus constrain prices. For domestic consumers, competition is limited, so that electricity prices are considerably higher and gas prices probably higher than they would have been without privatisation (Yarrow 1992, p.25; Yarrow 1993, p.29). The large profits made by the utilities since privatisation have added to calls for lower prices, particularly for the poorer members of society, from consumer groups (NCC 1993, NACAB 1993).

Another effect of privatisation has been the introduction of the Fossil Fuel Levy (FFL). This is levied at 11% on domestic electricity bills, equivalent to £30 per annum for the average family. The money is used, almost exclusively, to subsidize the provision of nuclear power. The FFL is only levied on electricity and is another reason for the greater cost penalties faced by electricity users. The European Commission has required that the FFL going to nuclear electricity is phased out by 1998, as it is anti-competitive. At the moment, Nuclear Electric is receiving £1.25 bn in subsidy a year from domestic consumers.

The constraint of prices through privatisation is at odds with the Government's objective of raising prices, ostensibly to encourage greater energy efficiency. The prime example is the imposition of value added tax (VAT) on domestic fuel at 8% in April 1994 and 17.5% from April 1995. These very substantial price increases will be regressive and penalize poor households the hardest, for several reasons. First, the poor are paying a larger proportion of their weekly budget on fuel already (Table 4 below). Secondly, the poor are on tight budgets and cannot increase expenditure to maintain consumption (Table 2). They will cut back the most on the amount of fuel they use, although this is already the lowest. Richer households can afford to absorb a large proportion of the price rise. Finally, the poor do not have the capital resources to invest in energy efficiency improvements and thus maintain standards of energy service. For them, this route depends on outside investment.

Table 2: Effect of a 15% price increase on domestic energy consumption, UK 1989

	Quintile of income				
	Poorest	**2**	**3**	**4**	**Richest**
Before tax (£ pw)	8.55	10.45	10.96	12.01	13.9
Tax paid (£ pw)	1.17	1.44	1.48	1.60	1.80
Change in energy use	–9.9%	–8.5%	–6.5%	–5.0%	–1.9%

Source: Pearson and Smith 1990, p.12

The effect of imposing VAT on domestic fuel will be very little reduction in consumption as a result of improved energy efficiency. For this to happen, there would have to be substantially increased capital expenditure on insulation materials and other energy efficiency improvements, and there is no evidence that this has happened, or been promoted, for instance by new advertising campaigns.

Thus, the environmental benefits (as belatedly claimed by the Government) of imposing VAT are mainly being achieved through additional hardship in low-income homes, rather than real energy efficiency improvements. For the latter to occur, without increasing hardship, there needs to be direct capital investment in low-income homes (Figure 3).

Figure 3: The effect of policy initiatives on the fuel poor and environmental pollution

INITIATIVE	HOMES	PLANET
Increased income	Warmer	Worse off
Fuel price rise	Cooler	Better off
Investment in energy efficiency	Warmer	Better off

The Government announced a compensation package in the November 1993 budget, but this will cover up to 75% of the average, added costs for pensioners (all income groups) and up to 50% of the costs for other, low-income households. This support is only for the first three years. The compensation is not related to actual fuel costs and therefore will be of least help to those in the coldest, most inefficient properties who already have high bills. An additional part of the package, for three years, is a further £35 million for the Home Energy Efficiency Scheme (HEES) which has been extended from the main benefit recipients to include all those over 60 years of age. The additional money is added to the pool, so that it will be up to the discretion of the local installers to ensure that the same proportion of low-income families benefit. Otherwise, there is a risk that demand for the non-poor over-60s will absorb the majority of the money.

Another impact of concern for the environment is likely to be an increasing focus on the use of electricity, because this is the most polluting fuel (Table 3) – a unit of electricity at the meter (delivered energy) produces four times more carbon dioxide than a unit of gas at the meter. The ratio is reduced when the efficiency of the appliance is taken into account (useful energy), but can still be up to 1:4 with the most efficient gas appliances.

Table 3: Carbon dioxide emissions from main domestic fuels, delivered energy (at the meter), UK 1989 and 1992 (kg CO_2/kWh)

	1989	1992
Electricity: general tariff	0.83	0.73
Electricity: off-peak	0.75	0.65
Coal	0.33	0.34
Oil	0.30	0.29
Gas	0.20	0.21

Source: BREEAM

Here it is useful to distinguish between the use of electricity for cooking, space and water heating (where other fuels compete) and for lighting and the main appliances, which are electricity specific. The lack of competition from other fuels means that traditional market forces will not deliver increased energy efficiency and reduced consumption. Hence policies to stimulate more efficiency in electricity-specific appliances will be introduced externally, for instance through the Regulator, the Energy Saving Trust or the European Union.

As the thermal efficiency of the housing stock increases, the energy (particularly electricity) used in appliances will represent a greater proportion of total household demand. Most of the evidence cited refers to heating, because this is the largest energy expenditure, particularly in inefficient homes. Low-income households are deprived of other energy services, such as hot water and lighting as well, but the level of disadvantage is more difficult to define (Boardman and Houghton 1991, p.62).

Income and Poverty issues

The households on the lowest incomes are, by definition, those eligible for an income-related benefit (the renamed means-tested benefits). For fuel poverty purposes, the main benefits are: income support, housing benefit, council tax benefit, family credit, disability living allowance and disability working allowance. According to the Chancellor of the Exchequer, these are received by 8 million households (Hansard 1.4.93, WA col 492). Therefore, 36% of all households in the United Kingdom can be defined as poor.

A major part of the growth in fuel poverty is the increasing number of poor people in the UK from 3.9m households in 1973, to 6.4m in 1986 and 8 million in 1992 (Hansard 1.4.93, Boardman 1991). For consistency of comparison though, an average is taken of the 30% of households with the lowest incomes.

The 30% of households with the lowest incomes spent 9.3% of their weekly income on fuel in 1991 – nearly twice the average (Table 4). Better off households only had to spend 4.1% of the weekly budget, but this amounted to nearly a third more (£3.19) in absolute terms. These figures reflect the importance of fuel, as a basic necessity.

Table 4: Expenditure on fuel, by income, UK 1991 (£/week)

	30% of households with lowest incomes	70% other	Average
Gas	3.52	5.48	4.89
Electricity	5.16	6.47	6.08
Coal & coke	0.81	0.64	0.69
Other	0.53	0.62	0.59
Total fuel	10.02	13.21	12.25
All expenditure	108.11	323.72	259.04
% on fuel	9.3	4.1	4.7

Source: Based on CSO 1992

The amount spent as a proportion of income is dropping slightly over the years, but it is difficult to identify the relative importance of energy efficiency and both increasing poverty and greater wealth as incomes in the UK become more unequal. The expenditure level is rounded up to 10% as a rough indication of 'affordability' in low-income families (Table 5).

Table 5: Budget proportion spent on fuel, by income group, UK, 1981-1991

	30% of households with lowest incomes	70% other	Average
1985	11.0	5.4	6.1
1988	10.0	4.4	5.1
1991	9.3	4.1	4.7

Source: various, based on the relevant Family Expenditure Surveys

One further reason for greater fuel poverty is the demise of heating additions. Prior to April 1988, £500 million was paid annually to the majority of claimants to help with heating costs. Those heating additions that had been based on the social characteristics of claimants (mainly age) were, in theory, incorporated in the new income support premiums. The remaining £200m was being paid largely on the basis of the heating system and fuel used and no attempt was made to replace them, so the money was lost to claimants. There is now no regular support for claimants' heating or energy costs in the social security system. The VAT compensation to be introduced in April 1994 will provide up to £400 million a year, but is only for three years and neither fully compensates for VAT nor addresses the problems that existed prior to April 1994.

As explained, capital investment is needed to improve energy efficiency. By definition, someone on an income-related benefit has little capital or savings. Many households are so poor that they have no savings or capital at all and may well be in debt. In 1981, the proportion of Supplementary Benefit claimants with no capital was 62% and this had risen to 69% by 1987; claimants had less resources in 1987 than in 1981 – further evidence that poverty is deeper. This means that the poorest households are unable to change the energy efficiency of their own dwellings with their own money.

A further constraint relates to tenure. Two-thirds of the 30% of households on the lowest incomes are in rented accommodation (Figure 4) and the bulk of the remainder are elderly people who own their homes outright.

Figure 4: 30% of households with the lowest incomes, by tenure, UK 1991

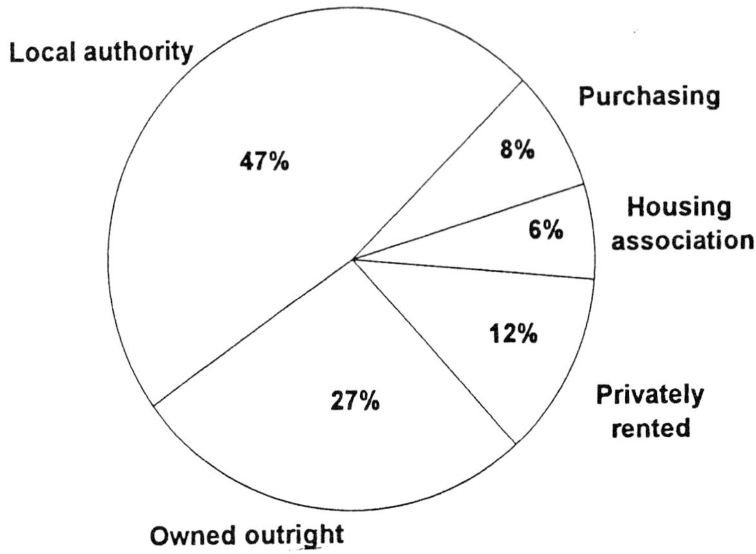

Source: CSO 1992, p.8

A household living in rented accommodation has few rights to, and less interest in, improving the property and expects the landlord to do so. The landlord, however, has no responsibility for running costs and limited ways of recouping the capital expenditure through rents. Some local authorities have enabled tenants to choose improvements, such as central heating and insulation, provided that the rent is increased. Where the tenant is on housing benefit, this effectively provides a saving in private fuel bills on heating and replaces it with an additional public cost through higher rents and benefits. Similar schemes have been instituted by housing associations, using private finance. The Department of the Environment issued a consultation paper in November 1993 designed to restrict these schemes and minimize the cost to the Department of Social Security.

Recent research at BRECSU has shown that there are greater benefits to landlords, through reduced maintenance, voids, and so forth, than the value of the benefits accruing to tenants in reduced fuel bills and greater warmth (Ward 1992). The over-riding importance given to expenditure constraint by the present

Government will, therefore, reduce investment on energy efficiency, even with private funds. This will cause further deterioration of the housing stock and be detrimental to revenue expenditure by social housing providers.

Insulation, Heating and Energy Efficiency

The 1986 English House Condition Survey defined dwellings as the 25% least efficient, 50% average and 25% most energy efficient, using relative values, unrelated to defined standards such as affordability. The top and bottom quartiles are shown by household income in Figure 5 demonstrating that low-income households are disproportionately likely to be in the least efficient dwellings.

Figure 5: Energy efficiency by household income

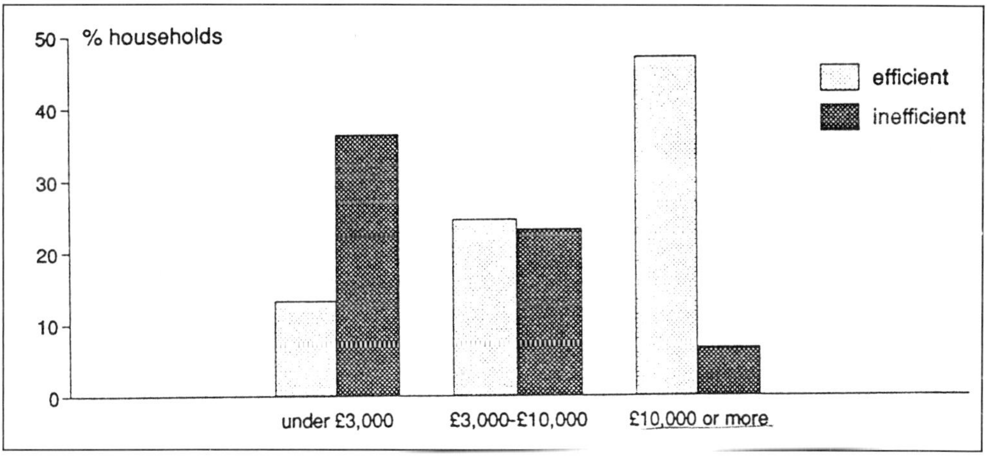

Source: DoE 1991b, p.31

Between 1970 and 1989, the largest improvements in the energy efficiency of the housing stock and heating appliances occurred in 1979 and 1985. These appear to be unrelated to oil price rises and the associated policy responses or the major advertising campaign of Monergy in 1986. As a minimum, these figures question the efficacy of Government energy efficiency programmes and reliance on consumer responses to prices and advertising. From 1986 to 1991 there has been minimal improvement in the efficiency of the housing stock (Shorrock et al. 1992, pp.26-32; Shorrock and Bown 1993, pp.4-7) and there has been a 28% decline in insulation sales between 1989 and 1992 (HC648-II, p.40). Even though the energy efficiency of the housing stock is improving slowly, ownership of insulation measures and central heating are strongly correlated with higher incomes (Table 6).

Table 6: Ownership of insulation measures and central heating, by income, England 1986

Household annual income	<£3,000	£3,000–£6,500	£6,500–£10,000	>£10,000
Loft insulation	86	89	91	91
Wall insulation	25	20	25	31
Double glazing	16	28	33	46
Draught-proofing	43	48	52	64
Hot water tank cover	85	90	85	98
Central heating	59	64	74	89

Sources: Based on Barker and Johnstone 1993; DoE 1991b, Tables A3.7, A4.2, A4.4 and A4.6
Note: these are approximate income quartiles

The ownership of central heating is important because it is correlated with warm dwellings for two reasons. First, the central heating system provides the mechanism for getting heat around the house easily, and probably into most rooms. Secondly, because of the cost of installation, central heating is more likely to be found in the homes of better-off families, who are also able to afford to use it extensively. This is confirmed by the evidence that, in cold weather, the temperature is maintained in centrally heated homes: expenditure can increase to offset the extra cold. The temperature in non-centrally heated homes tracks the weather more closely: expenditure has to stay constant, so the internal temperature drops. When it is below freezing outside, 38% of non-centrally heated homes are 'cold' homes, which means the living room is below 16°C and the rest of the house below 12°C (Moore 1991). These conditions are severely prejudicial to health. The Department of Social Security will provide additional help for selected claimants during periods of exceptionally severe weather, but it has to be below freezing for seven consecutive days before the recipients are entitled to £6.

Assessment of Government Policies

Energy inefficiency, low levels of insulation, the heavy use of on-peak electricity and below average ownership of gas central heating are all correlated with low-incomes. This was true in 1991 (Boardman 1991, p.223) and continues to be so, in the absence of Government policies to redress the imbalance. How has this come about?

Many Government policies have more than one objective and with energy and housing the desire for improved energy efficiency is usually a secondary factor, at best. Raising revenue through VAT and training the unemployed through community insulation projects are just two examples of the interplay of objectives. As the anti-VAT campaigns demonstrated, the Government's response to consumer pressure still tends to treat the symptoms, not the causes. Hence, £400 million is being put into income compensation for VAT, but only an additional £35 million for new capital expenditure.

Assessing the level of public expenditure on energy efficiency improvements is problematic, not least because of the split between capital and revenue programmes and between energy-efficiency and, the wider, energy-related headings (Boardman 1993, pp.317-8). Thus, replacing a rotten window with double glazing in a local authority dwelling could be listed as £60 (the additional cost of an extra pane of glass) as an energy-efficiency repair, or the full £600 (the cost of the entire window), as an energy-related capital investment in the Housing Investment Programme.

One trend in Government programmes has been to limit expenditure over time. This was the experience with loft insulation grants. After the first oil crisis in 1973-4, the scheme was initially for all income groups and then in 1988 became dependent on a means test. The rationale is that targeting assistance on the poorest makes the best use of Government resources and gives real 'additionality' by funding work that would not otherwise have been undertaken. This is perfectly accurate, but the net effect has been a diminution of investment by more affluent households who also need the incentive of a partial grant. Eligibility for HEES has now been extended to all those over 60 years of age, whatever their income, as part of the VAT compensation package, but only as a temporary measure.

A further policy has been to limit identifiable budgets, in the name of increasing local decision-making. The Green House Programme was announced in 1990 with an initial budget of £60 million. Despite its very considerable success, the programme has not been extended and there is no more money available. The

Green House Programme funds were top-sliced from the Housing Investment Programme, it was an identifiable fund, and the remaining HIP distributed across all authorities. To encourage the spread of best practice, responsibility has been transferred directly to each local authority to bid through the HIP. In reality, the same amount of money may be available, but the net effect is likely to be less investment in energy efficiency now, because of pressure from other investment programmes, particularly at a time of reduced expenditure generally.

The Home Energy Efficiency Scheme (HEES) is the main low-income programme, as it has national coverage and is the continuation of schemes that have been in existence since 1978. The present administrative format dates from 1.1.91. The 1993-4 budget of £35m mainly provides draught-proofing in local authority dwellings, with lift, tank and pipe insulation and advice added in varying proportions. Over 1 million households have been draught-proofed since 1981. The peak of activity was in 1988 (NEA 1991, p.14) with present levels almost as high (Gillis, 1994). The majority of draught-proofing materials do not last longer than 5 years, so that much of the past investment now needs replacing and is no longer providing any benefit.
The history of assistance with draught-proofing is interesting as the main policy incentive was to provide work experience through temporary employment and training programmes (e.g. Community Programme and Employment Training). The emphasis on this measure has remained, despite evidence that, in energy efficiency terms, it is not the most cost-effective use of money, if only because of the limited life of the materials. There is no disputing that draught-proofing does benefit the recipients, who take 80% of the improvement as additional warmth and only 20% as energy saving (Oseland and Ward 1993, p.33).

No new insulation measures have been grant-aided for low-income households since 1981. Cavity wall insulation is one of the most obvious omissions as this is more cost-effective than draught-proofing (DoE 1993e, p.19). Leicester City Council provided 5,000 dwellings with cavity wall insulation under Green House Programme, at less than £100 per property (HC 648-II, p.392). This is less than the cost of draught-proofing a dwelling under HEES and is more cost-effective and longer lasting. The other major omission is the lack of support for the installation of new heating systems that are cheaper to run. Whilst both of these measures can be included in local authority bids under the Housing Investment Programme, neither measure has been identified for assistance across all sectors by a grant. As outlined in chapter 3 the reduction in local authority capital expenditure programmes in the last few years has resulted in an almost complete cessation of new public sector housing construction. New buildings are more energy efficient than old, because of the effect of the gradually-improving Building Regulations. The decline in total construction means that an average of 200,000 new dwellings have become available each year for the last 10 years (DoE 1992b, Fig 5.17),down to 50% of the pre-1970 rate. Most of these new properties are in the private sector now, so they are bought by richer households and do not benefit the poor. The average energy efficiency of low-income homes is not improving as a result, whereas more affluent families gradually have better standards.

Capital constraints on public sector housing, certainly over 30 years, means the construction that does occur rarely includes additional insulation and the heating system installed is often chosen because of a low capital installation cost, regardless of high running costs. The latter is a reason for the concentration of electric heating systems in social housing. For long-term landlords, such as social housing providers, this is misplaced economic constraint: there are minimal extra costs at the time of construction of providing a high standard of energy efficiency. Government policy towards the different fuels and associated heating systems has been confused. In 1976, the Labour Government had to institute a special programme to assist authorities with the problems caused by electric heating (Boardman 1991, pp.97, 186). The present Government is again condoning the installation of electric night storage heaters, by allowing local authorities to raise the funds through leasing. More efficient, but fixed, forms of heating and insulation cannot be funded in this way. The practice has been condemned by the Environment Committee:

> *"We believe it is nonsensical that the DoE is encouraging local authorities to install inefficient forms of heating..."* (HC648-1, para 148).

Even more worrying is the decline in demolitions and slum clearance to about 10,000 a year. At this rate, all the present 23.6 million UK dwellings will not have been demolished for another 2,360 years. The normal expectation is that a house is built to last 60 years. This is no longer true, the average dwelling in the UK is now 50 years old. A major policy readjustment is going to be required soon, to make the millions of homes built in the nineteenth century, and still inhabited, suitable for twenty-first century living.

The total cost of a programme to provide affordable warmth in the existing homes of low-income families is estimated to be £20 billion over 16 years. This is equivalent to an average of £2,500 for each of the 8 million households on income-related benefits. The expenditure is to bring each house up to an NHER of 8 and would be the equivalent of the current Building Regulations, plus double glazing and an efficient heating system (Boardman 1990, p.10, updated). At an annual expenditure of £1.25 billion, this is equivalent to the amount currently raised through the Fossil Fuel Levy to subsidise nuclear power.
The Government has no clear strategy for maintaining, let alone improving, the housing stock in order to provide for the expected higher standards of living and energy efficiency. There are limited attempts to make investment in energy efficiency part of mainstream policies, for instance through HIP, but these lack conviction and resources at the moment. The evidence indicates that the energy

efficiency improvements occurring in low-income homes are minimal in comparison with the extent of the work required.

New Initiatives: the Utilities and the Energy Saving Trust

When the gas and electricity industries were privatised, their profits were strongly linked to increased sales and there was no incentive or opportunity for investment in reducing energy demand through the more efficient use of energy. Since April 1993 for gas and from April 1994 for electricity, the pricing formulae have been adjusted to provide that opportunity. The majority of the resultant expenditure will be in the domestic sector. In 1993-4, British Gas had earmarked £6m and about half of this was spent. There is uncertainty about the future of these programmes as the new Gas Regulator, Ms Clare Spottiswoode, is reconsidering the approach. From April 1994-98, the Regional Electricity Companies will collectively have about £20m to spend annually, with energy reduction standards set by the Electricity Regulator.

The money spent on these initiatives will have been raised from all consumers through a small increase in the unit price of gas or electricity. One of the crucial issues is how the money will be spent across the different income groups. Some of the money will be spent through the Energy Saving Trust, a non-Government body established in November 1992, with a specific role to save carbon dioxide emissions. The first programmes, some actual, some proposed, are summarised in Table 7.

The Local Energy Advice Centres are the only EST initiative funded directly by Government. There are 30 pilot centres around the country and each has had to provide equivalent matching funding. The brief for these LEACs is to focus their advice on the socio-economic groups I, II, and III, in other words, not the poor. The justification is undoubtedly that it is these better-off families that have the capital to respond to the advice with new purchases of insulation materials and more efficient appliances. In practice, the LEACs were launched in October 1993 at the same time as there was a peak in concern about the imposition of VAT. Hence, the initial calls have been from all income groups.

Of the other programmes launched by the EST, the most successful has been the gas condensing boiler rebate. The discount is needed because, although more efficient, these boilers are at least £400 more expensive than a conventional boiler. Thus, it is only better-off householders that will be obtaining them as a replacement and benefiting from this rebate. The first EST scheme can, therefore, be described as a reverse-Robin Hood approach: the money has been raised from all consumers, but distributed solely to richer households.

How would an appropriate level of investment in low-income households be

Table 7: Energy Saving Trust programmes in the domestic sector, UK 1993/4-1994/5

Programme	Target group	Value per recipient	Total EST budget for programme *	
			1993-4	1994-5
Condensing boilers	Homeowners	£200 rebate	Up to £2m	Ends 30.4.94
Combined heat and power	Housing providers	Reduce payback to 3 years	£1m	Up to £2m?
Low energy lightbulbs	Purchasers of first 700,000 bulbs	£2-£5 per bulb	£0.75m	?
Energy efficiency in social housing (EESH)	Claimants on main means-tested benefits, in social housing	£500	Nil	£10m?
Homes 2000	Homeowners	£250	Nil	£8m?
Local Energy Advice Centres	Householders and small businesses	£70 worth of telephone advice for free	£1.8m	£2m

* including EST administrative costs, but no matching funding from external sources

defined? The two factors involved are the proportion of expenditure required as grant and the proportion of benefit taken as reduced energy consumption. Low-income households do not, by definition, have capital, so that the total cost of improvements to their homes has to come from external sources. The EST may have to pay the whole cost of an improvement, or find matching funding from central or local government. With better-off households, the investment can be triggered much more cheaply, perhaps as a result of a 10% or 20% discount from the Trust, with the household providing the rest of the expenditure. Thus, programmes targeting the rich enable the Trust to obtain more carbon dioxide savings per pound of Trust money than in poorer homes.

Many households take some of the benefit of energy efficiency improvements as

added energy services (e.g. warmth) rather than as a smaller fuel bill, though with some measures, for instance low-energy lightbulbs, all the saving is reduced energy consumption. It is thus crucial whether the success of a programme is measured in the drop in actual energy consumption – the smaller fuel bill – or includes the value of the additional warmth as well. Unfortunately, additional warmth does not help to save carbon dioxide or cut costs for the utilities.
To ensure that an appropriate proportion of the benefit from utility investment goes to low-income households, a standard needs to be set. For instance:

* if 30% of all households are fuel poor, then 30% of all the energy savings (not including the benefit taken as warmth) must be in their homes; or,
* that 30% of all the benefit (energy savings and warmth together) are in low-income homes.

The first is the more beneficial for the poor as it requires greater expenditure in low-income homes and the second is the minimum acceptable to enable the Regulators to comply with their obligation that there is no discrimination: only the equal distribution of the benefits will ensure this. If the Regulators, the Energy Saving Trust and the politicians do not sign on to this commitment, these growing investment programmes could further disadvantage the poor.

The EST has a remit from Government to go for the most cost-effective approach to carbon dioxide reduction and target programmes on rich households. For this reason, the EST is most likely to support a maximum of 30% of *expenditure* being on low-income homes. As poorer families require a large discount this would result in a perhaps 85% of the energy saving occurring in richer homes, an approach that would clearly disadvantage the poor. Interestingly, if this 'E' factor money from the utilities is spent by the gas and electricity industries themselves, there is a greater likelihood of an emphasis on low-income households for two reasons. First, the utilities have considerable overheads as a result of slow or late payment of bills, predominantly in lower-income families. With improved efficiency, the bills should become more manageable and the debts reduced. Thus, a focus on low-income households has already been announced by Manweb for its investment programme. The second reason is that the utilities do not want to reduce their sales more than they have to. The original British Gas proposals promoted gas heating systems rather than improved insulation, to maintain or increase market share. Where gas displaces electricity this tactic, fortuitously, reduces pollution.

As these examples demonstrate, there will be a growing political debate between those, such as the Government and the Energy Saving Trust, who want primarily to reduce carbon dioxide emissions, and other members of society who are concerned about social equity, for whatever reasons. At the moment, the emphasis on environmental objectives is diverting resources from energy efficiency improvements, even in the least efficient homes, such as those of the poor.

Other Initiatives: a Wider Perspective

Other initiatives expected to reduce carbon dioxide emissions in the domestic sector are:

- the imposition of value added tax;
- revisions to the Building Regulations;
- compulsory energy labels and minimum standards on some appliances.

The bias against low-income households from the first measure has already been explained and the revised Building Regulations would affect new dwellings only and these are rarely occupied by the poor. However, as homes become more energy efficient buildings, the emphasis will shift to the lighting and appliances. Traditionally, Building Regulations and housing standards have focused on the durable elements: walls, floors, windows and roof. Should the energy efficiency standard for new construction automatically include less durable items, such as light fittings and heating systems and fridges, provided that the quality of the building elements is not reduced? The recent Environment Committee Report (HC 648-I) included considerable evidence on this debate, which has yet to be resolved in revisions to the Building Regulations. The likelihood is that acceptable housing standards will be based on energy audits, including most, if not all, appliances.

The effect of appliance-based programmes could be more equitable, but this is not certain. From January 1995, energy labels will enable consumers to identify more efficient appliances, first fridges, freezers, and then washing machines, tumble driers and dishwashers. The effect of imposing minimum standards will be to remove from shops the least efficient models. Both of these schemes will assist all consumers, but predominantly those able to purchase new equipment. Low-income consumers own less appliances and are more likely to obtain second-hand replacements (Boardman and Houghton 1991, pp.57-8), partly because of the constraints of the Social Fund rules.

One possible, but failed initiative was the Energy Conservation Bill. The Government refused to allow this private member's bill to be passed. It would have required local authorities to audit the energy efficiency of all the houses in their area, not just their own properties. As good information is the prerequisite of effective action, this Bill would have been an important advance. The Government's killing of this Bill demonstrates a lack of concern for energy efficiency.

These known initiatives may reinforce the disadvantages experienced by the poor, particularly those designed to achieve carbon dioxide reductions, for instance through the Energy Saving Trust, and because of the imposition of VAT. This risk will increase if present policies prove ineffective and the UK appears unable to meet our commitments for carbon dioxide reductions in the year 2000. A likely consequence is that new proposals will be introduced that achieve a quick response, particularly through better-off households.

The Government has given a commitment to develop policies that will constrain carbon dioxide emissions from 2000 onwards (DoE 1994c p.68). These longer term commitments on greenhouse gas emissions, at present unquantified, and the general needs of the housing stock will require a wide range of policies and substantial investment. For instance:

* Energy consumption is greater in larger dwellings, particularly if they are poorly insulated. At present there are thousands of dwellings that are underoccupied by families of one or two people, particularly elderly people. New construction programmes and conversion policies should focus on how to enable the elderly to achieve affordable warmth, partly through living in smaller dwellings. Some social agencies shrink the dwelling around the occupant, through Staying Put grants or similar. This is a sound, social policy with much to commend it, but what are the energy implications? Should the focus be on more imaginative forms of sheltered housing, with more generous space allocations, in order to provide a real alternative to the old family home for elderly people?
* The debate about adequate improvements to the existing housing stock will shortly have to include more explicit discussion about the cost of upgrading the present stock versus its replacement, with all the social upheaval that this can cause. Is society prepared to pay large sums of money to make the existing housing stock fit for the 21st and 22nd centuries, rather than rebuild extensive areas in our inner cities? For instance, the cost of getting a pre-war solid wall house up to 9 NHER is currently greater than the cost of getting a new building to 9 (HC648.III, p.390).
* New building, in inner city areas, allows for a new emphasis on public transport and local shopping, all of which will be needed to reverse our rising transport demands and fits in with recent Government restraint on out-of-town shopping centres (PPG 13);
* A further advantage of urban refurbishment is that it creates the opportunities for district heating from combined heat and power schemes, with substantial improvements in the efficiency of power stations (DoE 1994c, p.19).

Conclusion

The poor live in the most energy inefficient homes and these are being improved more slowly than the homes of other families. In addition, there are now more people in poverty. For both these reasons, fuel poverty is a growing problem in the UK and is likely to continue to increase with current policies. Insufficient policy attention has been given to the energy efficiency of low-income houses and this must be redressed in proposals to reduce environmental problems. The fuel poor live in cold, damp houses already. The condition of these properties should not be made worse in order to reduce the risk of climate change. Both objectives can be achieved, if the approach is through more capital expenditure.

The role of capital expenditure in differentiating fuel poverty from ordinary poverty has been barely recognized by Government. This is surprising, as reducing poverty requires indefinite provision of support, whereas capital expenditure programmes are finite. Once the housing stock has been improved, the effect of the expenditure lasts for as long as the measures installed. Therefore, the single most effective approach to minimize hardship for the poor is to increase capital expenditure. That lesson has yet to be learnt by Government, so that the present worsening inequality is unlikely to be reversed in the short-term. The fuel poor will continue to be cold.

CHAPTER 8: The Greening of the Housing Market

Yvonne Rydin

Stating an intent to examine the 'greening of the housing market' begs the question of 'what is green housing?' Just as there are shades of environmentalism (Dobson, 1990; Pepper, 1984), so there are many answers to this question. The purpose of this chapter is to examine the different ways in which environmentally-acceptable practices within the housing market may be achieved. It begins with a brief review of alternative definitions of 'green housing' and then moves on to consider the pressures for change which arise within the housing market itself. This leads on to consideration of the different forms that government policy could take: regulations, market-based instruments and more radical restructuring of the market. While much concern within the housing market and government circles has focused on residential development, the importance of addressing the existing housing stock is also emphasised. The chapter concludes with a discussion of the trade-offs involved in environmental policy for the housing market, between the depth of the greening process and the ease of achieving change.

Shades of Green Housing

As discussed in chapter 2 eco-centrics are at the darkest green end of the environmental spectrum, and can be severely anti-urban, espousing a kind of rural self-sufficiency, directly living off the land. Urban development is viewed with hostility and tight population control is advocated to avoid the need for development. Such views tend to lie outside the mainstream of debate on green housing. Further along the spectrum, but still within an ecocentric perspective, are the soft technologists. They take a more positive view of urban life and talk of 'reviewing the city' (Elkin et al., 1991) or 'eco-city' (Engwicht, 1992). Here there is scope for urban dwellers to live in relative harmony with the environment, provided that they make radical shifts in lifestyle and forms of social organisation. This involves rethinking the city as a network of urban villages incorporating plentiful green (agricultural, wildlife, amenity and recreational) space. It also means making limited applications of technology: low energy intermediate technology such as using bicycles rather than cars, and recycling waste water within the home and garden rather than using expensive sewerage infrastructure and water treatment facilities; or more advanced and environmentally benign technology such as optical fibres cabling to enable telecommuting. Housing has an important part to play in this urban vision, integrating work and home, enabling decentralised social organisation, providing for local food production and recycling of wastes, and conserving local wildlife; chapter 11 in this volume on self-build housing reflect this viewpoint.

Moving from an eco-centric to a techno-centric perspective brings us into the mainstream of governmental, professional and indeed market-based discussion of green housing. Here the proposed adjustments to prevailing patterns of housing are relatively modest. There is an emphasis on energy efficiency, on local habitat conservation and on the choice of alternative building materials. The claim is that sustainable urban development is a feasible option, preserving environmental assets for future generations while maintaining an active development process and housing market. There is little discussion of social reorganisation here; rather the goals of sustainable urban development are re-cast in technical terms such as increasing the U-values of walls, undertaking more careful site surveys or introducing new technology for re-using construction waste. Management from above, the top-down approach, is recommended to achieve these goals, both within the public and private sectors. Thus architects are urged to rethink their professional practice:

> *"In the energy crisis of the 1970s the RIBA coined the slogan 'Long life, loose fit, low energy' to describe the approach that architects should adopt to design. This slogan is still valid."* (Vale & Vale, 1991a, p.11).

Land-use planners should play a role, at strategic and site-planning level:

> *"Conserving an environment capable of supporting human life. This is a basic requirement for all land use planning."* (Beer, 1990, p.18),

and:

> *"It can be the site planner's role to identify any scarce resources on a particular site and work to meet the strategic planning objectives, by maintaining the possibility of access to the resource if it is mineral, and conserving it if it is a living resource. It can also be the site planner's role, when the resource is to be exploited, to indicate how this could occur within minimum damage to the environment."* (Beer, 1990, p.24).

And Stephen Owen, in discussing how to plan settlements naturally, talks of:

> *"an exploration of the benefits to people living in cities, towns and villages, and to the natural environment itself, can be secured from an improved understanding of that natural environment in settlements."* (1991, p.xi).

This techno-centric approach dominates the debate on green housing and is assumed to be the most pragmatic way forward, the best way of achieving an increased level of environmental protection.

Eco-centric approaches are, by contrast, seen as idealistic, unrealistic. They certainly imply more of a challenge to existing structures of economic, political and social organisation and a vigorous debate continues within the environmentalist literature over whether technocratic approaches increase the likelihood of political acceptability at the expense of diluting the environmentalist message too far (Dobson, 1990). The immediate concerns of housing policy practitioners will, however, rest more readily within a techno-centric perspective. The aim will be to achieve change sooner rather than later, if necessary immediate marginal change rather than longer term structural change. The urgent question then is how to achieve change within this perspective, within prevailing structures, notably within prevailing economic market-based structures.

Sources of Change from Within the Housing Market

There is an argument, found particularly within business journals and corporate accounts, which claims that market processes themselves will respond to the current environmental agenda, a self-greening market (Cairncross, 1991). This is held to be because market actors have an interest in taking environmental concerns on board. Such self-interest can be analysed from the supply and demand sides of the housing market. From the demand side, there is the apparent growth of green consumerism. House purchasers, the argument goes, have developed a heightened concern for the environment and wish to purchase housing which is demonstrably 'environmentally-friendly', preferably from builders with a good environmental record. Indeed such consumers may be willing to pay a premium for such housing. In this case, it is in housebuilders' interests to target the environmentally-conscious consumer and alter housebuilding practice to meet the 'green demand'. Eco-labelling, energy rating schemes and marketing which emphasises environmental features are all strategies designed to meet the requirements of green consumerism, strategies which may be aggressively used by housebuilders but also have an influence in the secondhand market.

Unfortunately research indicates that the strength of green consumerism may have been overestimated. Public opinion surveys show that concern with the environment has risen during the latter half of the 1980s but this is from a low base and the level of concern is sensitive to changes in economic output; during a recession environmental concern falls and vice versa. Public concern with the environment also encompasses a broad range of salient issues with matters as diverse as radioactive waste and dog fouling topping the list (see Department of the Environment 1992b, chapter 16).

A pilot survey by the author of environmental concern within the housing market also raised doubts about green consumerism (Rydin, 1992a). A postal survey of estate agents was used to gauge the perceived concerns of prospective buyers and the attitudes of estate agents themselves as gatekeepers in the marketplace. The research found that housing features which could be considered environmentally friendly were given a low rating:

- recycling facilities;
- cycleways;
- green building materials;
- energy efficient lighting;
- water metering.

while those features which were rated highly included space for the car and a garden for recreation and visual pleasure. Some energy conservation measures such as double glazing were moderately valued but many other aspects of energy efficiency were not. Perhaps the complexities of assessing the overall energy efficiency mean that consumers would welcome the simplification that an energy rating scheme would bring and then incorporate this issue more centrally in their decision making.
The survey also indicated a perceived preference for low density residential areas, a preference which runs against the conclusions of much recent research into the most energy efficient urban form, which favours higher densities (Owens & Cope, 1992; Ecotech, 1993). Neither does there seem to be great potential within the housing market for reducing transport-based emissions by encouraging a shift from the car to public transport and walking, for the survey found that housebuyers were perceived as favouring space for car parking over public transport provision, rating traffic-free areas low and only a minority valued pedestrian access to facilities very highly.

If green consumerism seems a weak force within the housing market, there may still be reasons why suppliers, particularly builders in the new housing market, would wish to develop more environmentally acceptable practice. Promoters of 'green capitalism' argue that there are direct benefits to business in adopting eco-audits and changing their production practice. These include: reducing costs, through waste minimisation and re-use of materials for example; gaining an edge on competitors, even if there isn't a market niche for green consumers to capture; and minimising the risk of incurring liability for environmental damage. In general, in a situation in which standards of environmental protection are rising, green corporate practices allow the builder to adopt a more long term perspective which can reduce costs, aid internal management and provide a good corporate profile.

This can be significant to investors in the firm as well as consumers, perhaps more so. With increasingly stringent application of the principle of 'the polluter pays' and the likely introduction of full liability for environmental damage, shareholders are scrutinising the environmental performance of companies more carefully in making investment decisions. In the search for finance on capital markets, housebuilders also have to be aware of this trend, not just in relation to construction practice but also in the choice of sites, as shown by the recent concern over contaminated land and registers for identifying such land. It should be noted though that housebuilders and developers generally may still look to be attractive investment opportunities compared to the more pollution-prone industrial sector.

Some evidence for growing environmental concern among housebuilders can be found in the statements in annual reports and corporate accounts. The following provides some examples:

> "*...our concern for the environment is an integral part of our everyday business strategy, providing an impetus to improve resource management, efficiency and competitive advantage.*" (Beazer Homes Ltd. 1992 Annual Reports and Accounts).
>
> "*...high standards of good environmental practice are in the best interests of our businesses, our people, our customers and society at large.*" (Bovis Homes Ltd. 1992 Annual Reports and Accounts).
>
> "*...care for the environment is the responsibility of the whole of society including industry.*" (Ideal Homes 1991 Annual Reports and Accounts).
>
> "*Tarmac cares for the environment – not just because it is right to do so, but because it is a fundamental aspect of our business.*" (Tarmac Plc 1992 Annual Report and Accounts).

However, the proof of corporate statements lies in corporate practice; housebuilders may claim to be environmentally friendly but are they building housing differently, in different places, to mitigate the environmental impact from living in this housing? There is clearly much greater discussion within the housebuilding industry on environmental topics. The trade publication 'The Housebuilder' showed a substantial increase in environmental coverage, a sixfold increase in column inches over 1987 to 1990 (Rydin, 1992a, p.235). There is a Construction Industry Environment Forum, organised by Construction Industry Research and Information Association (CIRIA) BSRIA and Building Research Establishment (BRE), which has over 130 members and a survey by this forum in 1991 identified the following as priority areas for research out of a detailed list of 48 items (CIRIA, 1992):

* Construction waste: recovery, reuse and recycling; disposal; toxic waste; waste minimisation;
* Alternative building materials; eco-labelling;

* Land contamination; protection of water sources; environmental audits;
* Policy and regulations; forthcoming legislation; summaries of advice on legislation.

The Building Research Establishment's Environmental Assessment Method (BREEAM) is well established for various sectors, though not social housing, (see chapter 10) and is likely to form the basis for an EC-wide version (Tighe, 1993 p.11). More firms are considering the implications of BS7750 on environmental management systems and environmental blacklists of building materials are now so extensive as to be causing some concern in the industry (Construction Industry Environment Forum Workshop 23.7.92).

Yet pilot research by the author raises doubts about the extent of actual changes in corporate practice, although further work is needed to confirm this, particularly into the volume housebuilders (Rydin, 1992a). A random sample of housebuilders were surveyed by post and the analysis of returns identified only a limited number of areas where changes in practice were occurring: increasing insulation standards, mainly in response to the revised 1990 Building Regulations; minimising waste from the construction process (which currently amount to 400 m. tonnes p.a.); protection of wildlife on sites; and treeplanting. There was some movement towards providing more energy efficient space heating systems. However, there were also numerous areas where little action was occurring:

- energy consumption in construction;
- water consumption in construction;
- use of recycled building materials;
- revising dwelling design to increase solar gain;
- reducing the distance to facilities;
- providing traffic-calming measures or cycleways;
- including wilderness areas;
- providing recycling facilities
- and providing space for bicycles.

The list is a long one!

The reliance on market process to produce a substantial change in the housing market can seem cornucopian, a term used to describe a variant of the techno-centric perspective which sees environmental problems as readily solved within the context of market-led growth. From this viewpoint, all that is needed is increased information to enable housebuyers to discriminate between builders and houses (both new and secondhand) and to enable builders to find alternative building materials, to manage construction sites more sensitively from the point of view of waste, pollution and nature conservation, and to choose appropriate sites in the first place. But examination of the extent of change in housebuilding practice and preliminary research into the decision making of buyers and builders suggests that there is little evidence of 'greening' from these sources. Rather there is a need to turn to a more environmental managerial perspective and the varieties of government environmental policy that could be applied.

Regulatory and Market-based Approaches to Greening

The dominant approach in environmental policy to date has been a regulatory one, using standards and procedures of assessment to set a bottom line for environmental protection. The use of development control within the planning system and building regulations are well established features of the residential development process. The revised Building Regulations 1990 give a recent example of how more stringent regulations can improve the environmental performance of new housing, in this case greatly increasing the insulation levels and energy efficiency of the building fabric. Of course, it can always be argued that the standards are set too low: the 1990 Building Regulations bring us in line with Swedish practice of the 1930s!

Building regulations provide a tight set of criteria to which new housing generally must conform. A more discretionary form of regulatory control is provided by the planning system, which is based on negotiation as much as the strict application of criteria laid out in development plans. The land use planning system is now taking a broader range of environmental issues on board, not just local amenity but global climate change. Reducing transport-based emissions, promoting energy efficiency and conserving wildlife have all moved up the land use planning agenda and form a more central part of decision making on land use and development. The introduction of environmental assessment for major residential developments and at the strategic planning stage will further strengthen this trend.

The success of the regulatory approach depends on two factors. First, there is the stringency with which regulations are applied, the extent to which discretion in the application of environmental standards is used to water down those standards. One problem with relying on the land use planning system to raise environmental standards is that environmental protection, as understood in this volume, is only one of several goals that the system seeks to achieve (Rydin, 1992b, pp.58-60). The planning system also seeks to promote local economic development and to meet the social needs of the local population and specific groups within that population. There is also the potential for conflict between local environmental quality, often defined in terms of amenity, and global environmental concerns, focused around the need to reduce energy consumption.

Second, such regulations are essentially responsive mechanisms for controlling certain pressures, here for residential development, once they have arisen. But the form that those pressures take will be shaped by other factors, notably commercial concerns. So that the environmental regulations are reacting to market-based pressures for a certain type of development. It is these commercial pressures that drive the selection of site, the development density, the choice of building materials, the details of site layout and building design. Beyond this, there is the fact that these regulations apply only to new housebuilding. A key problem in greening housing for analysts and policy makers alike is the distinction between the existing housing stock and new residential development. Existing housing constitutes the overwhelming bulk of the housing stock (see chapter 3 and 6 in this volume), with new build or conversions adding only a few percentage points to total stock in any year. Improving the energy efficiency of the existing housing stock could reduce delivered energy consumption by at least 40% (Department of Energy, 1990, p.224) while the contribution from new housing will be many times less.

However, it is clearly difficult to make substantial changes to the existing stock: many physical alterations to the fabric of standing housing are virtually impossible or, at least, prohibitively expensive; altering the layout of estates or settlements is similarly problematic; a large number of existing occupiers must be influenced to implement even a fairly simply change, such as retrofitting more insulation. Hence there is a strong education emphasis to policy for the existing stock, encouraging changes in behaviour often with fairly minimal alterations to the housing itself. While new housebuilding is numerically much less important within the total stock, a much greater degree of change can be achieved. There is clearly a trade-off here in policy terms between developing regulations primarily focused at new stock, which might create a small but growing pool of housing with high environment performance, and putting the policy effort into making a marginal improvement to existing stock with a potentially large aggregate effect.

Market-based Instruments

Neo-classical economics has long been an important paradigm in housing studies (for example, Stafford, 1978, Needleman, 1965) and it is currently undergoing a renaissance in environmental policy analysis as indicated in the work of David Pearce and colleagues (for example, Pearce & Turner, 1990; Markandya & Richardson, 1992). This is leading to proposals for a greater emphasis on policy instruments such as taxes and permits rather than regulations or subsidies on the basis that they are more economically efficient. Placing a tax on the consumption of carbon-fuel-based energy should reduce the level of fuel consumption and, because it operates within a market framework, it should allow each consumer to trade-off the extra costs of energy consumption against the benefits to be gained, resulting in the internalisation of the external costs imposed by such energy consumption and hence economic efficiency. Again the imposition of an additional cost on the use of building materials which have adverse environmental impacts (such as pollution, habitat loss, landscape scarring, substantial or toxic waste generation) would mean that the environmental costs would be incorporated into builders' and eventually housebuyers' decision-making. This would result, not in the cessation of use of such materials, but in a reduction in their use to an efficient level. This would balance the economic benefits of material use against the full range of costs incurred, including environmental costs.

To date, the environmental factors which have been considered within neo-classical housing analysis have been quite limited. Generally it is local externalities that are incorporated into the analysis, of the type that local land use planning seeks to regulate: visual amenities, access to public recreation areas; local pollution. However, the growing body of environmental economics literature is expanding the range of environmental concerns to which the neo-classical approach can be applied. Most environmental economics examples have focused on the more 'newsworthy' topics such as wetlands, tropical rainforests and global warming but there is clearly the potential for applying this expanded neo-classical approach to housing.

However, the existing evidence suggests that price and cost differentials associated with improving the environmental performance of housing do not always produce the outcomes that the neo-classical framework would identify. For example, in relation to the energy efficiency of new housing, timber-framed housing costs 25% less to heat than conventionally built housing but accounts for only 12-14% of the new build market. Again features to gain maximum ratings in BREEAM for housing cost only 0-3% of development costs (Tighe, 1993, p.11) and the costs of gaining a high rating in the Energy Foundation's schemes are similarly modest (Brennan, 1990, p.vi) yet the majority of new housing continues to rate low on environmental criteria. This means that the fiscal incentives needed to encourage investment in energy efficiency measures in new housing would have to be very substantial to get any effect at all. Either consumer influence is very weak in housing markets, or housebuyers are not swayed by environmental concerns, or suppliers of housing, particularly new housing, are not responsive to consumer pressure. To generalise from this example, the problems with this use of the neo-classical approach relate both to the general assumptions and procedures of the approach and to its applicability to the case of housing.

One basic concern with the framework is the definition of housing that it works with. Essentially housing is defined as a good, usually a physical good in a way which downplays the role of property rights in the housing sector and the social relations between parties. It can also be difficult to cope with the great variety of housing that exists within the sector, in tenure terms, physically and locationally; the approach seeks to identify sub-markets but these can be difficult to operationalise. Within the neo-classical framework, supply and demand schedules should be derived from the marginal costs of supply and marginal utility of consumption and these two schedules should be independent. However, it is doubtful whether, within an oligopolistic housebuilding industry, supply is decided on the basis of marginal costs, whether consumers do operate with a concept of marginal utility in any meaningful way, or whether supply and demand are independent given the way housing markets in any locality work. Certainly the limited nature of choice offered to any household in purchasing housing makes the notion of consumer sovereignty highly suspect, both in the private and public sectors.

Further concerns can be raised over the way in which the approach conceptualises the interaction of supply and demand, leading to an equilibrium position. This idea of equilibrium sits uneasily with the existence of severe housing shortage and points to the way in which the framework is essentially agnostic on equality in market outcomes and tends to value on the basis of willingness to pay in the market, a basis which favours high-income over lower-income households. The idea of an equilibrium achieved through market processes also greatly underplays the importance of the state in structuring and maintaining markets and of intermediaries, such as estate agents or mortgage lender, in supplying information and finance. For these (and other) reasons, some analysts have looked for an alternative to the neo-classical framework.

Restructuring the Housing Market

An alternative to the neo-classical model of housing markets is provided by a range of models which reject the explanatory value of the neo-classical framework, question the relevance of the concepts of markets in understanding the provision of housing, and seek explanations which combine consideration of actors' behaviour, agency, with the context for and constraints on such behaviour, structure. Some of the more interactive behavioural models identified by Gore and Nicholson (1991), effectively fall into this category. Also relevant is comparative work by Chambert (1992), operating from within an institutional framework (see Rydin, 1993, for an account of this framework) and the path-breaking writings of Ball (1983 & 1986), coming from a marxist framework.

Ball's definition of a structure of housing provision gives one example of the focus of this work:

> *"a structure of housing provision describes an historically given process of providing and reproducing the physical entity, focusing on the social agents essential to that process and the relations between them."* (Ball 1983, p.158).

No attempt is made at providing an overarching theory applicable to all types of housing; rather it is explicitly stated in each case that the interactions between the different agents are quite distinct in the case of speculatively developed owner-occupied housing, public sector rented housing built by private housebuilders, or self-promoted and self-built housing, to give some examples. While understanding the production of new housing stock was the original impetus to such models, they could readily be extended to consider rehabilitation or even maintenance activities and even, by including investment institutions such as building societies and landlords, the decisions surrounding existing housing stock.

This said, the current accounts of such models do not explicitly take on board the environmental dimension. There are asides in the existing literature which indicate how the environmental dimension could be built on. Duncan (1989), makes the argument that the way in which housebuilding is organised in Sweden compared to Britain means that Swedish housing is both more technologically advanced in terms of insulation and energy efficiency, and has greater provision for collective environmental features, such as play areas and public space. The role that profits from land dealing continues to play in the financial structure of British housebuilding and the resulting focus on the struggle for development gains from land between builders and landowners, prevents technological development in housebuilding and diverts resources from meeting environmental policy goals. It could also be argued that the land dealing role drives the search for maximum profits through manipulating density on sites, and thus can undercut policies designed to achieve the most energy-efficient densities and urban forms.

This example suggests that the approach could be fruitfully used to consider how the existing structures governing the provision of housing in various sectors impinge on the generation of environmental impacts and how adjustments to those structures could mitigate the environmental damage associated with the production and use of housing. Such an approach could be used to consider the role that financial institutions play in preventing the adoption of more energy efficient construction methods and building designs and suggest a solution to the paradox of the cost-effective yet rarely used energy conservation measures, in that the relation between the mortgaging decision and the purchasing decision may effectively bypass consideration of such measures.

The approach could also explore the relationship between the builders and building materials suppliers with its influence on the choice of materials and associated environmental impact, both in terms of the use of the materials in the dwelling and in the production process for those materials. It could also take on board the role that gatekeepers such as exchange professionals play in filtering information about the environmental dimension of different dwellings to prospective occupiers and thus explore the gap between general public awareness or consciousness of environmental problems and the nature of purchasing decisions. The approach can also move between the private and public sectors with relative ease. Chambert (1992) notes how many functions within the development process are often taken on by the state and the need to be able to accommodate this within a conceptual framework. An example of where this approach could be applied is in the case of public sector refurbishment where there is the potential for greater increasing energy efficiency through retrofitting. Yet such refurbishment is facing constraints from the financial arrangements surrounding not only local authorities but also self-managed schools and hospitals (notes on Construction Industry Environment Forum workshop, 12.10.92). The inter-relation of actors in different public sector organisations, and also with the private sector firms who will be tendering for such work, are central to understanding the constraints on improving the energy efficiency of the public stock.

Thus the structure-agency models suggests ways in which environmental impacts arise from the way in which housing provision is structured. The resulting policy prescriptions are based on the identified need to re-organise some of the relationships between agents involved in the process of provision. This would involve the restructuring of the housing market: transferring property rights as in a form of nationalisation of development land; or the introduction of new agents, whether state intermediaries or community-based organisations, to intervene in the current structures of production and exchange. It is argued that the environmental impact of housing arises from the way in which production and consumption are organised and structured and that 'greening housing' would involve fundamental change in these structures. Anything else runs the risk of producing merely cosmetic change.

Clearly such policy recommendations would be controversial. They arise from an understanding of the way in which structures of interests in the development process produce the current pattern of environmental impacts. Intervening in these structures would be conflictual, confronting vested interests and altering entrenched property rights. Again there is the trade off between the ease of implementing policy with environmental goals and the depth of the greening process that results. This also raises the question of potential problems in achieving a policy consensus for the greening of housing.

Conclusion

This chapter has suggested a number of different approaches to considering how and why environmental impacts arise from residential development and also the resulting policy prescriptions. There appears to be a tension between the ease with which certain approaches could be adopted, both in empirical research and by policy makers, and the extent to which these approaches really tackle the causes of environmental impact and the resistance to effective environmental policy. The structure-agency models, for example, seem to provide a promising analytic framework yet are likely to suggest radical policies which may be considered politically infeasible in the current context. One question that researchers in academic and policy circles need to ask themselves in addressing the greening of the housing market is the extent of the trade-off that should be made between achieving an extended scope of environmental policy and the significance of those policy changes. This relates to the tension between techno-centric and eco-centric approaches, highlighted in the chapter 2 of this volume.

This distinction between techno-centric and eco-centric approaches also raises the issue of public participation or community involvement. These are integral to an eco-centric approach, yet the emphasis on structures of market-based provision and development processes tends to result in techno-centric or top-down policy recommendations. One difficult but important problem remaining is how to marry intervention in the economic processes of the housing market with a more participatory approach to controlling, planning and organising such development. In particular the problem is to find a participatory approach which does not merely favour organised vested interests and protect middle-class localities, as the land use planning system sometimes stands accused (Rydin, 1993), but takes on board issues of equality alongside participation and environmental protection in trying to reform or restructure the residential development process. This is essentially the problem that the Brundtland report (WCED 1987) and its aftermath struggled with, brought down to focus on the housing sector. Combining the first two issues has been a central concern of housing studies over the past three decades; the environmental dimension now reformulates the problem anew as a challenge to researchers and policy makers.

CHAPTER 9: Greening Architectural Practice in Housing

Fionn Stevenson

> *"Ultimately the right decisions are not made by one person or even one group. They arise out of the situation. The more closely we can listen to the situation, the better will be the result."* (Day 1990a p.143).

'Learning from nature' is a theme that is often misunderstood in the current debate on greening architecture. There have always been builders and architects who draw heavily on natural forms and processes to evolve their housing designs; with their ideas growing out of a tradition of knowledge about local materials, lifestyles and climate (for example, Lloyd-Wright undated, Alexander 1976 & 1977). That tradition has been re-articulated in Britain to define sustainable design by current 'Green' architects such as Christopher Day (1990b, 1993), David Pearson (1989) and the Vales (1991a, b). Whilst the debate on sustainability is only now being promoted in housing, the discussion in architectural practice is still relatively polarised between 'community architecture' with its emphasis on promoting user control, and the 'starchitects' who tend to promote architecture within the confines of a traditional professional framework. At the same time the emerging green architecture movement appears to lack critical analysis of social and economic relationships (Dickens, 1993). When a housing professional engages with an architect they will be faced with someone who understands that sustainability is an issue in housing design but who discusses it only from within a traditional framework. The architect's approach to the housing design *process*, rather than simply the design itself, may well be aligned with the approach of the 'starchitects'. It is important that housing professionals recognise this from the outset so that the architect's approach to the design process can be properly questioned and contextualised in the housing arena through informed debate.

One dimension of sustainability, as introduced in chapter 1, emphasises the ability to draw on natural resources for our current requirements in such a way that those resources are not diminished or polluted for future generations. Sustainability in housing means going further than technical aspects of design and making sure that we have a process, as well as a product, that ensures that we 'design in' resource management and reduce the impact of the home on the natural environment in every way possible and at every stage. This requires that architects understand the housing process from the 'community architecture' viewpoint with its appreciation of user involvement and specific sets of social and economic relationships, as well as the 'green' architecture viewpoint with its appreciation of 'soft' technology and lifestyles. Housing design is a product of the interaction between housing policy, technology and economics. If housing design practice is to genuinely promote sustainability it must integrate all three of these elements using structures that allow for full participation of all parties including the end user at any point in the process. At present these activities operate in discrete cultures with ideologies that overlap, but cannot be integrated easily due to approaches that prevent satisfactory partnerships from being created between policy makers, implementors and their technical counterparts.

This chapter is intended as a contribution to the understanding of architectural practice as it relates to housing from a broadened 'eco-centric' view point. It attempts to provide a context for current green architectural thinking by locating it in socio-economic relations that currently inform the housing design process. Examples and illustrations are drawn from the architect's role in housing development of two major schemes. In order to understand some of the obstacles to sustainable design practice the first section examines the architect's cultural assumptions in relation to design and technology as well as the design team, which includes the user. By locating these assumptions within an economic system that privileges certain technical choices over others, we can begin to understand the problematic liaison between economics, housing technology and policy. Finally, the chapter offers an analogy with natural eco-systems as a tentative framework for integrating sustainability in to the housing design process itself.

The Role of the Architect: Artistic, Technical or Enabling?

Architects in Britain undergo an arduous seven years of training to become professionally qualified and it is through this that they continuously learn what their role is in relation to the client and users. The induction process is a subtle but a powerful one; many of the lessons learnt stay unquestioned with architects throughout their professional life and so it is appropriate to begin by looking at the nature of their training.

Training

Architects are not trained to work in an environment that reflects the teamwork that is required in housing practise between client, user and designer. Indeed students are often positively encouraged to see design as their sole prerogative with little or no teamwork between students, let alone teamwork with their future professional team members such as engineers, surveyors and housing managers. The emphasis in the majority of training institutions is on the individual excelling in their chosen field of specialisation. The frame of reference for this specialisation will be that of Artist or Technical Wizard. There is very little crossover between the two and no real attempt to link these two skills with the skill of communicating. Moreover these specialisations operate within a structure that gives the student no real understanding of the social and economic relations within which they must work. This is clearly pointed out in the current feminist critique of architectural training:

> *"Collaboration has not been a defining characteristic of 'good' architecture, even though it lies at the very foundation of design, development and construction. Collaboration contradicts a belief in personal choice and individual, creative freedom, that is, becoming a success on one's merits – a standard of excellence in a field defined by 'Starchitects'."* (Ahrentzen and Anthony, 1993 p.15).

Specialisation contained within a relevant structure that integrates the wider processes is potentially very valuable, but specialisation that operates within its own frame of reference is limited and less useful. If architects are not trained to 'talk' to their clients and work in a team with them, it is not surprising that 88% of clients interviewed in a recent survey (RIBA, 1993) felt they had a poor relationship with their architects and one wonders what the percentage might have been if the users of the buildings had been asked!

Architects are also trained to believe that their major contribution to housing design will be one of visible alterations to the environment. This was pointed out over twenty years ago by Robert Goodman:

> *"with architects' rewards determined by whether or not their work appears in visual media such as books, magazines and museums, there is a stronger incentive for them to focus on visual aspects of building design than, for example, to consider how comfortable the buildings are for the people that use them."* (Goodman, 1972 p.160).

In fact one of the greatest contributions that architects can make in the housing process is helping client and user alike to understand the spaces they live in, in order that they may then be able to more fully articulate their requirements in this domain. This has been particularly evident in the Housing Co-operative and Community Housing Association movement in Scotland where tenant participation is well established and not just tokenistic (Clapham and Kintrea 1993). However, it is not just in this area that Scottish tenants have made progress; sometimes they have resorted to direct activism to achieve considerable change.

Easthall is in one of Glasgow's most problematic peripheral housing estates, Easterhouse, on the east side of the city. In 1986 the local tenants were motivated by the appalling conditions of dampness and fuel poverty to try to improve their housing conditions through their own efforts having recognised the inability of the local authority to fund any major improvements. The local residents' association joined a local user controlled technical aid centre that in turn had strong academic links. As a result of this networking a unique event in Scotland took place; called 'heatfest', it was an ideas competition held over a long weekend in January 1987. Heatfest brought together tenants, architects, quantity surveyors, students and housing officials working in teams lead by the tenants. The winning team produced a low key passive solar retrofit design that used a combination of conservatories and high insulation on the existing four storey tenements to give a predicted reduction in heating bills from £22.50 to £6.50 per week.

Because of the competition a pilot project was set up using urban aid monies to retrofit a single tenement block comprising of six flats. The project was managed jointly by local tenants and councillors using design services provided by the technical aid centre. In this scheme the tenants defined the very nature of the project from the outset by voicing their concerns about dampness and fuel poverty. The architects involved responded sensitively by articulating the problem in design terms and thoroughly discussing the possible solutions with a strong tenant committee. The Association of Community Technical Aid Centres (ACTAC) is modelled on this principle with architects being directly accountable to the user in Scotland. In practise many architects see this type of enabling work as interference in their design process and are thoroughly suspicious of so-called community architecture (see Darke and Darke 1979 chapter 7).

A further anomaly in architectural training is the belief that only the architect has the technical understanding of housing functions and that the user and client have little to contribute in terms of design. They are seen as passive recipients in the design process (Sneddon and Theobald 1987). Technical knowledge in the training process is again taught out of context with little emphasis on the effects of applied technology on the *user* in terms of usability, maintenance, or sustainability. The following example shows how involving the users from the start can aid 'technology transfer'.

Technology Transfer

James Nisbet Street is situated on the north side of Glasgow next to the arterial M8 motorway, an inner city council housing estate but with all the problems of other peripheral estates designed in the 1960s boom era of mass housing programmes. Again tenants here were faced with the harsh reality of the City's housing capital investment being effectively cut. Faced with deteriorating homes and little prospect of money from the Council, the tenants set themselves up as a self-organising Housing Co-operative funded by Scottish Homes. There was also a key decision to be made over whether to demolish the houses and redevelop the estate, or opt for rehabilitation. The tenants chose to retain and improve the building fabric recognising that the social fabric of their local community was still relatively intact. A steering committee from the fledgling co-operative employed a local community architectural co-operative practice to undertake a feasibility study for the 400 odd houses. As a result a rolling programme of six phases was identified with Scottish Homes setting aside some £16 million over a six to ten year period for the work to be carried out. The architectural practice's commitment to tenant participation in design as well as the tenants' intimate involvement in decision making through the new housing co-operative structure ensured that all tenants were interviewed about their views on the design proposals and their often insightful observations were incorporated into a revised design which was in turn scrutinised fortnightly by the tenant committee (Edwards, 1991).

Until very recently little emphasis has been placed on the 'Cradle to Grave' approach to design with the close involvement of tenants' groups. Very few schools of architecture undertake 'live' projects with continuous feedback as a significant part of the syllabus. Indeed one celebrated architect has been quoted as saying that he would never return to visit a building he had designed once it had been completed preferring instead to move onto the next one! (James Stirling, informal interview with architecture students). With this attitude design problems can be ignored for a long time.

Teamwork, or Lack of it

Once an architect is employed they are soon introduced to team working and discover that 90% of practice is management and administration with only 10% being devoted to pure design matters. There exists an uneasy relationship with other members of the design team whom the architect has been trained to see as of secondary importance. This can be seen in the current debate about which professional should lead the design team with architects assuming themselves to be the natural leaders (RIBA 1993). This can result in a lack of co-ordination as an architect will often fail to perceive the need to consult their quantity surveyor or engineers until after an initial scheme has been designed. Then the other professionals just have to 'make it fit' no matter whether or not the initial design idea is wholly compatible with their requirements. The user often loses out in the whole process.

Work for an architect in the social housing field is often obtained through competitive tendering where tendering is based on ideas with only the winning firm being recompensed for time spent on the competition. This again disadvantages the user who will not be involved as a team member at this crucial stage of the design. Successful schemes will often be won by seductive images at the expense of a consultative design process. For example the recent 'Crown

Street Regeneration' Design and Build scheme in the Gorbals, Glasgow involved no tenant consultation in the housing competition between developers. A brief will have been issued by the client but, because the situation is not interactive the designer will have no real idea of the actual problems that the users wish to solve until after the competition entry has been submitted or, worse still, the scheme has been built!

Technical Problems

Architects in housing also rely heavily on an existing body of technical literature and accessible knowledge when tendering. Housing technology is capital-intensive, driven by the pressure to reduce labour intensive methods in order to increase profits in the construction industry. The architect is often the passive recipient of the latest in technological advances that incorporate factory manufactured products that involve energy intensive processing, often labelled 'high-tech'. Housing is becoming a kit of quick fit, large scale items. Wood is being replaced by plastic, stone and clay brick by concrete blocks and cement renders and internal finishes by ever more complex chemical processes. This is an attempt by contractor and manufacturer alike to cut down on the labour side of building housing (see chapter 11 on how self-build can reverse this process). Architects unwittingly participate in this process by specifying more and more of these highly energy-intensive, non-renewable, non-reusable and unbiodegradable housing products simply because they seem to be an 'efficient' way of building.

The use of Upvc windows is a good example. They have gradually replaced wooden windows on spurious 'maintenance free' grounds. In fact a Upvc window is virtually unmaintainable and can only be dumped in a landfill at the end of its thirty-year lifespan, whereas a wooden window, if maintained properly, can last sixty to a hundred years or more. Plastic roof edging to tiles has also replaced the traditional timber boarding under the guise of quick fixing on site. The specifier is seduced by these new materials and practices through contractors' lower prices, reflecting the apparent time saved on labour by using additional and precious non-renewable resources in manufacturing; the prices of which are kept artificially low because they are deemed to be endlessly available.

It is unlikely that architects will challenge the dominance of manufacturers of these products because these commodities are often seen as a secondary consideration to spatial quality in design practice. A rare exception to this rule is the architect David Lea who searches out sustainable materials to combine seamlessly with his spatial designs (Blundell-Jones, 1989). There is usually little time to investigate alternative materials given the fixed fee constraint within which architects operate, with precious design time being devoted to spatial solutions because this is more visible and gives greater short-term impact.

The Development Process: Working With the Architect?

This section examines the actual working arrangements of the various professionals involved in the social housing development process in order to show that far from promoting sustainability, current practice positively discourages it through inadequate briefing, budgeting and timing as well as a confusion of roles. The users, designers, and housing managers all suffer in this alienating process, leaving behind them a product often unfit for its purpose; requiring reinvestment, which defeats the original purpose of the exercise. Several threads in the development process can be picked out that essentially define how an architect grapples with this process in practice. An examination of the brief, the first attempt at defining the housing project to be undertaken and its associated requirements, reveals some of the assumptions frequently made that mitigate against sustainability. The brief can then be placed in the context of finance, timing and structural practices to illustrate the major obstacles to sustainability.

The Brief

The brief is the fundamental communication between the architect and the client. The scope for the brief is partly defined by the services which the architect is offering which are in turn defined by the architect's appointment conditions, and there are problems with both devices. The brief is generally put together by a team in the client group (that is housing professionals) which will draw on development staff, area housing managers, and sometimes maintenance staff, and hardly ever intended users. Because decision making is based on a linear, hierarchical process, the briefing team will not draw on the multi-disciplinary expertise available from the design or building team. How many housing departments have an architect present in the think tank first considering area renewal strategies or stock assessment? How many architects deem their services to include working up a brief with their client and users? The feasibility of the brief is thus untested until it reaches the design team by which point briefing factors such as budget or timescale are fixed. The design team are left to deal with these as best they can with whatever minimal contingency sums have been built into the brief. An essential feedback loop therefore is missing in this process.

From the point of view of the client, the brief will probably barely touch on issues of sustainability. This is because housing professionals are only now beginning to address problems of sustainability in a tentative fashion, e.g. life cycles, CFCs, etc., and tend to be content with looking at energy use rather than total energy required to build, use, maintain and demolish or recycle the housing in question. The Easthall scheme in Glasgow for example, focused heavily on reducing energy in use in an attempt to end fuel poverty but used energy intensive materials in the process. The James Nisbet Housing Co-operative scheme has, in addition to low energy in use, attempted to reduce the use of energy intensive materials choosing timber finishes where possible and avoided the use of CFCs. Neither scheme, however, has looked at the possibilities for re-cycling or evaluated the total energy involved in the process.

Besides the physical assumptions about resources made in the brief, there will be many cultural assumptions that mitigate against sustainability. These might include car-orientated design requirements rather than public transport; living arrangement requirements for individual cooking and washing facilities, and housing design mixes that cannot be adapted, (for alternatives to this see Ahrentzen and Frank 1989). Certain fashionable ideas such as selective demolition of housing over two storey height, or 'front and back doors' for all housing will be built into the brief predefining it with ideas that may be untested from the viewpoint of sustainability. The architect will be required to produce a solution based on these perceived aspirations without recourse to redefining the brief from the environmental perspective.

Sustainable technical requirements such as biodegradability or re-use will largely be absent from the brief, this being left in the domain of the architect. Given that architects have had little training in sustainable design, many will not have a grasp of the issues involved let alone have the technical competence to provide solutions. But if the right questions are not asked in the brief then the housing professionals concerned will not realise that they can deal with these environmental issues at all. Many housing briefs tend to concentrate on the social and spatial requirements with little reference to technicalities felt to be covered by technical standards and architectural services. There is no mechanism for feedback in a brief that might allow the client to appreciate omissions by the architect. The alternative is demonstrated by Ferguslie Park Housing Association who are commissioning architects to specifically consult tenants over green issues at the briefing stage of a development in Glasgow; it will be interesting to see what effect this has on the social and spatial requirements.

In response to an ill-defined situation the architect will respond with their own agenda. They may attempt to redefine the brief as best they can given the constraints now imposed by time. Or they may interpret a brief that is relatively slack on the technical side with strong architectural agenda. Radical plan and elevational treatments may be proposed for visual effect to imprint a certain style on the project that will then mark out the housing as 'belonging' to that architect. Sustainable design will be a low priority unless the client has specifically requested it because there is no visible effect associated with the effort required to consider such issues.

Indeed, the ecological aspect of sustainability is often not even recognised as a design issue by architects but is relegated to the status of 'technical requirement' rather than a holistic concept that informs sustainability in design from the outset. This can be seen in the 'style' school of architecture where the emphasis is firmly on creating interesting spaces and elevations. The discussion of built form in the mainstream architectural journals usually excludes an assessment of the ecological consequences of this approach to design although some attention might be paid to 'low energy' requirements. In contrast to this there are architects who take the holistic ecological approach as their primary motivation (Pearson, 1989) allowing this to dictate the very form of their housing design. Depressingly, there are very few architects practising primarily in the housing field who have broadened out their concerns with 'low energy' design to include ecological concerns in any meaningful way because the debate between two approaches previously mentioned is so underdeveloped.

The Budget

Under the current stringent financial climate the budget for low cost social housing will be the minimum perceived possible. In all likelihood it will exclude the use of sustainable accounting mechanisms such as revenue trade offs against capital for long-life products or low-energy products such as solar panels or condensing boilers. The yardsticks currently used to assess the 'value for money' of a scheme will use relatively short pay-back periods (2–5 years is not uncommon for energy efficiency measures, though the lifespan of the measure might be 30 years) and will operate on minimum space standards that exclude adaptability. However it is possible to incorporate environmental features. For example in the case of James Nisbet Street Housing Co-operative, both the tenants and architect were united in arguing with the funder that passive solar glazed-in balconies and condensing boilers were energy and cost effective in the long term, and should not be excluded as 'unnecessary extras'. The Easthall residents opted to augment funding altogether, using sponsorship and community funding for the first scheme and European Community funding topped up with local authority funding for the second, larger scheme. This allowed them to transcend some of the traditional barriers to funding green measures enabling them to include 'buffer zone' spaces which function as additional amenity space as well as saving energy (Vale and Vale 1991a).

But financial squeezes are likely to be placed on developing the essential tools for sustainability such as life cycle analysis of building products. Often environmental impact analysis is deemed an 'extra' that requires justification. Unless the client carefully defines these extra services when appointing the architect from the outset it can be difficult to add on the cost of these at a later stage. It would also help if the architects' appointment conditions drawn up by the Royal Institute of British Architects recognised that these services are an essential part of an architect's contribution to housing design and incorporated them into the basic 'conditions of services' rather than the 'additional services' section of the document. The overall basic fee should then reflect the additional cost of carrying out this work.

The Timing

This is one area in the social housing design process that has potentially the most disruptive effect on continuity and sustainability. Should the design team wish to invest additional time in understanding sustainability issues involved in their scheme and involve the users in this process, they will be subject to the usual vagaries of government financial planning. This might involve having to suddenly speed up the design process to adapt to a spending shortfall for the next financial year or due to a surplus in the current financial year. The problem can be overcome to some extent. In the James Nisbet scheme the architects were re-employed for three successive phases and so could build up considerable knowledge about the effects of green measures taken over a number of years. In the case of Easthall also, a monitoring project has been set up with funding from the government to assess the measures there with the same architects also being re-employed for the second project.

Without flexible long term planning we often end up with what is known in the trade as 'road repaving schemes in March', where work is carried out simply for the sake of spending the money in order not to lose it that year. Annual government budgeting encourages an inherently unsustainable way of thinking where unnecessary ballast is built into schemes to cushion the essentials from unpredictable cuts. If the cuts don't materialise, the design team is left with a scheme that is profligate in its use of natural resources on non-essential items. Furthermore timescales rarely account for thorough user consultation and feedback with the architect often having to take a short cut on time set aside for design or specification to adapt to this requirement from the client when it is stipulated without any additional fee. This may be one reason architects generally are so disparaging of participatory community architecture, feeling it to be an imposition on rather than a stimulus to design. The architects for James Nisbet Street and Easthall were community-orientated firms that were well used to working directly with the users and made an allowance for this at the outset of the projects. This attitude contrasts strongly with the local authority architects who have carried out refurbishment adjacent to these schemes with only the minimum of consultation with users, often in the form of intimidating mass meetings rather than individual interviews, in an effort to save time and money.

Structural Barriers

Accountability in architectural practice becomes problematical when the funding source is remote from the user/client/architect interface. This occurs typically in publicly funded housing where design decision implementors are well down in the hierarchy of strategic decision making. There are very often tensions between local housing offices or associations and their centralised government funders. The interaction between the two tends to be 'top down' with local bodies feeling alienated from decision making, with a result that the users are nearly always marginalised. In addition traditional structures for the procurement of housing tend to be organised on an individual professional basis rather than a functional basis that might involve several different professionals at once. The sequential nature of these structures means that decisions are passed down the line until the user has to accept the consequences. Very often the head of the structure doesn't know what the feet are doing. From a sustainability viewpoint this is bad design practice. The architect is often required to respond quickly to such an unintegrated structure. Also architectural firms have to be adept at switching quickly from one job to another trying to keep all the balls in the air simultaneously. There is often a lack of continuity in the office as certain jobs progress so far and then suddenly become dormant while others leap into life because of a remote decision; these are not the most enabling conditions for the implementation of sustainability in design. Furthermore, price changes on products cause unforeseen changes to the design. For example a three to six month delay can see price increases of between 10-20% on certain items. Because of the lack of feedback structures between client and architect, the significance of this may be lost on the client who may be unaware of the subtle changes that have been made. This in turn can lead to a built form that does not have its own tailor-made design which is an essential ingredient of sustainability in housing.

A Model for Sustainable Housing Design and Practice

Having examined some of the factors which underlie architectural practice in the housing field and located them in working practices, we can see clearly some of the limitations involved in trying to promote sustainability. This section tentatively suggests an ecological approach which may provide a radically different model for better practice. It has been suggested elsewhere in this book that the structure-agency model is a useful way of analysing the housing process (see chapter 8). An appropriate analogy of this is the eco-system methodology provided by ecology, and it may be appropriate to evaluate green housing design in these terms to assess its potential for sustainability (Hawes 1993).

Housing as a Native Eco-system

Drawing on our understanding of how the natural world functions Jane Jacobs defines housing as:

> "*Specific and particularised buildings always involved in differing, specific processes.*" (Jacobs, 1961 p.454).

She goes on to suggest that an understanding of the city as 'organism' can be derived from life science disciplines using the following principles:

* to think about processes (as opposed to products);
* to work inductively, reasoning from the particular to the general;
* to seek for 'unaverage' clues, involving very small quantities which reveal the way larger and more 'average' quantities are operating.

A social eco-system methodology, given its systems analysis basis, can function as a form of structure-agency modelling process which recognises relationships between different agencies. To understand this more fully let us think of the housing system as native woodland ecosystem. This woodland must be self regenerating if it is to survive. It is a life supporting system that functions incrementally over time. The woodland seeds itself locally, grows, is used by various inhabitants and decays incrementally. Even in its decay are the seeds of reconstruction and at any one moment different elements are replacing themselves, almost imperceptibly as new mingles with old, mutually supporting each others' process. There is no idea of 'waste' and everything is renewable. The woodland gives back everything it takes from the local soil, air and water.

Housing must be like this if we are to maintain a balance with the earth's resources. Nothing must happen too quickly; sustainable practices take a long time and we can use time to save physical resources. For example, each housing stage must be thoroughly considered, compared and evaluated before moving on to the next stage, in the same way that ecosystems rely on feedback to form varied but dynamically stable and sustainable forms of life. Housing programmes must allow for assimilation of previous ideas and feedback from built schemes as part of the brief, which must be far more considered and detailed than is usually the case. Time is money, but we do not 'save' any time by using high-tech fixes or quick building programmes; we merely steal from the future the time and resources the next generation will need to clear up our hasty mistakes.

Nothing must happen on too large a scale or in an unintegrated fashion. Small incremental building should be encouraged on infill sites, with local repairs and adaptations as necessary. Large scale demolition and new-build should be avoided because the social and physical environment cannot easily absorb such rapid change. Every end should serve another end; waste can become compost, literally and figuratively, with materials being re-used or recycled in the ecosystem. Materials can be adapted to local climates and ecosystems effectively 'growing' from and decaying back into the land at the end of their life. It should also be possible to give back to the locality, all the energy extracted from it, if we use renewable energy and material sources. In a social ecosystem we should attempt to give back as much of the human potential as we extract, through local jobs and locally managed resources.

Ecological Housing Technology

There is a pressing need to seamlessly combine sustainable technologies with a cultural evaluation to avoid the costly technological mistakes of the 1960s and

1970s, that gave us sick building syndrome and damp housing. There is also a need for more holistic appraisals that assess the complicated interaction between the inhabitants, their physical homes and their changing lifestyles. Housing technology must also be redefined as a symbolic process that evolves with the user and not for the user. Without a feedback loop built into the system that allows architects to work with knowledge about the holistic impact of their designs and products, emerging technologies and materials will be developed as isolated specialisms unintegrated in our proposed housing ecosystem.

Any new products and technologies should be carefully tested and evaluated for both usability and sustainability. Housing professionals should stipulate in the briefing process that the onus be on the architect to 'prove' new products. Existing building products and techniques should be constantly re-evaluated in the light of these criteria to help eradicate the use of those that are unsustainable, eco-labelling will be useful here. Testing of products and technologies should be measured against life cycles required in practice for housing. A roof product should last for at least 60-100 years; many late Victorian slate roofs where properly maintained are still perfectly serviceable. Why should we accept life cycles of 20 or 30 years for products?

Structures for a Housing Ecosystem

Concurrent with holistic analysis is a danger of 'option paralysis' where the professionals are faced with so much inter-related information and feedback that many simply turn their back on sustainability and opt for the unsustainable status quo that they know. The architect is particularly at risk from this disorder being at the interface of culture and technology. The antidote is detailed and clear decision-making by the housing client during the briefing stage, well before the design stage. In the case of the James Nisbet scheme, for example, the architects had been appointed to carry out the feasibility study that incorporated a social survey. This gave them a clear understanding of the issues involved, well before the design stage, enabling them to comment on the client's brief as it evolved. To avoid professional myopia in this respect housing bodies should be structured to incorporate a multi-disciplinary mode of working. Strategies for housing renewal and individual scheme briefs should be evolved through working groups that have professionals from all the fields concerned with housing and the environment. The user must also be incorporated with their highly professional understanding of what it is, or will be, like to live in the housing under consideration. At a very basic level this might mean a local office with a housing development officer, maintenance officer, architect, local planner and housing user with other professionals drawn on to the team as required.

The competition structure for procuring 'good' housing design must be questioned at this point. While competition produces incentive in architects and a plethora of ideas, it is questionable how effective these ideas are in solving the actual problems stated in the brief in a meaningful way. Negotiated appointments with design teams are more able to ensure that the clients' requirements will be met in full and have the potential for a degree of continuity that competiton processes lack. Through this continuity the architect can build up detailed and effective knowledge about the housing that they are dealing with and a strong relationship with the rest of the team. At present much of this potential is destroyed as government policy forces competitive tendering on housing bodies often irrespective of how many advantages there might be to a negotiated contract. This is not to say that competition is inherently unsustainable. On the contrary, all ecosystems operate on the basis of competition as well as co-operation but they do so in an appropriate manner, carefully assessing which mode is more effective in promoting sustainability.

Eco-budgeting

Equally important in terms of structure for sustainability in housing is the ability of these integrated design teams to have some degree of control over timescales and finances that are closely inter-related anyway. Central government and local authorities must reckon with five year financial budgets with built in moveable financial ballast to account for slippage in the system, rather than the annual hurdles race which uses resources as a ballast instead. Housing budgets should also allow capital costs to be traded off against revenue savings where this proves to be more sustainable. This would allow some pump-priming in the market for green products that have long life cycles or long term energy savings but short term overheads not experienced by competitors. Yardsticks should accept the argument for higher space standards, where it can be proven that long term savings can be made in the future through having the extra space to adapt or convert housing easily for changing life cycle needs, rather than forcing users to move if they acquire a family. Sustainable housing means long term planning that will ensure houses last for at least a hundred years but be fully adaptable, to derive maximum benefit from the financial resources put in to them.

Tenant Participation: Essential Feedback System

In housing terms self regeneration would mean that projects and demands are driven by the inhabitants rather than outside agencies. The life support system refers to the symbiotic relationship between the inhabitants and the housing 'enablers', be they managers, funders or designers. Unlike the community architecture lobby, which over emphasises the 'bottom-up' approach (Sneddon and Theobald, 1987), a true housing ecosystem recognises that feedback is a two-way process with different components of a housing project, or 'organism', mutually supporting each other and giving each other information about the current state of play at the macro and micro levels of organisation, local and regional. The 'us and them' disappears as both parties recognise their reliance on each other for survival. The essential ingredient for change here is that the present managers and professionals must recognise how much they already rely on users. As Mark Bhatti (1993) points out:

> *"How many council house repairs could be done successfully if the householders did not monitor their houses, report the repairs, were not in when the workers came round, and did not keep an eye on future problems?"* (p.104)

Bhatti goes on to argue that tenant participation enables users to have control over their local environment. This would certainly shift the power base and redistribute it more equally but on its own it does not ensure that the 'us and them' syndrome of mutual suspicion and withholding of information will disappear – this can be clearly seen in some of the dialogues in Sneddon and Theobald (1987). At best professionals treat tenants who have obtained power with a cautious distance; at worst a 'cold war' sets in, with both parties evenly matched but unwilling to make a move because of ideological differences. True participation means all parties recognising that each group requires the other in order to *survive* and that the sum of the whole is always greater than its parts in housing systems as well as natural ecosystems.

Conclusion

The proposal for a 'housing ecosystem' approach as a way of promoting sustainable housing design is radical in that it undermines current structures totally. It is a new paradigm and one that will not be easily absorbed into the existing system. However it is possible to introduce incremental changes towards a consistent way of working at every level, with the goal of achieving an overhaul steadily, with plenty of time for feedback on the changes; the means must be the same as the end to achieve sustainability. Decision structures must be flexible and as close to the ground as possible so that given the appropriate resources our housing 'woodlands' will develop their own unique ecosystems particular to each location. The users and 'enablers' must be fully responsive to global and local requirements as well as each other. Paradoxically professionals must 'let go' just when it would appear that they most need to 'hold back' at a time of rapid environmental change. We need to view the housing design process not as a human appropriation of resources towards specific ends, but as a continuously self-modifying ecosystem that allows for human participation, which can in turn modify itself when nature requires it to.

CHAPTER 10: Environmental Assessment and the Development Process

Sue Barker-Wolff

Environmental assessment is a means of authoritatively appraising the achievement of alternative 'green' building practice in housing based on concepts of 'sustainability'. It is also a means of raising the awareness of these issues and encouraging the implementation of alternative building methods, designs and materials in the development process. In this chapter three aspects of the use of environmental assessment, and their implications for changing building methods, are considered and illustrated with a case study of a 'green' housing development. The first aspect consists of methodological problems of defining 'sustainability' and the absence of consensus as to the building measures that should be encouraged. A wide range of global, local and indoor issues can be included and there is technical debate over the importance of some of them. The only national scheme of environmental assessment is the Building Research Establishment Environmental Assessment Method (BREEAM), which has deliberately selected well documented environmental risks on which there is broad consensus. Appraisal schemes such as BREEAM involve combinations of different issues with qualitatively dissimilar risks as well as widely varying financial costs. This raises the problems of multi-variate analysis and how the importance of different items in a 'green' specification should be weighted.

The second issue addressed in the chapter is the usefulness of environmental appraisal as a means of encouraging the implementation of green building methods. Most housing development does not presently require statutory environmental impact appraisal or safety appraisal. Schemes such as BREEAM are voluntary and rely on the enthusiasm of clients and their perceived benefits in terms of an improved green image, better saleability, or reduced running costs to make them attractive. The impact of BREEAM to date has been disappointingly low, although it is argued that the number of assessments underestimates the true influence of the scheme and much larger green developments are in the pipeline. Housing associations in particular appear to be taking the initiative in promoting green building on a wider scale.

Thirdly what lessons can be learned from the implementation of environmental assessment so far? Developers and clients must consider cost, build-ability, and reliability and some of these issues have been obstacles to the implementation of green specifications. The case study of the Greenwrythe Lane project by South London Family Housing Association indicates that green building can be achieved at a reasonable extra cost; provided green principles are applied from the outset. Some green features are easy to achieve including improvements in energy standards over current Building Regulations (BRECSU 1993). Environmental appraisal on its own does not solve the problem of which measures are to be included and in particular what information the designer or builder needs to implement alternative methods. Even so, obstacles to implementation of 'green' building measures include cost; the absence of authoritative guidance as to how to select and specify green measures; lack of familiarity in the building industry with some methods proposed; lack of standards and, in some areas, lack of research.

Criteria for Green Building

Green buildings can generally be defined as those which go well beyond the prescriptions of current UK Building Regulations, British Standard Codes of Practice and statutory health and safety regulations. In particular they would:

* achieve much higher standards of energy efficiency and reduced carbon dioxide emissions both in use and embodied in construction materials and processes;
* avoid the use of materials and packaging manufactured with CFCs or HCFCs;
* avoid the use of materials, processes or designs hazardous to the health and safety of either the builders, occupiers, or people in the locality or which involve pollution or health risks in their manufacture;
* avoid the unnecessary consumption of scarce resources both in construction and use and recycle or provide for the recycling of materials.

Up to the early 1980s most efforts in the UK at environmentally conscious building have concentrated on the energy aspects, based on the need to reduce carbon dioxide emissions. Energy appraisal schemes for housing have been developed by the National Energy Foundation (a public charity), and Star Point based on the Building Research Establishment's (BRE) energy calculation procedure for housing, BREDEM (Building Research Establishment Domestic Energy Model, see Anderson 1989).

More recently in the late 1980s concern has been developing over the other environmental problems; notably ozone depletion and the use of CFCs and HCFCs in buildings resulting in the Montreal Protocol enforced by a European Community directive; the destruction of tropical rain forests and the use of tropical hardwoods, health, water economy and pollution. In Germany environmental concerns have led to the Baubiologie movement (1) and the introduction of 'Blue Angel' DIN standards for building and services components. In Sweden research by the Swedish Council for Building Research has developed guidelines on building health. Green buildings can no longer simply be energy efficient ones, although some building developers continue to advertise their houses as such.

In 1990 the Building Research Establishment together with a firm of architects and energy consultants published the first system of environmental appraisal in the UK: *Building Research Establishment Environmental Assessment Method.* BREEAM New Homes (Prior et al, 1991) is a voluntary environmental appraisal scheme intended to encourage green house building and give authoritative recognition to developers who incorporate green issues in the selection of materials and processes. The scheme is operated by independent assessors who check compliance with targets and issue certificates, under the supervision of the BRE. There is a check-list of 25 items or targets to be included in the specification. These cover global issues such as global warming and the ozone layer, and give credits for achieving set levels of estimated carbon dioxide emissions and avoiding CFCs and HCFCs; local issues affecting use of resources and impact on the local environment and indoor issues which effect the health and safety of occupiers. The scheme gives approved methods of validation of carbon dioxide emissions, and issues credits as illustrated in Figure 1. A number of these issues are not strictly 'green' but represent good design practice, for example the safety and security items that derive from 'Secured by Design'. Although there is no 'pass' mark, an unofficial grading system distinguishes between excellent, very good and fair. Since the type of issues differ qualitatively and vary greatly in the ease of implementation these grades specify minimum achievement levels in each sub catagory (Table 1).

Table 1. Minimum BREEAM Green scores in each category

This multi factorial check-list system deals with some of the problems of multi-variate analysis: energy is given a higher weighting by being given up to 6 credits.

Rating	TOTAL	Global	Local	Indoor
Excellent	24	5	7	9
Very Good	18	3	5	7
Good	12	2	3	7
Fair	7	1	1	2

The above issues have been conservatively selected on the basis of well documented risks and easily accessible and well tried solutions. The BRE

Figure 1. BREEAM Credits: (Applied to Futureworld scheme MacKay and Baker Brown)

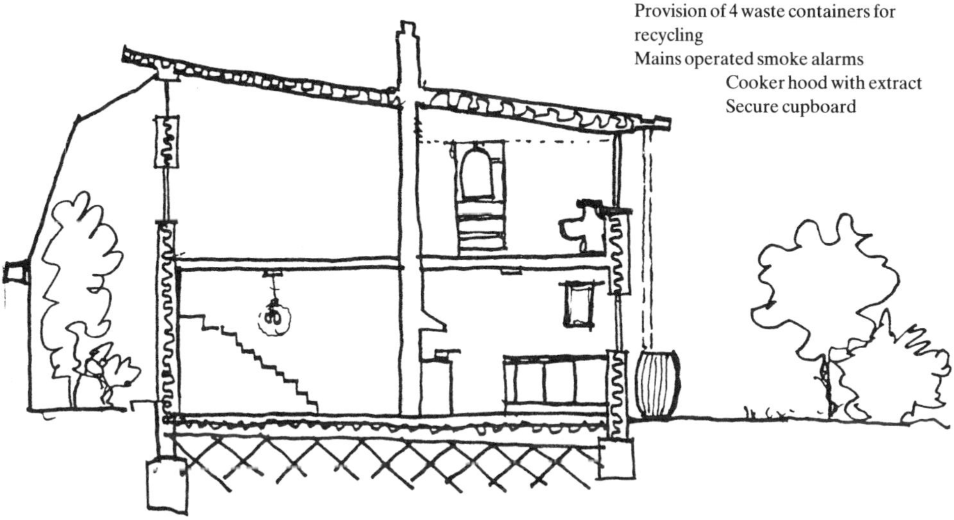

recognise that the selection is cautious and itemise, as issues for future development, other environmental issues some of which are already common practice in for example, Germany and Sweden. There are other local schemes for environmental appraisal such as the South London Consortium Energy Group's 'Green label' for existing housing (Ince 1991) which includes water based paints, low formaldehyde building boards, indoor condensation control and a range of ecological enhancement items in addition to the BREEAM issues.

Building Standards

There is still debate about the full range of environmental problems that should be addressed by green buildings. There is technical debate about whether certain items are indeed hazardous, as well as disputes over safe levels. There are also conflicts between measures which may eliminate a safety hazard but involve an energy penalty. BREEAM 3/91 does not currently regulate Volatile

Organic Chemicals (VOCs) apart from naphthalene, produced by coal tar products, and urea formaldehyde foam insulation. Other VOCs have been identified as causing ill health, irritation and are, in some cases, carcinogenic. VOCs are increasingly used in buildings as components of wood products, furnishings, wall coverings, paints, glues as well as cleaning materials. The effects of a 'cocktail' of chemicals are suspected of causing immune suppression, but are not yet medically established. These concerns have led to recommendations to avoid building materials containing these products by the World Health Organisation (1987), the Commission of the European Community (CEC 1992) and the Swedish Board of Building Research (Johnson, 1991) and to control both emissions and indoor air levels.

Formaldehyde, for example is a very common VOC and is extensively used in ply, chipboard and medium density fibreboard. Exposure to formaldehyde is known to cause irritation, aggravate asthma, and at high levels in animal tests be carcinogenic. The regulation of permitted levels of formaldehyde in indoor air (Table 2) is much lower in the USA, Germany and Sweden for example, than in the UK according to the London Hazards Centre (1990, p.44).

Table 2 Maximum Permitted Formaldehyde Concentrations in PPM (parts per million)

UK	USA	Sweden/Germany
2	1	0.1

Furthermore timber products in the USA, Germany and Finland have 'low formaldehyde' labelling and at lower levels than British Standards (2). The emission of NOX, oxides of nitrogen produced by high temperature burning appliances, which is not controlled in the UK, is regulated in Germany under the 'Blue Angel' kitemark scheme. Thus both tighter standards together with statutory requirements for labelling enable green designers to select appropriate products. CIRIA's review of environmental issues in the building industry highlights the problem of lack of knowledge about material pollutant emissions in the UK:

> *"... The designer needs to know what is coming off, at what rate and for how long."*

and indicates that:

> *"If Eco-labelling of building materials is adopted by the industry then emission characteristics must be considered a central issue."* (CIRIA 1993, p.42).

PVC is the subject of some dispute. Originally considered a hazard to workers due to the toxic nature of the vinyl chloride monomer, there is now debate about whether it should be excluded on other grounds, pollution and production of dioxin when incinerated, which is challenged by the manufacturers. Elimination of PVC in all building products, for example electric cabling, would result in an energy penalty because mineral insulated copper clad cable (MICC or pyro) would have to be used instead. Analysis of the energy content of materials and total life cycle costing is not yet feasible in the UK since research on equivalent comparisons is still under way and as yet unpublished.

Usefulness of Environmental Assessment

The penetration of BREEAM into development practice in the social housing sector is a major problem, and the number of schemes assessed under BREEAM encouraging. 120 units have been assessed to date of which 14 were 'excellent', and the majority 'very good'. Half were by housing associations and half by builders. Although the number of schemes assessed is not very encouraging there is evidence however that the buildings assessed form only part of the total number of buildings whose construction has been influenced in whole or part by green principles. Developers will assess a sample showcase building and apply the methods to others. At least five housing associations are developing green briefs for future developments which do not appear in BREEAM statistics. Two major housing associations, Gwalia and North British are now developing proposals for large scale green schemes supported by the Commission of the European Communities' THERMIE programme funding for the 'Environmental Network' of European housing groups. A project supported by the Joseph Rowntree Foundation, 'Twenty-First Century Homes', managed by the Urban and Economic Development Group (URBED, 1992), is promoting a series of demonstration projects illustrating the application of green principles to a range of widely replicable types of housing including: 'Homes for Change' a block of 50 flats in Hulme, Manchester; 2 storey housing at 'Futureworld'; Milton Keynes and Ta Coed Village, Swansea. Local authorities in Birmingham, Bristol, Leicester and Newcastle upon Tyne and Gwyned County Council, Humberside County Council, Falkirk District Council and others have developed environmental policies which include energy efficiency and green building principles.

Statutory Context

To some extent the lack of implementation of green principles can be attributed to the costs of BREEAM assessment and the wider knowledge of the National Home Energy Rating (NHER) scheme for energy appraisal which developers see as being 'green'. However the lack of take up can also be seen as resulting from a lack of government regulation or incentives. Most housing development, unless it forms part of a large scale development does not fall into the category of projects for which environmental impact analysis is required (3). Statutory controls such as planning permission are mostly concerned with land use, density, and aesthetic issues and Building Regulations similarly do not regulate many of the features commonly seen as green, although they do influence energy use and noise.

The CIRIA Environmental Forum have identified a wide range of environmental issues in building where the development of alternative building practice either requires research, demonstration or publicity. Furthermore regulation of standards and labelling to ensure their compliance is needed. As mentioned in chapter 4, The European Construction Products Directive, which obliges manufacturers to 'provide material fit for purpose with minimal emissions of toxic gases, dangerous particulates and radiation', could form the basis of an eco-labelling system (4). This is yet to be fully developed in the UK. The ambit of BREEAM stops at the boundary of the building and the builder's range of responsibility. Housing related environmental measures which are under the control of other authorities include water economy, waste management, development planning and transport. The foregoing discussion has neglected these infrastructural issues but these should also be considered.

Lessons to be Learned

Of the houses which have been appraised under the BREEAM scheme, most dwellings have managed to comply with the following green issues: avoidance of asbestos, lead and urea formaldehyde; restriction of timber treatment to necessary areas under BS Codes; provision of smoke alarms and cooker hood; and carbon dioxide emissions to achieve 4 credits when gas is the heating fuel. Most of these items are negligible in cost and correspond to good building practice anyway. The items which are more difficult to achieve, and some of the reasons for this, include:

* **Avoidance of all HCFCs:** a timetable for the phase out of HCFCs (Hydrochlorofluorocarbons are less damaging to the ozone layer than CFCs) is not included in the Montreal Protocol and thus materials labelled 'CFC free' may include HCFCs. Choosing insulation materials which do not include them requires checking with the manufacturer and in some situations such as 'inverted' flat roofs alternative insulants may not be suitable. Hot water cylinder insulation is often overlooked and until recently most factory applied insulation used HCFCs although there are now a limited number of manufacturers who produce HCFC free hot water cylinders.
* **Higher carbon dioxide standards** (5–6 credits): these higher levels of energy efficiency, equivalent to about 9 to 10 on the NHER scale, require both substantially higher levels of insulation together with very efficient heating systems and controls, such as gas condensing boilers or electric heat pump ventilation units. The extra capital cost (although revenue savings result in reasonable pay-backs of 5 to 9 years) deters

developers to whom initial cost is critical.

* **Hardwood from regulated sources:** since there is no internationally agreed and monitored system of timber labelling and tropical hardwoods may be included in composite timber products such as ply, it has proven difficult to find reliable sources of sustainably managed hardwood.
* **50% of roof coverings recycled:** re-use of old slates and tiles is often not possible due to their condition. There are a small number of manufacturers whose tiles include recycled materials, such as fly ash, but these may not be satisfactory on grounds of appearance and suitability.
* **50% masonry from recycled sources:** second hand bricks are considerably more expensive than new ones. Whilst a few manufacturers make blocks using blast furnace slag ash a limited range is available.
* **Whole house ventilation:** both whole house systems with heat reclaim and heat pump ventilation units are considerably more costly than a conventional heating system with passive ventilation and extract fans. With mild English winters less tightly built dwellings can achieve acceptable indoor ventilation levels with simple trickle vents and extract fans and it can be argued that whole house ventilation is unnecessary.
* **Passive stack ventilation:** these are PVC pipes installed in kitchen and bathrooms instead of extract fans and require specific consent by the local authority as an alternative to the Building Regulations. It has been reported that some local authorities are resistant.
* **Six litre flush WC:** these are not commonly available and only one supplier in the UK is known.

The obstacles to implementation described above include both cost, difficulty in finding alternative suitable materials, a limited range of suitable alternative products which may not meet other constructional and reliability requirements and restrictions imposed on choice by aesthetic and planning requirements.

Case Study: Housing Association Development

The following case study illustrates what can be achieved by an enthusiastic developer, in this case a housing association, and some of the lessons to be learned. Green Wrythe Lane was developed by South London Family Housing Association as a small (28 unit) general family needs estate with 22 terraced houses and 6 flats on an infill site (part of a redundant school) in Carshalton. Development staff of the association, encouraged by their local authority, Sutton, initiated the proposal to develop a 'green' scheme and to use this exercise to appraise the costs and wider applicability of green measures. Based on the association's outline sketch scheme and with the architect and environmental consultant, Roy Grimwade, two alternative briefs were tendered simultaneously for a design/build contract: a conventional and a green brief. In design/build contracts the contractor is responsible for the detailed design and

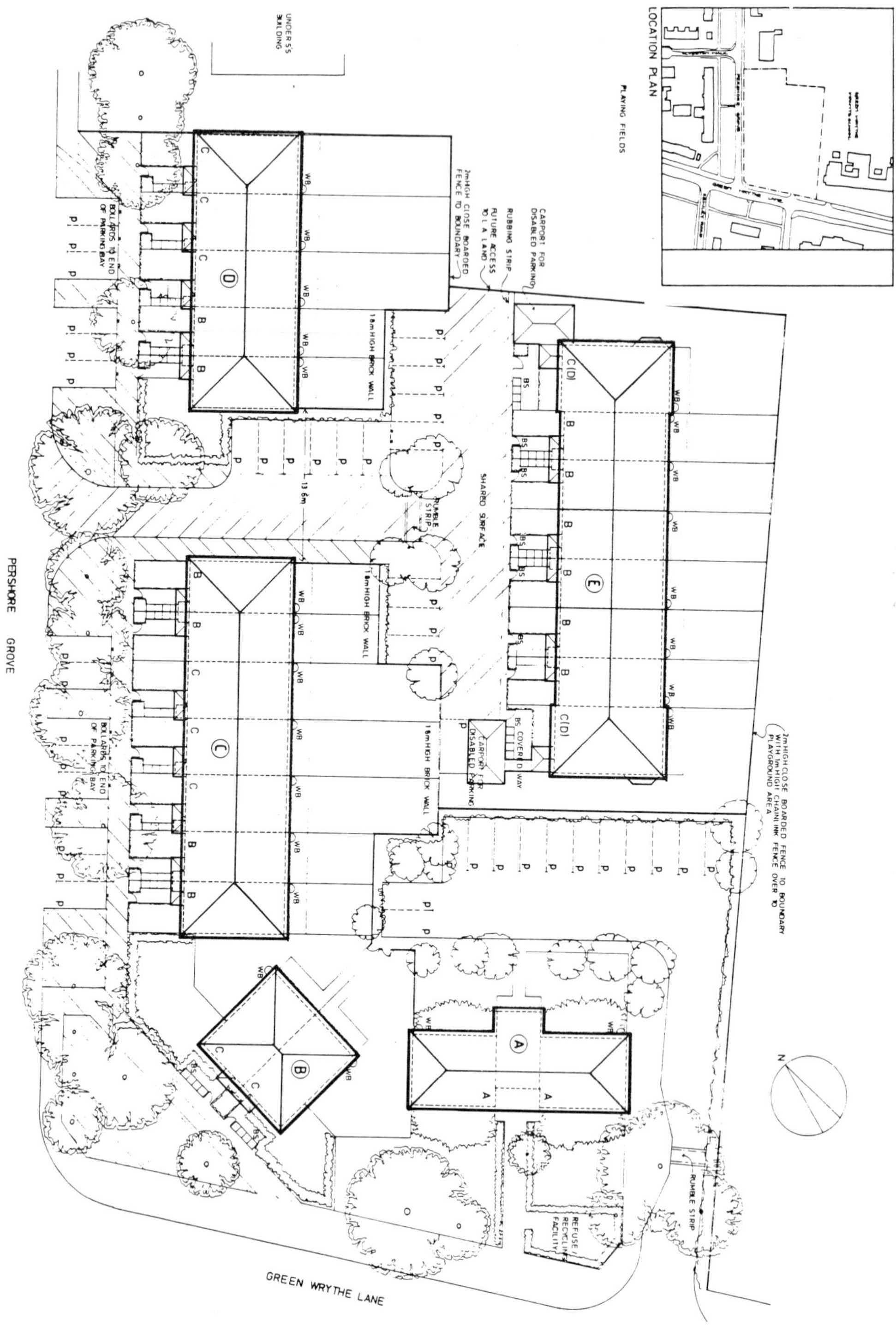

Figure 2: Site Plan Green Wrythe Lane, Carshalton (Courtesy ECD Architects and Energy Consultants)

may select how they chose to satisfy the terms of the client's tender specification which may be of varying levels of detail. In this case the brief combined both a performance specification and some detailed suppliers or construction methods. The green performance specification included the obtaining of BREEAM 'Excellent' standard as well as a number of other items not covered by BREEAM:

* avoidance of formaldehyde
* avoidance of other VOCs
* daylight and natural ventilation to bathrooms
* avoidance of PVC
* use of cellulose insulation

A 'green' tender was, with some modifications and negotiation on cost, accepted from builders Willmott Dixon, and overall came within cost limits. An initial overcost compared to a conventional specification of approximately £3000 per unit was negotiated down to £1500. Savings in energy running costs to tenants are predicted to be on average about £6 per week or about £300 per annum. This would indicate a simple pay-back period of 5 years which would usually be considered a good investment decision. It is anticipated that the rent set will include an element of repayment to offset the higher initial costs.

SLFHA's original design had a layout conforming to passive solar principles with compact terraces, south facing living rooms and more extensive glazing to the south and was not amended by the builders. Internally some minor re-arrangement and modification of window sizes was necessary to ensure that bathrooms had natural daylight and all rooms conformed to the day lighting recommendations. Items which had to be amended due to cost or practicality included:

* timber frame walls (factory assembled as panels) were constructed using 150mm insulation as opposed to 225mm on grounds of cost;

* solid timber kitchen units were substituted by cheaper low formaldehyde board units;

* ground floors (over a concrete suspended beam and block sub-floor) used a low formaldehyde particleboard (Type C4);

* PVC was not entirely excluded (although external gutters and wastes are cast iron and conventional PVC clad electrical cable and PVC internal drainage was used since alternatives are more costly;

* heating system. A gas warm air with heat recovery (Johnson Starley) and extract cooker hood was used throughout instead of a wet system (boiler and radiators) due to cost;

* cellulose insulation was not used in walls due to absence of Agrément certificate for this type of use;

* six litre flush WCs were not used since the BREEAM credit for water economy was already satisfied by the provision of external water butts.

The fact that an overwhelmingly 'green' brief was achieved at little extra cost is, in part, a reflection of the competitive tender climate, tender costs indices declined in 1991 and 1992, as well as the tendering method which allowed a truly competitive comparison between the two alternative strategies. It also reflects, within the design parameters allowed in design/build contracts, some detailed trade offs between different elements of construction to be able to afford the some undoubtedly more expensive green features. The association's agent noted that unsuccessful tenderers appeared to have priced the green tender as a series of 'add-ons' to the conventional specification with resulting very high extra costs. Integrating the green items in the original cost planning by the builder allowed economies to be made.

As a result of this exercise SLFHA have commissioned ECD Architects and Energy Consultants to develop a green specification to be applied to all future new build development. This performance specification is lower than the Green Wrythe Lane brief, achieving a 'very good' BREEAM rating, but retains high energy standards: NHER of 9. Green items which are most likely not to be included, as a performance specification the precise choice is up to the builder, based on value for money, are: the use of recycled materials for walls, hardcore and roofs, mechanical or stack ventilation, cooker extract hoods, and compliance with CIBSE daylight criteria. This brief was tendered as part of a volume procurement tender, in which builders were asked to tender for a programme of 1000 units over 3 years in order to achieve cost savings by bulk orders. Extra costs are estimated at between 1–2% of a typical contract sum for London.

The lessons that can be learned from SLFHA's experience are:

* green design if initiated at the start can be cost effective. Passive solar design for example, can only be incorporated, and for no extra cost, at the beginning;
* clients need to commission a green and energy efficient performance specification together with their own construction, design and maintenance requirements and will need to employ an experienced environmental consultant at the earliest point in brief development;
* whilst a green specification will cost more, economies can be achieved by thoughtful trade-offs and by introducing more effective tendering procedures;
* most elements in a green specification are achievable in terms of cost and buildability.

Care needs to be employed in the selection of builders tendering to ensure that they are familiar with the methods used. The contract needs to ensure that duties of both performance and testing are effectively passed on to sub-contractors.

Conclusion

One barrier within the industry appears to be that some materials are not yet proven in use or lack accreditation. Development and testing of new building materials is required. Suitable alternative materials particularly those using recycled components are either simply not available or in a limited range or with limited suppliers. Investigation of materials and processes suitable to comply with a green specification is time consuming and often requires the advice of environmental consultants. Difficulties are presented by the lack of information given by manufacturers on the contents or emission rates of their products with respect to VOCs, NOX, and HCFCs for example. There is also an absence of standards against which to measure them and legislation regulating permitted levels. These problems require both statutory intervention in the form of labelling requirements and permitted levels and development of new standards and testing methods.

The conclusions from SLFHA's Green Wrythe Lane project, the BREEAM experience and the CIRIA review suggest that there are a number of ways in which government policy, building practice, research and information need to be developed to promote wider application of green building principles on to a reluctant industry. Without government encouragement through fiscal incentives or statutory requirements it is up to enthusiastic developers to promote green building. Cost is another barrier; green building measures do cost more, although a very small fraction of total building costs, but may be reclaimed by future savings in fuel running costs, (particularly with the introduction of VAT on fuel). Overall savings to the community are not yet considered. The environmental value of refurbishment is actively discouraged through the imposition of VAT compared to new build. Tightening of public funding cost limits for housing associations will discourage the initiatives now being persued unless future revenue savings can be taken into consideration.

Finally, the environmental appraisal through the BREEAM scheme is voluntary. The extension of environmental impact appraisal to this category of development and its incorporation into the statutory planning system could enable local government to encourage green building practice. Standards both for energy efficiency and indoor pollution are low compared to Germany, the Netherlands, and Scandinavian countries. The author's recent study shows that energy standards could be reasonably improved at little extra cost (BRECSU/NFHA, 1992). Furthermore standardisation of energy measures could be expected to result in economies of scale. The implementation of statutory energy labelling would bridge loopholes in the present system of Building Regulations by taking into account the energy performance of the whole building including the heating system and not just elements of fabric as at present. In summary, for green building practice to make any significant impact on the housing stock a combination of measures involving financial incentives, regulation, information and advice and research aimed at providing that information is required.

Notes

(1) The Institute of Building Biology, White Horse House, Crown Hill, Ashdon, Saffron Weldon, Essex CB10 2ET.

(2) German Standard of 100mg per 100g for particleboard compared to 25mg per 100g in BS5669.

(3) Under the Town And Country Planning (Assessment of Environmental Effects) Regulations 1988 and Department of the Environment Circular 15/88 an assessment is only needed if likely to have ‘significant’ effects on the environment.

(4) BS 7750 for Environment Management Systems Standard, which accredits successful environment policy, does not deal with the requirements for environmental practice.

CHAPTER 11: Greening Housing: the Role of Self-build

Jon Broome

In Britain the self-help sector accounts for just 6 per cent of completions, the lowest proportion for any developed nation for which statistics exist. Many people involved in housing regard self-build housing as an irrelevance, with little to offer towards improving current housing conditions. Britain has a disabling framework for self-help housing and compared with other countries very few people actually build their own houses – they do so in the face of considerable obstacles arising out of the current housing system. In other parts of the world the situation is different. In 'developing countries', sheer necessity has impelled countless homeless people to provide for themselves (Ospina 1987) whilst in Germany self-help completions accounted for 60 per cent of the market during the 1980s. In the example of Sweden, 12,000 families built their own houses under the auspices of Stockholm City Council during the period from 1927 to 1976. Completions are currently running at between 200 and 250 houses per annum. The self-build organization has been and still is entirely self financing. Sometimes the infrastructure is installed as part of a larger council development alongside the self build scheme. The houses are all timber framed and arrive on the site as factory-made components. Only one self-builder in 1,000 has failed to complete their house once started and less than one in 100 has been more than two months late in completing – a much better record than the professional building industry in this country can boast. There is a waiting list of 10,000 families and in this way the City Council has enabled around 30 per cent of all the single-family houses in the city to be built by the people who live in them.

This chapter outlines an approach to housing which deals with increasingly important environmental concerns such as energy conservation, healthy buildings and sustainability. The theme of self-build housing and its relationship to the environment is developed in four parts: the first sets self-build within the context of current housing issues and outlines a community approach aimed at people in housing need. The second section concentrates on environmental aspects of self-build including energy in use and in construction; the local environment; the internal environment; healthy buildings and 'green' specification of materials. The final section discusses the opportunities for self-help housing and the contribution it can make to a green housing policy. A case study of a self-build project shows how some of these issues can be implemented in practice.

Why Self-Build?

It is the case that self-build addresses many current concerns in housing. For example self-build housing is cheap to build, offers good value for money and therefore can provide housing which is affordable. Indeed self-build houses tend to be built to higher standards of space and specification. These higher standards usually include energy conservation measures which lead to housing which is cheap to run. Furthermore, the participation of the self-builders in the process enables people to suit their needs and wishes. This leads to high levels of satisfaction and builds a community as well as houses. Because control is in the hands of self-builders this leads to good maintenance, long term improvements, and flexible extensions. Finally, and most importantly in the context of housing and the environment, the method of self-build housing described below is adaptable with a long useful life. It is designed to suit people's needs and wishes and has a low impact on the environment. In short this is an example of 'sustainable housing'.

There are other issues which are largely ignored in housing circles at present. The most significant advantage of self-build is not just to do with the houses themselves, but with the less immediately apparent beneficial effects for the people taking part. People have gained great self-confidence achieving something of lasting value, organizing together as a group, dealing with the authorities and professionals and working together on site. Also self-build developments tend to avoid the dreadful monotony of most mass housing, public or private. This aspect is likely to assume a greater importance in future years as the public becomes more discerning with higher expectations as seems likely under the increasing influence of other countries in Europe.

Britain has a very small self-help housing sector because of a number of difficulties in the operation of the housing market. Some of these could be improved if the self-help sector was encouraged in Britain.

* self-help housing activity is not as susceptible to economic cycles as other forms of housing development. This would give greater stability to the housing market as a whole;
* self-build costs are based on the cost of materials and land and not on the level of profit that the market will stand. A significant self-help sector would offer price competition for speculative housing and tend towards lower and more stable prices;
* lower, and most importantly, flexible costs reduce the need to borrow. This increases people's security and reduces repossession;

* self-builders energy and invention represents a hitherto largely untapped additional resource for housing investment;
* if self-builders were more influential in the housing market there would be a greater emphasis on use values rather than financial ones.

This chapter describes only one approach to self-build, that is, 'community' self-build housing, which forms a relatively small part of the self-help housing field. It is characterized by the self-builders carrying out the majority of the actual construction work themselves in contrast to those who only retain responsibility for the management of the building project – the building work itself being carried out by a number of subcontractors. The majority of self-builders want to obtain a bigger, better house at a reduced cost and have access to the money necessary to do so. Community self-build involves people working together as a group, and can be described as 'social' housing because it is aimed at households who would not generally be able to raise the finance necessary to buy land and the materials for a house. Finally, this approach has been employed for a number of schemes incorporating ecological design principles based on a particular form of timber frame construction and self-build organization known as the Segal method (Broome and Richardson 1991). The two essential ingredients of the idea are firstly, people having a simple building technology at their disposal which allows them to design and build their own homes without previous building experience; and secondly, the fact that the self-builders are at the centre of the whole process.

The Walter Segal Building Method

This self-build approach was devised by the architect Walter Segal in 1962 (see Broome and Richardson 1991). It is an approach to how to build rather than a system of construction and is based on combining standard building products which can be bought at any builder's merchants within a timber frame of posts and beams using simple 'dry' jointing methods such as screws and bolts. The building is organized on a dimensional grid derived from the sizes of standard components. One of the features of the Segal Method is that the documentation for building is simple and forms an integral part of the whole approach. The information is contained within a manual which deals with each step in the construction in sequence listing the materials required alongside the instructions and diagrams of how to assemble them. It contains:

* layout drawings which show the positions of the wall panels, partitions, windows and doors related to the planning grid together with elevations showing the heights of windows;
* framing drawings showing the structure together with diagrams of the structural frames themselves and details of the joints, all with dimensions;
* diagrams of typical junctions where a partition joins the external wall, where a window joins a wall and so on;

* a schedule of materials which lists all the materials that are needed, specifying type, quality, quantity ready for pricing;
* step by step instructions of how to put the elements together to build the house.

The main advantage of the Segal approach is that its simple construction method can be quickly mastered by someone without any previous building experience. Skilled wet trades such as bricklaying and plastering are eliminated. It is also an economical form of construction. This is the result of two main features: the extent of foundations is much less than for most buildings and the need to employ costly subcontractors is eliminated by the simplicity of the construction. Because the construction is relatively quick, materials are used in their stock sizes as far as possible, straight off the lorry and into the building. The construction has a low impact on the local environment and disturbance to the site is minimized. The building is raised above the ground on posts which eliminates the need to level the site and thus greatly reduces the amount of heavy groundwork that is required. The reduced extent of foundations enables buildings to be built close to trees. Finally, the buildings are very adaptable. Because the walls do not support the weight of the building it is possible to change around their position to suit changing circumstances. It is very easy to extend a Segal house. The way the building is put together is easy to understand and the dry construction makes it easy and inexpensive to upgrade the specification and to replace defective parts.

This approach to building construction has been employed to build one-off houses in Britain and Ireland over the last 30 years. Many of these have been self-built and the Segal method offers particular advantages for self-builders. The first of what could be described as a 'social' self-build scheme was initiated by the London Borough of Lewisham and completed in 1981. Fourteen households from the Council waiting or transfer lists designed and then built their own houses. The self-builders were mostly from working class backgrounds, generally established families although a few of the houses were built by young people and by people nearing retirement age. About half were previously living in council accommodation and half in privately rented flats. None could afford to buy a house and the financial arrangements were devised so that people on relatively low incomes without any capital assets could take part. Nobody knew whether ordinary people without any previous building experience, given access to land, money for materials and technical assistance could successfully build their own houses. The scheme was a success and a second similar development was completed in Lewisham in 1985. This time the group was more varied and included black people and a single mother who built her house with help from friends. Another scheme of 8 houses started being built in Lewisham by a co-operative of young black people in 1992. In mid 1993 there were more than 100 Segal self-build houses under construction on 12 sites in London, Brighton and Birmingham. The method has also been used to build a number of community buildings.

Environmental Issues and Self-build

The Segal method of construction has been developed over the last few years to incorporate 'green' thinking. In 1987 a demonstration low energy self-build house was built at the Centre for Alternative Technology at Machynlleth in Wales and the following year a similar house was built by a team of unemployed young people at the Glasgow Garden Festival as a living exhibit. Both these houses incorporated energy saving measures such as high levels of insulation and a passive solar conservatory. In 1990 a community nursery building was completed for the Calthorpe Project in Kings Cross, London that incorporated measures to reduce the use of toxic materials in the construction. The following year an educational facility for the London Wildlife Trust in Camberwell, South London took this thinking much further by addressing the issue of the amount of primary energy 'embodied' in the building construction itself, in addition to the other issues described above. Many green concerns have been incorporated into the practice of Segal self-build construction, and these are being applied in five main areas explored in the rest of this section.

Energy in Use

These self-build developments currently under construction reduce energy consumption in use in the following ways:

* **high levels of insulation.** Commonly U values are around 0.25 w/sq m °C for the walls and floor and 0.15 for the roof. This compares with a building regulation standard of 0.45 w/sq m °C for walls and floor and 0.25 for the roof;
* **well sealed double glazed windows.** Sealed double glazing units in weatherstripped frames;
* **orientation for passive solar gain.** Wherever possible windows in all main rooms face between south east and south west;
* **airtight construction.** In addition to having well sealed windows it is also important to ensure that the fabric of the building as a whole is not too leaky. Common faults are around penetrations such as a boiler flue or around a window where it is built in to the wall. Particular care has to be taken to prevent excessive air leakage through the building fabric in a dry type of construction where gaps in the construction are not plastered over as in a masonry building. Cellulose insulation which is wet sprayed into the walls is employed and it has the additional benefit of sealing the construction against air gaps;
* **efficient heating systems** using a condensing gas boilers with a responsive control system will reduce energy consumption on heating by about a further 5%;
* **a passive solar conservatory** has a number of benefits. It acts as an environmental buffer between the inside and outside. It traps the sun's heat when it is shining and reduces heat losses at other times. It provides

preheated air for ventilation. Finally, a conservatory provides relatively inexpensive extra space in a house which is comfortable without any heating for nine months of the year;

* planning to **minimize heat loss.** All entrances are planned with a lobby. This is separate from the hall arangement usual in many houses in England but similar to the separate vestibule common in Scotland. The disadvantage of the conventional entrance directly into a hall is that when the front door is opened cold air from outside is directed right into the core of the house including upstairs. Designs for self-build houses incorporating these measures have been assessed under the National Home Energy Rating Scheme [NHER] and scored up to 9.8 out of 10. The annual cost of heating such a house is estimated at just £30.

Energy in Construction

The building industry consumes about 7% of the primary energy consumed in Britain and of this it is estimated that about one third or between 2 and 3% of the total is used in domestic construction. By comparison, domestic energy consumption is about 30% of total energy consumption. In other words something of the order of 10 to 15 times as much energy is consumed heating and lighting houses as is consumed in building them in the first place. However, the greater the reduction of energy consumption in use, the greater the significance the energy used to build a house. By way of illustration, it is estimated that it takes around 100,000kWh to produce the materials in a typical 100 sq m house and 19,000kWh to put them together on the building site. (A kilowat-hour, kWh, is the energy consumed by a one bar electric fire burning for one hour and is familiar to us as one 'unit' of electricity). A low energy house might consume around 5,000kWh per annum. In other words, the energy used to build the building is as much as is required to heat it for nearly 24 hours. The energy 'embodied' in the building itself is a significant part of the total.

Although the energy content of building materials should not be the only criterion by which we make choices, it can give us a useful idea of the relative amount of pollution that may be created by their use. Some common materials are listed in Table 1 showing their energy content and an estimate of the energy content in a typical brick built house.
Timber construction replaces heavy, energy intensive materials such as bricks which are fired in a furnace at high temperature, with a renewable material which is largely made by energy from the sun. Most of the energy involved in the use of timber is in the transport because most of the timber used in the UK is imported from Canada and elsewhere. A timber framed building might be constructed of materials with an embodied energy content of around 70,000kWh and it has been estimated that it can be self-built using less energy intensive, but more labour intensive, methods on site with the expenditure of just 1,500 kWh. Furthermore, if the building is built of UK grown timber and is insulated using

Table 1. Energy Content of Common Building Materials

MATERIAL	kWh/tonne	kWh/house
facing bricks	860	25,600
clay tiles	800	4,000
concrete tiles	300	1,500
local slates	200	860
single layer plastic roof membrane	45,000	18,800
cement	2,200	15,300
plaster/plasterboard	890	5,300
steel	13,200	16,400
copper	15,000	3,390
imported softwood	1,450	4,700
local air seasoned timber	200	
glass	9,200	2,400
plastics	45,000	5,100

Source: Chapman (1975), Gartner and Smith (1976) and information supplied by Pat Borer.

cellulose fibre fill made from recycled newspaper, then the energy content of the building is reduced still further to around 57,000 kWh or around half that of a brick contractor built house.

One or two interesting points emerge from the Table 1. Comparing the energy embodied in the roofing materials listed demonstrates that natural materials have relatively low levels of energy embodied in them, natural slate is better than clay tiles and both much better than a plastic membrane from an energy point of view. Copper requires a large amount of energy to smelt it from its ores. However, the quantity of copper used in a house is relatively small and so its contribution to the total energy content of a house is still less than half that of timber for example. Copper is used for carrying electricity, a use for which there is not a suitable substitute at the present time. The whole issue has therefore to be approached with common sense.

Internal Environment

The fundamental consideration in producing buildings with a healthy internal environment rather than 'sick buildings' is to avoid the use of unhealthy materials and finishes. For example, many materials emit small quantities of toxic gases into the atmosphere. Materials that 'outgas' in this way include:

* the plastic PVC used in building for soil and waste and increasingly hot and cold water and heating pipe work, flooring and the insulation of electrical cables;
* foam plastics used for thermal insulation;
* joint fillers and mastics used for sealing around windows, kitchens and bathrooms adhesives used for flooring and other purposes;
* formaldehyde resins used to produce chipboard, plywood and MDF (Medium Density Fibreboard) amongst the many uses of which are flooring and kitchen fittings;
* paints and timber stains almost all of which contain fungicides.

The effects of timber treatments on the health of workers and householders are well documented. Timber treatments against rot and insect attack contain arsenic compounds and other powerful and poisonous insecticides and fungicides. The can cause brain damage and in some cases death. They are regularly used in buildings, however, and few workers and D-I-Y enthusiasts are aware of the hazards.

It is possible by careful design and specification to eliminate many of these potential hazards. For example, one of the conditions necessary for timber to rot is that it remains damp for a prolonged period. Timber will get wet on the outside of a building but if it is designed so that air can circulate around it enabling it to dry out again it will not rot and will not need to be treated with chemicals. One can use natural organic paints, stains and adhesives rather than the products of the chemical industry. These are the product of 'gentle' chemistry based on natural raw materials such as pine resin, linseed oil and beeswax. Also kitchen cabinets can be built of solid timber in preference to chipboard or MDF.

The problem is exacerbated by the impermeability of modern construction techniques. Modern timber frame buildings incorporate a plastic sheet which acts as a vapour barrier preventing the moisture vapour generated in a building by people breathing, cooking and bathing from entering the construction where it would cause a problem if it condensed within the wall or roof construction. This is all very well but it is as if the building is wrapped in a plastic bag which contains not only the water vapour but also the toxic substances produced by the outgassing of materials. There are also problems of local condensation and potential damage when the plastic bag is incomplete having been incorrectly installed or damaged during construction. An alternative approach is to use a permeable or 'breathing' construction similar to traditional building methods. The concept is one of vapour control layers rather than vapour barriers. Cellulose insulation made from recycled newspaper is used which can absorb moisture vapour and give it up to a ventilation space behind the wall cladding or roofing. Moisture and other waste gases can permeate through the construction at a controlled rate which prevents the build up of condensation and allows the building to 'breathe'.

Choice of Materials

The primary energy content of materials is useful as a guide to the pollution debt created by their manufacture. Other sources of pollution result from production processes; the environmental damage caused by the extraction of stone, clay, iron ore or the clear felling of forests for example. There are environmental problems associated with the disposal of materials when they are finished with; wood will biodegrade harmlessly whereas plastics will not. There are also polluting by-products of manufacturing processes as suggested in chapter 1, particularly chemical based paints. The effect on the ozone layer of materials containing CFC gases such as foam plastics and refrigerants used in air conditioning must be considered. Alternative gases are now employed to make many foam materials and ammonia based refrigeration can be used in air conditioning although this has its own problems. However a green building should be designed for natural ventilation thus avoiding the problem in the first place, which simultaneously reduces energy consumption.

Another consideration is the sustainability of sources. Tropical hardwoods have evolved to withstand a perpetually damp environment inhabited by aggressive insects and ever present fungi and for these reasons it is very durable and in demand for windows and doors. In spite of the propaganda of the timber industry, hardly any tropical hardwoods are from sustainable sources. It is estimated that around one tenth part of one per cent of tropical forests were being managed on a sustainable basis in 1985. Hardwoods from sustainable sources should be used instead, native hardwoods such as oak for instance. The selection of materials to minimize their environmental impact is a complex business made more so by the lack of available information. Materials are tested to determine their strength, density, porosity and so on. Products also have to show when they contain certain harmful substances but this information is largely meaningless to any one other than an industrial chemist. There is no labelling, however, showing environmental impact. Indeed, it is often impossible to ascertain because the composition of products is an industrial secret which manufacturers will not divulge. A great deal of investigation and research is therefore needed before we are able to take a comprehensive approach to green specification (as discussed in chapter 10). Only then will it be possible for clients and users to monitor the specification of materials and products in the buildings they commission or inhabit. Meanwhile, there are certain common sense rules of thumb that can be followed:

* use natural materials in preference to manufactured ones;
* use locally produced materials in preference to imported ones;
* consider the life cycle of the building; the potential for recycling materials and potential problems of demolition and waste disposal;
* consider the sustainability of sources as far as possible;
* consider the energy cost of products as far as you are able;

- be sceptical about suppliers' claims; most tropical hardwoods from supposedly 'sustainable sources' are not.

Although the careful choice of materials applies to all forms of building, the argument here is that self-builders will become more aware of wider environmental issues once they start considering the impact of the material they use.

Local Environment

There are four principle issues relating to the local environment and these self-build developments from the point of view of a sustainable approach to housing. The first is to minimize the impact of development on the local environment. Self-build is inherently much less disruptive to a neighbourhood during construction than a development built by a contractor. Self-builders are using small scale power tools rather than heavy equipment that creates noise and dust pollution. Self-builders may take longer and build at the weekends but the whole process is more benign. Second is the fact that, of necessity, self-build schemes tend to be relatively small in size. The largest group of households that can organize themselves effectively for planning and building is around 25 households. The developments described here are as small as 5 dwellings. Developments of this size can be integrated into the environment without the problems associated with large scale estates.

The third is to minimize the impact of the development on the site. These schemes make full use of the flexibility of the Segal method of construction to devise plans and forms that respect the context within which they are set. The Segal method minimizes the physical disruption of the site because it is not necessary to level the site as the buildings are raised above the ground on posts rather than sitting on the ground. The extent of foundations is much less, reducing the amount of excavation still further. It is also possible to build close to existing trees without fear of subsidence. The trauma of the machine ravaged site created by the typical developer's approach of bulldozing the site flat and everything on it is avoided. It is also possible to go further by considering the development as a positive opportunity for enhancing the local environment. In this way self-build schemes have been designed with grass roofs planted with wild flowers to provide new wildlife habitats. Finally, the long term future of housing will be assured if the control and management of the immediate surroundings is vested in the inhabitants.

The Environmental Opportunities of Self-build

There are two principle factors limiting self-help housing in Britain: difficulty of access to resources such as land and finance; and the professionals' mistrust of ordinary people. As Richard Norton-Taylor (1982) observes just over three per cent of the adult population owns over seventy percent of the land:

"The concentration of land ownership in Britain, encouraged by the enclosures and the Industrial Revolution, is unique in Europe." (p.23).

A free market in a finite resource makes it expensive; self-builders find themselves unable to compete in the market because of price and lack of knowledge of the market. Also the use of land is tightly controlled by planning legislation. Indeed Duncan and Rowe (1992) suggest that:

"Arguably, in countries with a tradition of autonomous self-development... the planning system will more easily accommodate self-help housing. In those with a tradition of closed decision making and authoritarian social structure (as in Britain) self-help will be excluded. This seems to be confirmed by the history of self-help in the British case". (p.19).

Hardy and Ward (1984) also show that recurrent surges of popular interest in self-help housing have been constrained by planners, speculative builders and local authorities. Individual self-developers also have difficulty borrowing money because they are regarded as a high risk by financiers. On the contrary, self-builders have a very personal stake in completing a development successfully. The greatest benefit will derive from self-build if self-builders assume a high level of responsibility. Only they can sensibly take control of the detailed day-to-day decision making and management of a project. Larger organizations one step removed from the process cannot deal effectively with the individual decision making involved. The self-builders will lose the benefits of choice if they do not take over this role. Many professionals and officials, however, are often unwilling to let go (as Stevenson argues in chapter 9). The underlying difficulty is one of mistrust of ordinary people by the elite of landowners and financiers together with politicians, planners and other officials. Again in the words of Duncan and Rowe:

"It is almost as if making it easy for people to provide their own homes would upset the social apple-cart." (1992 p.19).

A growing proportion of the population now express concern for the environment; individuals who are interested in building for themselves tend to be inclined towards doing something about it. Self-builders may well not initially be aware of the issues of the energy content of building, the environmental impact of materials, microclimate and healthy building; but experience has shown that many are very willing to embrace green ideas once these have been put forward. Indeed many green measures necessary do not cost anything, they are more to do with careful specification at the start of the project. Self-builders are often willing to make the relatively small investment in energy conservation, and savings achieved express themselves as higher standards. Having become involved with the process of self-build households may well become familiar with the idea of energy conservation and environmental improvement. Indeed some measures such as specifying untreated, naturally resistant, softwood instead of either treated softwood or tropical hardwood, actually cost less.

Information is very important, and indeed data is not even available to specialists in the area, still less to the general public. Much of the basic information on the pollution produced during the manufacture of products, for example, is not yet available and more research is needed. The availability of materials is crucial for progress in this area. In places such as Germany where ecological building is further developed, products are available on the market which can be substituted for potentially harmful products. Some of these are imported to Britain but they are not easily available and they are often expensive. Nevertheless, self-builders will often opt for ecologically sound products once the implications are explained. Environmental education and information is what is needed. Self-builders are generally keen to act with care towards the environment once they are made aware during the process of building their homes. Most of all this approach needs to be incorporated into the development of a green housing policy.

Case Study: Diggers Self-build Project

I am going to outline this project as an example of the self-build schemes under construction at the time of writing. It is singular in its inception, membership and design; all these schemes have a unique set of circumstances and designs and this diversity is one of the characteristics of this type of development. This project does, however, demonstrate some of the basic features which are shared with other projects. The scheme was the brainchild of a small group of young people many of whom live in a housing co-operative in Brighton. It has been developed under the name of Diggers and consists of nine houses. The Diggers co-operative includes teachers, practising and not, an artist, someone working in computers and several more or less unemployed people, one or two of whom work occasionally as jobbing builders. About half the households have children, some of them are single parents. Many of the group have a more or less 'alternative' outlook on life. As I suggest above, this group should not be taken as in any way 'typical', they are simply one group amongst many with a particular mix of people in it.

They had become aware of the idea of Segal method self-build and, as is often the way, it took two or three years for this idea to gel into a determination to pursue the notion of building their own houses. During this time they were in touch with the much larger Sea Saw Self-Build group in Brighton and were aware of the problems being faced by the Sea Saw group securing funding in the period before the Housing Corporation made Housing Association Grants (HAG) available for self-build. However, one member of the core group was on the management committee of CHISEL (a secondary housing co-operative) who were responsible for their existing co-operative. Jose Ospina of CHISEL developed the co-operative funding model for self-build and the Diggers decided to adopt this approach. As a group they were familiar with the idea of a co-

Diggers Self-build project

operative and were sympathetic to the ideals of a co-operative approach to life.

Fortunately the Diggers were able to persuade Brighton Council to offer them an option on a site. Brighton Council supported a number of self-build schemes during the 1960s and more recently the elected members and officers were familiar with the concept of Segal method self-build having supported the Sea Saw scheme and a self-build project for single homeless young people. The Council offered a site adjacent to this scheme which was half built at the time. This site is a steeply sloping pocket of land occupied by temporary timber buildings which housed the local Steiner school, who had to relocate, and the part of the site occupied by their buildings formed a plateau backed to the north and east by a steep bank. The site is surrounded by large trees and enjoys good views over the valley towards the south and west. Five two and three bedroom detached family houses are now sited on this bank. They look out over the roofs of four one bedroom semi-detached bungalows.

The houses are of a split level design which make the most of the sloping bank. All the dwellings have a conservatory and a verandah to the south to take advantage of the sun and the view. The passive solar conservatories

Diggers Self-build

contribute to the energy efficiency of the dwellings. Other energy efficiency measures include a high level of insulation, high performance double glazed windows with good solar orientation, condensing gas boilers controlled by a boiler energy manager and thermostatic radiator valves. The houses also incorporate ecological design thinking. Recycled newspaper was used for insulation in the roof, walls and floor. Natural organic paints and stains are being used throughout and the roofs are covered in turf with wild flowers planted in it. The turf roofs were a positive feature as far as the planners were concerned. Their attitude has been fully vindicated as the effect of the houses nestling into the hill side with their grass roofs and verandas has proved very harmonious. The construction and materials are covered by the insurance scheme operated by the Housing Association Property Mutual (HAPM).

The self-builders were fully involved in the development of the design. One unusual decision they took was to make all the open space around the buildings communal. The effect of the houses grouped around a common green in the centre works well and lends a very spacious feeling to the scheme. A small office for the co-op is planned in this space and additional funding is being raised for this purpose. The self-builders were also very keen in the environmental aspects of the design.

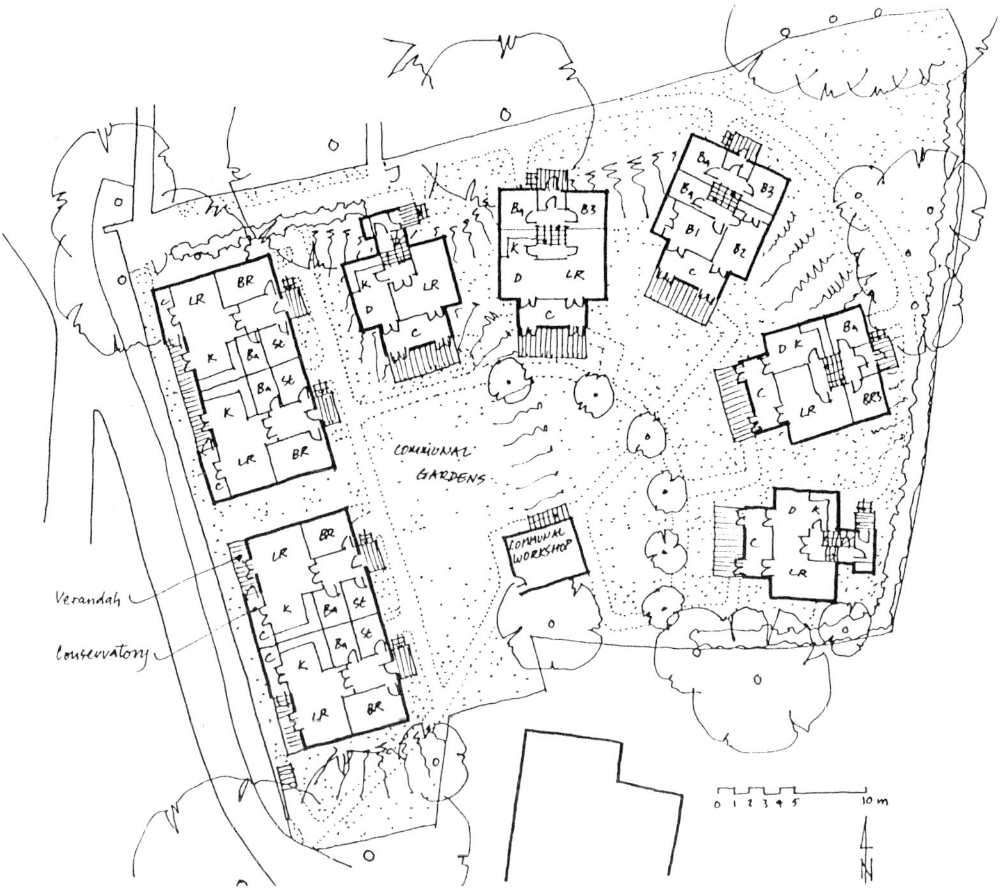

Diggers Site Plan

A number of training sessions were organized by the architects, Architype, a London based practice with particular experience in self-build, timber construction and ecological design. These included three full days before work started on site dealing with topics which included planning a building project on site, health & safety, ordering materials and understanding the drawings and schedules. These issues are the key to a successful building project. These pre-contract sessions also helped motivate the group prior to being able to start on the physical work. An experienced contract manager was appointed with a background in training, building and self-building. He was responsible for organizing the group and their work on site including demonstrating the operations in the building process. He also dealt with ordering materials and programming the work. Further full day training sessions were held on site. The building project was also being used as a training resource for building trainees who were able to gain site experience working on the job whilst helping the self-builders with their efforts.

Diggers section plan

Diggers construction process

The scheme started on site in May 1992, was given a shove by the then Housing Minister, Sir George Young helping to raise a frame in October 1992. The construction period of 22 months was longer than anticipated and was a reflection in part of the level of complication introduced into the project by the split level design of the houses and the extent of conservatory, verandah and balcony construction. The turf roofs have been featured in the media in Britain and also in the US, Japan and Australia.

The project was funded under the cash programme of South London Family Housing Association using the CHISEL model for self-build co-ops for rent. The works cost and rents are summarized below. Rent levels were two thirds of the National Federation of Housing Associations' indicator rent levels for 1993. In addition, the self-builders are granted a 'premium tenancy' which entitles them to a cash payment in recognition of their unpaid self-help labour if and when they decide to leave the scheme. In this particular project the cash payment will be around £4,000. The project demonstrates what can be achieved when people are given the opportunity to house themselves. With careful education, training and information, environmental features can become integral to the development process. Projects of this type may be small and limited, but they can show a way forward for sustainable housing.

Table 2 Diggers Self-build: Facts and Figures 1993

Number of units	Type of unit	Area sq m	Materials cost	Rent £/week
4	3 bedroom house	82	£29,000	£36.53
1	2 bedroom house	68	£25,000	£30.86
4	1 bedroom bungalow	48	£18,000	£27.17
	TOTAL material cost		£213,000	
	Groundworks subcontract		£50,000	
	Site manager		£18,000	
	TOTAL works cost		£281,000	

Conclusion

For housing to be sustainable it has to meet the wants and needs of the people who live in it, and be capable of adapting to those needs as they change; housing of the kind described above is one way of achieving this. Self-builders are in control of a method of construction which is inherently adaptable and environment friendly so that one way of building sustainably is to give control to people themselves. With the necessary information, resources, and encouragement they will build green. People would create small groups of charming, timber framed houses designed by the occupants to suit their needs and wishes; adaptable to changing needs and with a long useful life, with low environmental impact, and little energy required to construct and occupy. There could be a growing demand for housing of this kind if an imaginative and environmentally sensitive way forward is found out of the current impasse in social housing. Even so, it is also the case that not everyone thinking about building their home is concerned about the environment. However experience has shown that most self-builders will take it seriously given the education and information. Clearly not everyone can or wants to build for themselves, but the *opportunity* to do so should become a central part of green housing policy.

CHAPTER 12: A Green Future for Housing?

Mark Bhatti, Jane Brooke, and Mike Gibson

The environmental impact of housing activities is, as the scope of the contributions show, a large area to cover and much needs to be done. The chapters in this book demonstrate the importance of considering environmental issues in the policy and practice of housing. The range of the subject, from daily home life to the future planning of settlements, may suggest that the complexity of the problem makes it difficult to comprehend and solve. However we believe that this makes housing an important area for action, and a particularly interesting subject to study. We are now on the threshold of changes in housing policy and practice which puts housing provision centre stage in achieving immediate environmental objectives, particularly reductions in CO_2 emissions. However there are a number of tensions, barriers and opportunities that have been identified throughout the book; these are brought together in this chapter.

There is a tension throughout the book as to the value of a 'bottom up' or a 'top down' approach. Some of the contributions favour a 'low tech' approach, with small scale housing production, high labour input and decision making at the local level. Projects of this type can link together various areas of environmental concern, and promote technologies that are easily applied and understood by users. The ecological value of collective working arising out of a strong community movement can clearly be seen in many housing projects, and this is a crucial base for greener housing practices. As we have seen much of green thinking and innovative environmental housing practice have emerged in single organisations at the local level and clearly this needs to be encouraged. However even though the 'demonstration effect' of these projects cannot be denied, for they highlight a successful methodology for minimising environmental impact; this approach is marginalised in the housing system. The overall influence of the 'local' can be quite small and the new ideas may not penetrate the housing process in general. The 'top down' approach suggests that driving forward on environmentally sensitive housing policies and practices requires a clear direction from Central Government. For example, the structural conditions of housing production identified by Yvonne Rydin in chapter 8, may only be tackled through stringent standards and close regulation of the industry. Or, as Brenda Boardman points out in chapter 7, an equitable energy policy that ensures affordable warmth for the poor may only be formulated and implemented from the centre. In many areas of environmental policy central direction can be a key to unlocking resistance to change. However, the lack of any coherent national housing policy in recent years has major implications for driving forward on green housing policy. The local advances that have been made may not be sustained into the future and the national framework for an environmentally sensitive housing policy and practice has yet to be established. Indeed it is at the local and international levels that most activity is evident; environmental policy has yet to be taken seriously by Central Government, as the fall of the Energy Conservation Bill clearly demonstrates.

Given that both 'top down' and 'bottom up' approaches appear to be necessary, the question we are left with is: where and how do they meet? In the process of developing environmental policy for housing, the key consideration must be to find ways of combining central direction with local control. For example, the current development in energy efficiency measures highlight the choices to be made. If we are indeed on the threshold of major energy efficiency investment then a range of opportunities is opened up. On the one hand, Central Government initiatives like the Energy Savings Trust provide opportunities for meaningful action across the whole country. However, the way in which this is put into practice is crucial. It could be handed over to private sector companies using public subsidies to install energy saving products by applying the quickest and most efficient means at their disposal aimed at increasing profit. But on the other hand, this initiative could seek to operate through local community organisations. The 'top down' method is clearly inadequate if energy saving is to be understood as long term action linked to wider environmental objectives, and the benefits are to flow into the local community. The combination of central direction and local energy programmes could yield multiple environmental returns from public sector investment, particularly if it is linked to a well thought through and large scale environmental education programme delivered through the local agencies. There is ample evidence on how the use of local labour and training in energy conservation programmes can benefit run down neighbourhoods (see also Davidson 1988, NEA 1991). The lack of this kind of enabling framework in Britain means that it is very difficult for green housing projects controlled by the community to get off the ground. In this context funding agencies, governments, and housing managers must create the right conditions for people to make environmentally informed decisions in and around their homes, and in their daily lives.

Environmentally sensitive housing policy must be developed with considerable involvement from the users of housing. We are arguing here for 'empowerment' and participation so that communities are able to make decisions about the quality of the local environment they need and want, and decide how they are to achieve it. In part this involves rethinking the relationship between professionals and users. For example, a green approach to architectural practice, as Fionn

Stevenson points out in chapter 9, raises the question of who 'owns' the knowledge and technical skills, and who benefits. It also involves dissolving the barriers between the professions themselves; working as teams incorporating housing managers, architects, and funders on specific problems. Moreover as the community self-build approach, outlined by Jon Broome in chapter 11, shows it is possible to bring users fully into the housing process.

Resources are a major constraint on any strategic approach to environmental problems. It may appear that increasing resources are being allocated to environmental improvements, particularly energy efficiency measures, but this must be seen in the context of continuing cuts in capital investment for housing. Thus even though more money will flow through to energy efficiency measures it is likely to be at the cost of reduced funds for refurbishment and massive cut backs in internal improvements. The conflicts of policy in this area are shown by the imposition of VAT on fuel being followed by cuts of £600 million capital expenditure in November 1993. Central Government must free up resources and allow housing organisations to invest in alternative methods of working such as self-build, advance 'low' technologies, experiment with green design, and enhance capital programmes in order to increase the quality of local environments.

Another barrier is that housing is often seen in isolation; environmental problems do not occur in isolation, nor can they be tackled in a partial and fragmented manner. For example, environmentally conscious planning of housing can bring real improvements. Reinvestment in brown field rehabilitation, as demonstrated by Glasgow City Council, linked to employment and local facilities can radically change deteriorating environments. This requires, we believe, a 'holistic approach to policy making'. In short, the development of an integrating framework that covers a number of policy areas, allows input from users, and can be co-ordinated from the centre. Against this, the restructuring of the state intervention in housing over the 1980s has meant a reduction in the powers of local government over major environmental decisions. It is a paradox that state withdrawal from direct provision has come at a time when environmental deterioration requires more, not less, state action. It is difficult to see how de-regulation in the housing sector can be married with reducing environmental impact or increasing environmental protection. The solution that has been sought by Central Government is one of quangos and market based mechanisms such as the Energy Savings Trust, eco-labelling, energy ratings, and of course VAT on fuel. But this not only raises issues of accountability, it increases social polarisation (as Brenda Boardman points out in chapter 7), and pushes environmental responsibility on to individuals who must now pay for environmental improvements. The solution is to prevent negative environmental impacts arising in the housing system in the first place. In part this means strong regulation, as witnessed in countries like Holland, Denmark, and Germany, and a stronger role for local government in improving the local environment through housing based policies and practices.

Even though there are many structural constraints there are also some opportunities that may help in the development of green housing policy and practice. These involve the infiltration of 'green' technology into management practice, the evolution of an environmental culture, and growth of housing education. Over the last 15-20 years technological innovation in energy conservation, pollution abatement, and green design have made many new housing practices possible. For example, energy rating systems are now affordable and easy to use and are likely to spread quite quickly throughout the management of housing. There are also environmental management systems emerging such as European Union's Eco-Audit schemes, and BS 7750, (though they still require considerable development) which will assist in establishing both an operational and strategic approach to environmental improvements. The infrastructure for the use of environmental technology is slowly being created which can and should permeate everyday housing management practice. And some of it is now becoming user friendly, for example, do it yourself energy ratings.

These are the necessary conditions for the shift towards implementation of green housing policy and practice. However they are not sufficient. Even though an operational and strategic approach which links housing and environmental policy is now practicable, the main question is why it is not being taken up with any force inside the housing movement? The answers to this question are not clear, but preliminary survey results (Bhatti 1994a, Rydin 1992a) show that there is a low level of awareness of linkages between housing practice and environmental problems amongst housing policy makers and practitioners. Even though some individuals may have a strong grasp of the issues, there is little evidence of an environmental culture developing within the housing field. In many ways housing is falling behind other areas such as education. As Mark Bhatti argues in chapter 2, the development of an environmental culture in society presents an opportunity for housing to play an important part in tackling major environmental problems. Many of the solutions being proposed are centred in and around the home. For example, as tenant and owner occupiers realise the need for energy conservation measures, they also become receptive to green ideas. Indeed we believe that housing is right up front in the process of environmental change. The home is the starting point of environmental action.

Finally, housing education and training has expanded in recent years with a range of courses designed for people with varying experiences, abilities and aims. These present an opportunity for the 'greening' of education and training, whereby environmental issues become a significant part of housing courses. As the chapters show, a considerable amount of green thinking, policy making and actual practice is already happening. Hopefully the book has cleared some ground in relating housing problems and environmental issues. We have pointed to areas that need developing if housing is to respond effectively to the environmental challenge. The chapters offer a critique of current theory, policy and practice and suggest ways forward. Not all of these ideas can or will be implemented, but they show the growing importance of thinking imaginatively about housing and the environment. More importantly all the contributions help to progress debate in what has been up to now a neglected area.

Conclusion

What is clearly emerging is the need for a green housing policy that will pull together various strands and issues into a coherent framework. Most importantly we have stressed future housing debate on the environment must address issues of 'poverty' and 'inequality'. Questions of social inequality lie at the heart of a green housing policy; without equity there is likely to be a major flaw as the poor are forced to use whatever is necessary to get by, usually engaging in environmentally damaging practices. We believe that central and local Government must ensure a minimum standard of environmental quality, with everyone guaranteed equal rights to access good quality environmental services. Housing consumers must be free from damp, condensation and pollution; have affordable warmth with access to clean air and water as well as open spaces. A green housing policy involves 'living within the limits' imposed by the earth's resources and capacities to provide. It will not be easy to challenge commonly accepted ideas in housing, but we want to reappraise the conventional argument that thousands of dwellings should be built every year to meet demand or housing need. The focus must shift towards rehabilitation of existing buildings and the recycling of building materials. We are *not* saying that no new housing should be built, but rather that new development must be sensitive towards the environment, developed with maximum user participation, and linked to local employment and transport policy. Clearly some new units must be produced, but only after careful consideration, and they should be produced in a different way. The development at Greenwrythe Lane (chapter 10) shows the potential of minimising environmental impacts if green principles are designed in at the beginning of the process of commissioning and design.

In the long term the demand for new housing is determined by uneven economic development, the problems of which are central to achieving sustainable urban development. As we have argued expansion is built into the system leading to major environmental impacts, but a green housing policy must point us towards making much better use of what we have now and establish policies to this end. A green housing policy sets up tensions and conflicts that must be imaginatively overcome with new modes of assessment. For example, an environmental accounting system which takes account of embodied energy, or CO_2 emissions of housing construction and materials, changes the way we think about the perceived high initial costs of green development, the profits of the construction industry, affordability, and costs in use. We need to find ways of balancing the opportunities of new build where non-toxic materials, renewable resources and energy efficiency can be integrated from the start; with the limits and high cost of rehabilitation. We find these tensions healthy and useful because they highlight the critical debate that is needed at this time. A green housing policy must also capture the breadth and depth of environmental problems we face today. Thus policies and practices need to make connections between the impacts of daily life for the planet on the one hand, and on the other, emphasise the effect of global change on the household. This again means rethinking some of the reasons why certain measures are put into place. For example, energy efficiency measures can be justified on the grounds of cost alone. However, the environmental reasons, for example the reduction in CO_2 emissions, need to be given equal prominence. We may promote measures in such a way that it benefits households financially, but the overall message about global environmental change must not be lost.

Finally, further research is required if we are to fully understand and explain the links between housing and the environment. In part a green housing policy can only be developed once we ask environmentally informed questions and start exploring some of the answers. Policy makers often want quick and ready answers; there is a danger that housing researchers will respond to this. But without studying the underlying issues and problems that have been highlighted, instant solutions may cause untold environmental damage in the future. This means that a greener housing study has to be freed from the constraints of short term policy development. Housing academics must examine the long term and underlying links between housing and the environment. This book demonstrates the need for new areas of policy analysis and practice development which can lay the foundation for a green housing policy.

REFERENCES

Agyeman, J. and Bhatti, M. (1994) 'House, Home, and Garden: Towards an Environmental Culture'. Paper presented to the 'Ideal Homes' conference September 1994 University of Teeside.

Agyeman, J. and Evans, B. eds. (1994) 'Local Environmental Policies and Strategies'. London: Longman.

Ahrentzen, S. and Frank, K. (1989) 'New Households, New Houses. New York': Van Nostrand Reinhold.

Ahrentzen, S. and Anthony, K. (1993) 'Sex, Stars and Studios: A Look at Gendered Educational Practices in Architecture', in Journal of Architectural Education Vol 47 No. 1 11-29.

Alexander, C. (1976) 'A Timeless Way of Building'. New York: Oxford University Press Ltd.

Alexander, C. (1977) 'A Pattern Language'. New York: Oxford University Press Ltd.

Anderson, B. R. (1989) 'BREDEM: the BRE Domestic Energy Model'. BRE Report BR66, Watford: BRE.

Anderson, V. (1993) Energy Efficiency Policies London: Routledge.

Association of County Councils et al (1992) 'Environmental Practice in Local Government'. Luton, LGMB.

Association of Metropolitan Authorities (1987) 'Local Housing Strategies'. London: AMA.

Association of Metropolitan Authorities (1991) 'Housing, Energy and the Environment: A Strategy for Action'. London: AMA.

AMA (1993) 'The AMA and the Environment: position statement'. London: AMA.

Audit Commission (1991) 'Healthy Housing'. London: HMSO.

Audit Commission (1992) 'Developing Local Authority Housing Strategies'. London: HMSO.

Ball, M. (1983) 'Housing Policy and Economic Power'. London: Methuen.

Ball, M. (1986) 'Housing Analysis: Time for a Theoretical Refocus?' in Housing Studies. Vol. 1 No. 3: 147-165.

Ball, M. and Harloe, M. (1992) 'Rhetorical Barriers to Understanding Housing Provision: What the "Provision Thesis" is and is not'. in Housing Studies. Vol 7 No. 1: 3-15.

Ballie, K. (1994) 'The Pub and Local Co-op which take "Barter" Money'. in New Economics No. 29.

Barker, T. and Johnstone, N. (1993) 'Equity and efficiency in policies to reduce carbon emissions in the domestic sector'. Energy & the Environment, Multi-Science, Brentwood, Essex.

Basset, K. and Short, J. (1980) 'Housing and Residential Structure: Alternative Approaches'. London: Routledge and Kegan Paul.

Beck, U. (1992) 'The Risk Society'. London: Sage.

Beckett, P. (1993) 'Green Shoots at the Grassroots'. in Housing January: 27.

Beer, A. (1990) 'Environmental Planning for Site Development'. London: E. & F.N. Spon.

Bhatti, M. (1993) 'From Consumers to Prosumers: Housing for a Sustainable Future'. in Housing Studies Vol 8, No. 2: 98-108.

Bhatti, M. (1994a) 'Environmental Issues in Social Housing'. School of Land Management and Urban Policy Mimeo London: South Bank University.

Bhatti, M. (1994b) Lagging behind on Energy Conservation in Housing (May) pp.10-11.

Birmingham City Council (1993) 'The Green Action Plan – Strategy for the Environment and Corporate Action'. Programme 1993/94.

Blowers, A. (ed.) (1993a) 'Planning for a Sustainable Environment'. London: Earthscan.

Blowers, A. (1993b) 'The Time for Change', ch 1. in Blowers A. (ed.) 'Planning for a Sustainable Environment' London: Earthscan.

Blowers, A. (1993c) 'Environmental Policy: the Quest for Sustainable Development', Urban Studies, Vol 30, Nos. 4/5, pp.775-796.

Blundell-Jones, P. (1989) 'Woodland Retreat: David Lea's Cottage'. in Architects Journal 27 September.

Boardman, B. (1990) 'Fuel Poverty and the Greenhouse Effect', Friends of the Earth, Heatwise Glasgow, Neighbourhood Energy Action, National Right to Fuel Campaign.

Boardman, B. (1991) 'Fuel poverty: from cold homes to affordable warmth'. Belhaven Press.

Boardman, B. (1993) 'Energy Efficiency Incentives and UK Households'. Energy & Environment, Vol 4, No. 4, pp.316-334.

Boardman, B. and Houghton, T. (1991) 'Poverty and Power: the Efficient Use of Electricity in Low-income Households', Bristol Energy Centre, Bristol.

Boris, C. (1993) 'Construction and Planning Projects under a Framework of the EC Procurement Directives in JEPL'. pp.816-823.

Boyle, S. (1990) 'Getting out of the Greenhouse'. London: Association for the Conservation of Energy/Worldwide Fund for Nature UK.

BRECSU/NFHA, (1992) 'Affordable New Low Energy Housing For Housing Associations, Future Practice R&D 2'. Watford: BRE.

BRECSU (1993) 'Energy Efficiency in New Housing: Low Energy Design for Housing Associations, Best Practice programme, Good Practice Guide 79'. Watford: BRE.

Breheny, M. (ed.) (1992a) 'Sustainable Development and Urban Form'. London: Pion.

Breheny, M.J. (1992b) 'The contradictions of the compact city', in Breheny (ed.) Sustainable Development & Urban Form. London: Pion.

Breheny, M. and Rookwood, R. (1993) Planning the sustainable city region, in Blowers (ed.) 'Planning for a Sustainable Environment'. London: Earthscan.

Brennan, J. (1990) 'Energy savings = cash savings – Ways to conserve power and help the environment'. The Financial Times 6 October: vi.

Brooke, R. (1989) 'Managing the Enabling Authority'. Harlow: Longman.

Broome, J. and Richardson, B. (1991) 'The Self Build Book'. Totnes: Green Books.

Bryant, R. (1979) 'The Dampness Monster: A report to the Gorbals anti-dampness campaign'. Endinburg: Social Council of Social Services.

Burridge, R. and Ormandy, D. (1993) 'Unhealthy housing: research, remedies and reform'. London: Ed F N Spon.

Byrne, D. et al (1986) 'Health and Housing: the relationship between housing conditions and the health of council tenants'. London: Gower.

Cairncross, F. (1991) 'Costing the Earth'. London: Business Books.

Carter, N., Brown, T. & Abbott, T. (1993) 'The Relationship between Expenditure-Based Plans and Development Plans'. in Progress in Planning Vol 39 No. 1: 1-69.

Central Statistical Office (1992) 'Family Spending: a report on the 1991 Family Expenditure Survey'. Central Statistical Office, HMSO.

Chambert, H. (1992) 'A conceptual model for comparative analysis of housing systems'. paper for the Urban Networks International Research Conference, The Hague.

Chapman, P. (1975) 'Fuels Paradise'. London: Penguin.

Chartered Institute of Housing (1991) 'Housing: A Radical Consensus'. Coventry: CIOH.

Christensen, K. (1989) Home Ecology. London: Arlington Books.

Clapham, D., Kemp, P. and Smith, S.J. (1990) 'Housing and Social Policy': London: MacMillan.

Clapham, D. and Kintrea, K. (1993) 'Housing Co-operatives in Britain'. Harlow: Longmans.

Coleman, A. (1985) 'Utopia on Trial: Vision and Reality in Planned Housing'. London: Hilary Shipman.

Commission of the European Community Directorate General for Science, Research and Development (1992) 'Guidelines for Ventilation Requirements in Buildings, Report No. 11, Indoor Air Quality and Its impact on Man'. EUR 14449 EN, Luxembourg: CEC.

Connaughton, J. (1993) 'Real low energy buildings: the energy costs of materials'. In Roaf S. (ed.) Energy efficiency in Buildings. Oxford: Oxford University Press.

Construction Industry Research and Information Association (1992) 'Environmental Issues in Construction: a review of issues and initiatives relevant to the construction and related industries'. Paper prepared for the Construction Industry Environment Forum.

Construction Industry Research & Information Environmental Forum (1993) 'Environmental Issues in Construction'. in CIRIA July 1993 Vol. 1.

Corporation News (1991) 'Benson Presses for Closer Co-operation'. No. 8.1 London: Housing Corporation.

Council of Europe (1993) 'Privatisation in Local Government'. EC: Brussels.

Coventry City Council (1992) 'Draft Environmental Strategy'. Dean, R. (1992) 'Independent Funding for Tenants'. Coventry: Institute of Housing.

Cox, A. (1993) 'Public Procurement in the European Community: Is a fully integrated market achieveable?' in Public Money and Management. July-September pp.29-35.

Darke, J. and Darke, R. (1979) 'Who Needs Housing?' London: The Macmillan.

Davidson, J. (1988) 'How Green is Your City?' London: Bedford Square Press.

Day, C. (1990a) 'Building with the Heart'. Bideford: Green Books.

Day, C. (1990b) 'Places of the Soul'. Wellingborough: Aquarian Press.

Day, C. (1993) 'Ensouling Buildings'. in Architectural Design Vol 63 No. 11/12.

Department of Energy (1990) 'Energy Use and Energy Efficiency in the UK Domestic Sector up to the Year 2010'. London: HMSO.

Department of the Environment (1990) 'This Common Inheritance'. London: HMSO.

Department of the Environment (1991a) 'Energy Conservation in the Home'. London: HMSO.

Department of the Environment (1991b) 'English house condition survey 1986: supplementary (energy) report'. Department of the Environment, HMSO.

Department of the Environment (1992a) 'The Development of the Local Authority Housing Investment Programme Process – A Consultation Paper'. London: HMSO.

Department of the Environment (1992b) 'State of the UK Environment'. London: HMSO.

Department of the Environment (1993a) 'The Development of the Local Authority Housing Investment Programme Process – Note on Ministers' Conclusions on the 1992 Consultation Exercise'. London: HMSO.

Department of the Environment (1993b) 'Draft Planning Policy Guidance Note No. 13'. London: HMSO.

Department of the Environment (1993c) 'Environmental management and Audit Scheme for Local Government'. London: HMSO.

Department of the Environment (1993d) 'Green House Programme Annual Report'. London: HMSO.

Department of the Environment (1993e) 'Energy Efficiency in Council Housing: Interim Guidance for Local Authorities'. London: HMSO.

Department of the Environment (1993f) 'English House Condition Survey 1991', London: HMSO.

Department of the Environment (1994a) Sustainable Development: the UK Strategy Development'. London: HMSO.

Department of the Environment (1994b) 'Planning Policy Guidance Note 13 – Transport'. London HMSO.

Department of the Environment (1994c) 'Climate Change: The UK Programme' London: HMSO.

Department of the Environment (1994d) 'Energy Efficiency in Council Housing: Guidance for Local Authorities'. London: DoE.

Department of the Environment (1994e) Annual Report: The Government's Expenditure Plans 1994-95 – 1996-97. London: HMSO.

Department of the Environment/LGMB (1992) 'The Ecoaudit Regulation in Local Government: Draft Guide 5 Housing Services'. Luton: LGMB.

Dickens, P. (1992) 'Society and Nature: Towards a Green Social Theory'. London: Harvester.

Dickens, P. (1993) 'Architecture as Commodity Fetishism: Some Cautionary Notes on Green Design'. in Housing Studies Vol 8 No. 2: 148-152.

Dobson, A. (1990) 'Green Political Thought'. London: Unwin Hyman.

Dobson, R. (1993) 'Bringing the Economy Home from the Market'. Montreal: Black Rose Books.

Doyal, L. and Gough, I. (1991) 'A Theory of Human Need'. London: MacMillan.

Drake, M. (1992) 'Europe and 1992: A Handbook for Local Housing Authorities'. Coventry: Institute of Housing.

Duke of Edinburgh's Inquiry into British Housing – Main Report (1985) London: NFHA.

Dukes (1993) 'Digest of UK Energy Statistics'. HMSO.

Duncan, S. (1989) 'Development Gains and Housing Provision in Britain and Sweden'. Transactions of the Institute of British Geographers 14: 157-172.

Duncan, S. & Rowe, A. (1992) 'Self-help Housing: the first world's hidden housing arm'. Urban and Regional Studies Working Paper, Brighton: University of Sussex.

Dunmore, K. (1992) 'Planning for Affordable Housing'. Coventry: Institute of Housing.

Ecotech Research & Consulting Ltd/Transportation Planning Associates (1993) 'Reducing Transport Emissions Through Planning'. London: HMSO.

Edwards, B. (1991) 'Dilemmas of a Green Architect'. in Housing Today.

Elkin, T., MacLaren, D. and Hillman, M. (1991) 'Reviving the City Towards sustainable urban Development'. London: Friends of the Earth with the Policy Studies Institute.

Elkington, J. and Hailes, J. (1988) 'The Green Consumer Guide'. London: Victor Gollancz.

Engwicht, D. (1992) 'Towards an Eco-City: Calming the Traffic'. Sydney, Australia: Envirobook.

Environ Advisory Services (1993) 'Affordable Options for Green Housing'. Leicester: Environ.

Energy Savings Trust (1993) 'EST domestic energy efficiency schemes – Homes 2000 and Social Housing'. Consultation discussion paper, mimeo November 1993.

European Commission (1990a) 'Europe 2000'. Brussels: EC.

European Commission (1990b) 'Green Paper on the Urban Environment'. Brussels: EC.

European Commission (1992a) 'Towards Sustainability'. Brussels: EC.

European Commission (1992b) Green Paper on Sustainable mobility. Brussels: EC.

European Commission (1992c) 'Urbanisation and the Functions of Cities in the European Community'. Brussels: EC.

European Commission (1993a) 'Proposals for a Council Decision Concerning the Conclusion of the Framework Convention on Climate Change'. O J C44 16 Feb. pp.1-21 Brussels: EC.

European Commission (1993b) 'Opinion for Proposal on Council Directive to Limit Carbon Dioxide Emissions'. O J C19 25 Jan. pp.34-7.

European Commission (1993c) 'Growth, Competitiveness and Employment'. Brussels: EC.

Fitzpatrick, I. (1993) 'A Census Analysis of the Effects of the Community and Area Renewal Programmes of Glasgow City Housing Department'. Department of Management Science, Strathclyde University.

Fraser, R. (1991) 'Working Together in the 1990s'. Coventry: Institute of Housing.

Friends of the Earth (1989) 'Environmental Charter for Local Government'. London FoE.

Gartner and Smith (1976) 'Energy Costs of House Construction'. Watford: Building Research Establishment.

Gibson, M. (1986) 'Housing renewal; privatisation and beyond', chapter 4 in Malpass, P. (ed.) The Housing Crisis, London: Croom Helm.

Gibson, M. and Groves, R. (1990) 'Neighbourhood Revitalisation: Into the 1990s'. London: National Home Improvement Council.

Gillis, W. (1994) 'Domestic Energy and Affordable Warmth'. Paper 2 in Watt Committee Report, Chapman & Hall.

Giradet, H. (1992) 'The Gaia Atlas of Cities – New directions for Sustainable Urban Living'. London: Gaia Books.

Glasgow City Council: (1982) 'Making the City Work'.

Glasgow City Council (1984) 'Glasgow's Special Housing Initiatives'. Research Memorandum No. 3.

Glasgow City Council (1986) 'Inquiry into Housing in Glasgow'. The Grieve Report.

Glasgow City Council (1991) 'House Condition Survey'.

Glasgow City Council et al (1993) 'Glasgow Regeneration Alliance: Shaping the Future'.

Glasgow City Council (1993a) 'Action for Warm Homes Critical Path'.

Glasgow City Council (1993b) 'Annual Policy Statement'.

Glasgow City Council (1994a) 'Housing Plan'.

Glasgow City Council (1994b) 'Glasgow City Housing Special Needs and Community Care Strategy 1994'.

Glasgow For People (1994) 'Twelve Reasons for Cancelling the New Motorway Plans for Glasgow'.

Goodlad, R. (1993) 'The Housing Authority as Enabler'. Coventry/Harlow: IOH/Longmans.

Goodman, R. (1972) 'After the Planners'. London: Pelican.

Gordon, David (ed.) (1990) 'Green Cities: Ecologically Sound Approaches to Urban Space'. Montreal: Black Rose Books.

Gore, T. & Nicholson, D. (1991) 'Models of the Land-development Process: A Critical Review'. Environment and Planning A 23: 705-730.

Gosling, P. (1994) 'Rio summit gets down to earth'. Independent on Sunday, 27 March, p.21.

Hams, T. (1994) 'Local Agenda Moves On'. Planning, 1072, 10 June pp.24-25.

Hardy, D. & Ward, C. (1984) 'Arcadia for All: the Legacy of a Makeshift Landscape'. London: Morrell.

Harland, E. (1993) 'Eco-Renovation'. Totnes: Green books.

Harman, J. (1993) as quoted in Planning No. 1037: 1.

Harvey, D. (1985) 'The Urbanisation of Capital'. Oxford: Basil Blackwell.

Hawes, P. (1993) 'Eco-systems'. in Architectural Design Vol 63 No. 11/12.

Hayden, D. (1984) 'Redesigning the American Dream: The Future of Housing, Work and Family Life'. London: Norton.

HC648-I (1993) 'Energy Efficiency in Buildings'. Environment Committee, House of Commons, Session 1992-3, Vol I, Report, London: HMSO.

HC648-II (1993) 'Energy Efficiency in Buildings', Environment Committee, House of Commons, Session 1992-3, Vol II, Minutes of evidence, HMSO.

HC648-III (1993) 'Energy Efficiency in Buildings'. Environment Committee, House of Commons, Session 1992-3, Vol III, Appendices, HMSO.

Housing Corporation (1993a) 'Affordable New Low Energy Housing for Housing Associations'. London: Housing Corporation.

Housing Corporation (1993b) 'Scheme Development Standards Housing'. London: Housing Corporation.

Hunt, S. and Boardman, B. (1994) 'Domestic Energy and Affordable Warmth' Paper 1 in Watt Committee Report, Chapman & Hall.

Imrie, R. and Thomas, H. (eds) (1993) 'British Urban Policy and the Urban Development Corporations'. London: PCP

Ince, M. (1991) 'Design Environmental Impact Certificate: A Green Label for Existing Housing'. London: SLC Energy Group.

Inner City Commission (1987) 'Private House Building in the Inner City'. London: House Builders' Federation.

Jacobs, J. (1961) 'The Death and Life of Great American Cities'. Harmondsworth: Penguin Books.

Johnson, B. G. (1991) 'Building for Health-Indoor Climatye and Effective Energy Use',. Sweden Council for Building Research. CBRD20 (Available from BSRIA).

Kemeny, J. (1992) 'Housing and Social Theory'. London: Routledge.

Kemp, P. and Wall, D. (1990) 'A Green Manifesto for the 1990s'. London: Penguin.

Kruger, A. (1991) 'H is for ecoHome: An A-Z Guide to a Healthy, Planet Friendly Household'. London: Gaia Books.

Leather, P., Mackintosh, S. and Rolf, S. (1994) 'Papering Over the Cracks: Housing Conditions and the Nation's Health'. London: National Housing Forum.

Leicester City Council (1992a) 'Protecting the Environment'.

Leicester City Council (1992b) 'Leicester in Partnership – The Comprehensive Housing Strategy of Leicester City Council'.

Leicester City Council (1992c) 'City of Leicester Local Plan – Written Statement (Deposit Copy)'.

Leicester City Council (1993) 'Leicester in Partnership – The Comprehensive Housing Strategy for Leicester'.

Leicester City Challenge (1993) 'Code of Practice'.

Leicester City Challenge (1992) 'Leicester City Challenge Bid'.

Lever, W. and Moore, C. eds (1985) 'The City in Transition. Policies and Agencies for the Economic Regeneration of Clydeside'. Oxford: Oxford University Press.

Lloyd-Wright, F. (undated) 'The Usonian House'.

Local Government Management Board (1991) 'Guide to Eco-auditing for Local Government'. Luton: LGMB.

Local Government Management Board (1992) 'The Earth Summit, Rio 92, Agenda 21 – A Guide for Local Authorities in the UK'. Luton: LGMB.

Local Government Management Board (1993a) 'A Local Authority Guide to the EC's Fifth Action Programme'. Luton: LGMB.

Local Government Management Board (1994) Local Agenda 21: Principles and Process. Luton: LGMB.

London Hazards Centre (1990) 'Sick Building Syndrome'. London: London Hazards Centre.

Lovelock, J. (1979) 'Gaia'. Oxford: Oxford University Press.

Lowe, P. and Goyder, J. (1983) 'Environmental Groups in Politics'. London: Allen and Unwin.

Maclennan, D. (1991) 'Extending the Strategic Role'. in Donnison, D. and Maclennan, D. (Eds) The Housing Services of the Future. Coventry/Harlow: Institute of Housing & Longman.

McGinley, P. (1992) 'The greenhouse effect'. The Guardian 19 September: 39.

McGregor, A. et al (1992) 'A Review and Critical Evaluation of Strategic Approaches to Urban Regeneration'. Training and Employment Research Unit, University of Glasgow. Edinburgh: Scottish Homes.

McLaren, D. (1992) 'London as Ecosystem', in Thornley, A. The Crisis of London. London: Routledge.

McLaren, D. (1989) 'Action for People, a Critical Appraisal of Government Inner City Policy'. London: Friends of the Earth.

Malpass, P. and Murie, A. (1994) 'Housing Policy and Practice'. Basingstoke: Macmillan.

Malpass, P. and Means, R. (Eds) (1993) 'Implementing Housing Policy'. Buckingham: Open University Press.

Markandya, A. & Richardson, J. (1992) 'The Earthscan Reader in Environmental Economics'. London: Earthscan.

Meadow, D. H., Meadows, D. L., Randers, J. and Brehnens III W. (1983) 'The Limits to Growth'. London: Pan.

Means, R. (1993) Perspectives on Implementation in Malpass, P. & Means, R. (eds) Implementing Housing Policy. Buckingham: Open University Press.

Moore, R. (1991) 'Cold, damp and mouldy housing in England'. Paper presented at Unhealthy Housing Conference, Warwick.

Morphet, J. (1993) 'Councillors left high and dry'. in Planning 12 Feb. p.13.

Morran, G. (1993) 'Time for Dialogue on the Regions'. in Local Government Chronicle 19 Feb. p.18/9.

Mumford, L. (1961) 'The City in History'. London: Secker and Warburg.

Murie, A. (1983) 'Housing Inequality and Deprivation'. London: Heinemann.

Murie, A. and Williams, P. (1993) 'Directions in UK Housing Research'. Paper presented to the Housing Studies Association Seminar Reading University. 14th-15th September 1993.

NACAB (1993) 'Out of control?' London: National Association of Citizens Advice Bureaux.

Naess, A. (1990) 'The Basics of Deep Ecology'. in Button, J., ed. The Green Fuse London: Quartet.

National Consumer Council (1993) 'Paying the price'. London: National Consumer Council HMSO.

Neighbourhood Energy Action (1991) Ten Years in The Cold. Newcastle: NEA.

Neighbourhood Energy Action (1992) 'HEES: the First Fifteen Months, Newcastle: NEA.

Neighbourhood Energy Action (1993) 'HEES: Barriers to Access'. Newcastle: NEA.

Neighbourhood Energy Action (1994) 'Fuel for Thought Annual Review 1993'. Newcastle: NEA.

Needleman, L. (1965) 'The Economics of Housing'. London: Staples Press.

Norton-Taylor, R. (1982)'Whose Land is it Anyway?' Wellingborough: Turnstone Press.

Nozick, Marcia (1992) 'No Place Like Home: Building Sustainable Communities'. Canadian Council on Social Development. Ottowa.

Oseland, N. A. and Ward, D. D. (1993) 'An interim evaluation of the Home Energy Efficiency Scheme (HEES)'. Watford: BRE.

Ospina, J. (1987) 'Housing Ourselves'. London: Hilary Shipman.

O'Riordan, T. (1981) 'Environmentalism'. London: Pan.

Owen, D. (1980) 'What is Ecology?' Oxford: Oxford University Press.

Owen, G. (1989a) 'Room for Improvement. Progress with prospects for energy efficiency grant to low income households', NEA Policy Discussion Paper Number 1. Newcastle: NEA.

Owen, G. (1989b) 'Access to Improvement. The involvement of housing agency services in energy efficiency' NEA Policy Discussion Paper Number 2. Newcastle NEA.

Owen, S. (1991) 'Planning Settlements Naturally'. Chichester: Packard.

Owens, S. (1992) 'Energy, Environmental Sustainability and Land-use Planning'. in M. Breheny (ed.) Sustainable Development and Urban Form. London: Pion.

Owens, S. & Cope, P. (1992) 'Land Use Planning and Climate Change'. London: HMSO.

Pearce, D., Markandya, A. & Barbier, E. (1989) 'Blueprint for a Green Economy'. London: Earthscan.

Pearce, D. & Turner, R. K. (1990) 'Economics of Natural Resources and the Environment'. Hemel Hempstead: Harvester-Wheatsheaf.

Pearson, D. (1989) 'The Natural House Book'. London: Conran Octopus.

Pearson, M. A. and Smith, S. R. (1990) 'Taxation and Environmental Policy: some initial evidence'. IFS Commentary No. 19, London, Institute for Fiscal Studies.

Peoples Asbestos Action Campaign (1988) 'Second London Asbestos Conference Report'. London: PAAC.

Pepper, D. (1984) 'The Roots of Modern Environmentalism'. London: Routledge.

Pepper, D. (1993) 'Eco-Socialism: from deep ecology to social justice'. London: Routledge.

Percy-Smith, J. and Sanderson, I. (1992) 'Understanding Local Needs'. London: Institute for Public Policy Research.

Pocock, R. & Gayland, B. (1992) Ecological 'Building Fact Pack'. Leicester: Tangent Design Books.

Porritt, J. (1986) 'Seeing Green'. Oxford: Blackwell.

Prior, J., Raw, G., Charlesworth, J. L., Burke, D. and Mitchell, J. (1991) 'BREEAM 3/91. An Environmental Assessment for New Homes, Ref BR208'. Watford: BRE.

Raemaekers, J. (1993) 'Corporate Environmental Management in Planning Practice and Research'. Vol 8 No. 3.

Royal Institute of British Architects (1993) 'Strategic Study on Architectural Practice'. London: RIBA Press Ltd.

Rydin, Y. (1992a) 'Environmental Impacts and the Property Market in M. Breheny (ed.) 'Sustainable Development and Urban Form'. London: Pion.

Rydin, Y. (1992b) 'Environmental Dimensions of Residential Development and the Implications for Local Planning Practice'. Journal of Environmental Planning and Management 35, 1: 43-61.

Rydin, Y. (1993) 'The British Planning System'. London: Macmillan.

Saunders, P. and Williams, P. (1988) 'The Constitution of the Home: Towards a Research Agenda'. in Housing Studies Vol. 3, No. 2: 81-93.

Saunders (1990) 'A Nation of Home Owners'. London: Unwin Hyman.

Scottish Homes (1993) 'Glasgow Housing Market Study'. Edinburgh: Scottish Homes.

Shelter (undated) 'Coventry Council Houses – The New Slums'. London: Shelter.

Shorrock, L. D., Henderson, G. and Bown, J. H. F. (1992) 'Domestic energy fact file'. Watford: Building Research Establishment.

Shorrock, L. D. and Bown, J. H. F. (1993) 'Domestic energy fact file 1993 update'. Watford: Building Research Establishment.

Singh, M. (1994) 'Backdoor'. Roof, March/April.

Smithers, R. (1990) 'Go for Green Houses: two schemes which will benefit the energy-efficient home'. The Guardian 16 June: 37.

Sneddon, J. and Theobald, C. (1987) 'Building Communities. The First International Conference on Community Architecture Planning and Design'. London: Community Architecture Information Services Ltd.

Socialist Environment and Resources Association (1993) 'Environmental Action in Local Government'. London: SERA.

Stafford, D. C. (1978) 'The Economics of Housing Policy'. London: Croom Helm.

Stewart, J. and Stoker, G. (Eds) (1989) 'The Future of Local Government'. London: Macmillan.

Stoker, G. and Young, S. (1993) 'Cities in the 1990s'. Harlow: Longman.

Talbott, J. (1993) 'Simply Build Green: A Technical Guide to the Ecological Houses at the Findhorn Foundation'. Forres: Findhorn Foundation Development Wing.

Taylor, L. (1993) 'Energy Efficient Homes'. London/Coventry: Association for the Conservation of Energy & Institute of Housing.

Thake, S. and Staubach, R. (1993) 'Investing in People: Rescuing Communities from the Margin'. York: Joseph Rowntree Foundation.

Thompson, R. (1993) 'Economic Regeneration: Trickling down or Growing Upwards'. Town and Country Planning Association Summer School, TCPA February.

Tieman, R. (1994) 'Spottiswoode scents victory on £1b levy', Times 27 May.

Tighe, C. (1993) 'Designer labels for buildings'. The Financial Times 5 May: 11.

Tomlinson, A. (1990) 'Home Fixtures: Doing-it-yourself in a Privatised World'. in Tomlinson A. (ed.) Consumption, Identity, Style. London: Comedia.

Townsend, P. (1979) 'Poverty in the U.K.'. London: Penguin.

Turner, J. F. C. (1993) 'The community basis of sustainable development'. in Rajan V. (ed.) Rebuilding Communities Totnes: Green Books.

URBED (1992) 'Homes for the 21st Century: review of the current state of the art'. London: Urban and Economic Development Group.

Vale, B. & Vale, R. (1991a) 'Towards a Green Architecture'. London: RIBA.

Vale, B. and Vale, R. (1991b) 'Green Architecture'. London: Thames and Hudson.

Ward, D. (1992) 'Housing Management and Maintenance Savings Through Energy Efficiency Refurbishment'. BRECSU, Building Research Establishment, Watford PD29/92.

Webb, A. (1991) 'Co-ordination – A Problem in Public Sector Management'. in Policy and Politics Vol 19 No. 4: 229-241.

Webb, A. and Gossop, C. (1993) 'Towards a Sustainable Energy Strategy', in Blowers (ed.) 'Planning for a Sustainable Environment. London: Earthscan.

Weston, J. (ed.) (1984) 'Red and Green: The New Politics of the Environment'. London: Pluto press.

Whitelegg, J. (1994) 'Driven to the end of the road', Guardian 28 March.

Widner et al (1992) 'Divided Cities in the Global Economy: Human Strategies. The 1992 European – North American State of the Cities Report'. Washington: German Marshall Fund.

Wilcox, S. (1993) 'Housing Finance Review 1993'. York: Joseph Rowntree Foundation.

Wilmot, P. and Huthieson, R. (eds) (1992) 'Urban Trends 1'. London: Policy Studies Institute.

Woodhouse, Peter R., Khaw, Kay-Tee and Plummer, Martyn (1993) 'Seasonal variation of blood pressure and its relationship to ambient temperature in an elderly population'. Journal of Hypertension, Vol 11, No. 11, pp.1267-74.

World Commission on Environment and Development (WCED) (1987) 'Our Common Future'. Oxford: Oxford University Press.

World Health Organisation (1987) 'Air Quality Guidelines for Europe'. Geneva: WHO Regional Office for Europe.

Yarrow, G. (1992) 'British electricity prices since privatization'. Regulatory Policy Institute, Studies in regulation 1, Hertford College, University of Oxford.

Yarrow, G. (1993) 'Regulation and pricing performance in the gas industry'. Regulatory Policy Institute, Studies in regulation 2, Hertford College, University of Oxford.